EXPERT SUCCESS STORIES

29 Inspirational Stories of **Transformation** from the **Expert** Success Academy

DANIEL WAGNER

First published in Great Britain in 2013 by Expert Success LLP

All contributors' photographs (except for pages 33, 62, 183) courtesy of John Cassidy www.johncassidyheadshots.com

British Library Cataloguing in Publication Data.

A catalogue record for this book is available from the British Library.

Paperback Edition	978-0-9576557-3-7
Hardback Edition	978-0-9576557-4-4
Digital Edition	978-0-9576557-5-1

V01

DEDICATION AND ACKNOWLEDGEMENTS

I am always fascinated to watch the credits roll at the end of a movie and I'm always amazed at the amount of people involved in making something happen.

And although this is not a Hollywood blockbuster, I'm similarly impressed and amazed at the amount of people involved in making this book a reality.

So thank you first to Kevin Bermingham, the project manager of this book. He has not just proven himself to be capable; he has shown tremendous tact and skill in pulling together and managing the work of so many people in an impossibly short time frame.

Next I want to thank the contributors to this book – my friends and tribe members of the Expert Success Academy who I got to know and respect over the last few years of my passionate journey. You're all heroes in my book (pardon the pun) and I applaud you for volunteering and standing up and leading the way. You have shown the world what can be achieved when you apply focus and clarity to a simple formula.

I also want to thank the contributors whose stories didn't make it into this book. We simply had too many and I had to make a choice. It's never easy, but it's part of life and leadership. I have done my best to show a wide variety of stories illustrating different levels of success and I hope that the experience of writing your story was worth it in its own right.

This book is dedicated to my mum and dad who, sadly, have both passed away in the last six months. They always believed in me and I know they would be proud to see that I'm helping to change people's lives and inspire them. I hope they would approve of what I stand for and what I fight against and I sure hope that they would forgive me for leaving Austria to find my luck in a foreign country.

I know that being in the UK was instrumental for my journey and I don't think this could have happened in any other place. This is a great country and I appreciate living here and taking advantage of the great market conditions this country offers to entrepreneurs. Thank you to all the teachers, coaches, fans, followers, students and friends who have made me feel so appreciated and welcome. I don't take it for granted.

I would also like to thank my business partner James Watson, my excellent team Corey Woolfe and Liz Brown and the rest of the Expert Success team. I could not have done this without you.

My gratitude goes also to my friend and business coach Paul Avins, my inspiration at the other side of the pond, Brendan Burchard and the many mentors and gurus who over the last eight years have helped me transform my life from delivering pizzas for Domino's in Slough to running a successful seven-figure business and helping hundreds of people break free from their J-O-B and become successful entrepreneurs.

CONTENTS

ABOUT DANIEL WAGNER

Daniel Wagner was born in Austria and moved to the UK in 1995. His varied journey across multiple careers and businesses led him to become one of the UK's most prominent teachers and trainers on Authentic Personal Online Branding, information product creation and tribe building. (The whole story is published in *My Journey & the Machine*.)

Daniel created and ran multiple six- and seven-figure businesses using online marketing strategies and is passionate about sales and marketing automation and influence and persuasion.

He is a frequent speaker on the national and international stage of business and marketing events and has inspired thousands to take action to start or grow their own businesses. The author of multiple books and founder of the Expert Success Academy, he passionately believes that running a successful business is within everybody's reach and he predicts a massive growth of small businesses in the next decade.

He believes that small businesses will move the UK and other countries out of recession and he empowers people to create financial freedom and independence through personal leadership.

A caring and passionate coach and consultant, he helps businesses of any size to achieve massive growth using proven marketing strategies combined with advanced influence and persuasion techniques.

This book is a testimony to Daniel's work and the life-changing effect of his teachings.

BY THE AUTHOR

My Journey & the Machine: How Internet Marketing Saved My Life, CreateSpace, 2011

Secrets of the Wealth Accelerators, Paul Avins Enterprises Ltd, 2011

Expert Success, Expert Success, 2013

INTRODUCTION BY DANIEL WAGNER

Founder of the Expert **Success** Academy

WHY THIS BOOK IS SPECIAL TO ME (AN INTRODUCTION YOU SHOULD READ)

DEAR VALUED READER,

What you are holding in your hands is a little miracle. Not just because for a book to be published means a thousand little things have to come together. Not just because of the strong desire of one person to see it through. I've written books before: three to be precise. My first was an autobiography outlining my journey to becoming a self-reliant entrepreneur (My Journey & the Machine); the second was as co-author with a distinguished group of people called the 'Wealth Accelerators' and the third being my bestseller and flagship book *Expert Success*. So what's so special about this one? I am glad you asked.

THE MIRACLE OF COLLABORATION

I call it a little miracle because it's a collaboration of so many people - a small selection from the plethora of success stories that my clients/students/friends/ tribe members can report and testify to. And it all came together in just a few short months. From a crazy idea sparked by a conversation, to an impossible deadline, to serendipitously finding the right people to help make this a reality – a wonderful example of the beauty of life in all its glory!

This book and the success stories you'll find within is also special because although each story is very different, they all have one thing in common. These success stories have been applying a simple set of strategies that I developed over the last few years which have literally changed thousands of people's lives. A bold claim, right? But if I asked you if having more money, more time and more purpose would make a difference to your life, what would you say? You might say yes, but how? And that is exactly what you are about to read.

IT'S NOT ALL ABOUT THE MONEY

Many of the people in this book have doubled or tripled their turnover and they are not exceptions! But it's not about the 'money'; it's about the better choices you'll be able to make because of it. And to paraphrase what the American entrepreneur and motivational speaker Jim Rohn used to say, 'it's not about the million; it's about the person you have to become to achieve it'.

And it's not just about 'more time'. I know that we all have 24 hours in the day, but I have observed that some folk seem to get a lot more done and still have free quality time to spend on things they love outside work. Good news – it's called leverage and it's learnable.

What this is really about is helping people to find their life's meaning and purpose. Boy – I can tell you some stories about this one. I was a true 'seeker'. I spent my youth trying all kinds of drugs, dropped out of school and tried many jobs, then spent many years in a religious group travelling the world looking for meaning; the list goes on. I even walked over fire just to try to work out what I should be doing with my life.

WE ALL KNOW DEEP INSIDE WHAT WE SHOULD DO WITH OUR LIVES

And all that time it was staring me right in the face. Deep inside we all know what we would love to do. We just don't believe we could make a living from it. We just can't see how anyone would value what we naturally have. In my example I always loved to create and invent things, share stories and make people laugh and have them give me attention. Now I have a wonderfully simple business where I get a lot of money for doing just that. That is just one example of what the 'Expert Industry' allowed me to do. Once I found my 'thing', my 'flow', my 'purpose', money simply followed. Now I understand why I hated my past jobs so much: they met none of my needs. Maybe you can relate to this. Maybe you are on your road to find out exactly what floats your boat – I sincerely hope that some of the stories in this book might inspire or encourage you to go out and get whatever it is you really want. It's out there for the taking.

The wonderful and highly successful entrepreneur BJ Cunningham, who spoke at my recent Expert Success Summit, has summarised a life of purpose in the following simple scenario. Love what you do, love who you do it for, love who you do it with and love where you do it. Got it? Yep – that's it. If you don't tick the four boxes yet, make a change!

A RADICALLY DIFFERENT WORLD OF THREAT AND OPPORTUNITY AWAITS

I'm pretty convinced that more money, more time and more purpose would improve anyone's life so I'm delighted to share a sample of our Expert Success Stories here in this little collection. May it drive you on to create a life you love.

One of the greatest challenges and opportunities of the world we are living in is that it is radically different to the one we grew up in. The last 20 years have seen the most profound changes in human history and the world economy imaginable. In fact if we are honest it's actually beyond most people's imagination. And the reason is simply that the internet has connected us all and made the world flat once more. The internet, and technology as a whole, are the stuff of science fiction. Everything changed. And there are two ways to deal with change. Ignore it or embrace it. You can guess what happens if you simply ignore it. So actually there is only one choice. Embrace the change or feel the pain! That is exactly what I and the other people in this book have done and are consistently doing. Discover opportunity in the change around us.

A WAKE-UP CALL

So let's do a quick reality check. We have got to wake up to what's really happening. Look around you. There has been a general breakdown in trust, the banks and governments are financially bankrupt, currencies are collapsing; it's all doom and gloom if you watch the news.

Do I think I'm immune to this? No, but I am not prepared to just sit there and wait for things to happen to me. I want to make things happen. I want to be in the driving seat. The job for life is gone (not that this was attractive to me anyway), taxes go only one way (and you can be sure it's not down), pensions go the same way (or disappear altogether). But most people are sitting there like rabbits in the headlights hoping for things to get back to normal. Well I've got some news for you: it ain't gonna happen. The old way is broken. Somehow you sense it, but you want to cling on to the belief that it might just be OK. Not just because it's more comfortable to hope it'll be alright, but also because you don't have a clue what else to do. But you have got to take it into your own hands. You are not alone.

THE POWER HAS SHIFTED AND IT CAN BE IN YOUR HANDS

Everything is different now. Marketplaces and power have shifted, social media has created a radical transparency that has brought down some big businesses, and the recessions of the last decade have seen a new breed of entrepreneur blossom from the ruins of broken promises. And you can join them. Never before has it been easier to get started. More millionaires have been made in the last 20 years than at any time in history. How can you become one of them? What secret knowledge or potion must you possess to become part of this? How can you take your place at the table where the billion dollar cake is being sliced up?

It's time to embrace the change. It's coming. It's been coming for a while. And the rules of the game have changed. Don't worry though – you're not too late. There is a new wave of people like those in this book, embracing the prosperous shores of the multibillion-dollar 'Expert Industry', and you can join them if you wish. For the price of a leap of faith and the sweat of your brow you can expect to join a world of new-found freedom, increased life purpose and the money you deserve and the respect you desire.

THIS MIGHT SOUND FAR-FETCHED OR CRAZY, BUT IT'S TRUE

If this sounds crazy or far-fetched, then maybe it's not for you. If life has made you so cynical that you can't dream any more or if you are too sceptical to believe and try, then there is no hope. But if you still believe that there might be a better way, then read on. Flick through the pages in this book to become a believer – proof dispels all doubt. Believe that you can change your life and destiny – that you can have what you want – and it might happen quicker than you can imagine.

So what is the magic behind these success stories? Are these exceptional people with special gifts? Nope. I can assure you that I and the Expert Success Academy members in this book are very normal indeed. Look at me. OK, I am pretty stubborn and (now) know what I want, but apart from that – pretty normal. And so are all the folks in this wonderful book.

IT'S MAINLY ABOUT A SHIFT IN MINDSET AND SELF-BELIEF

It's just a set of simple-to-embrace concepts that can change your position from 'chasing money and clients' to 'attracting money and clients'; from 'asking and hoping' to 'getting and knowing'; from 'confusion' to 'clarity'. I've seen so many people succeed in this industry through my teachings that I have an unshakable belief that literally anyone who puts their mind to it and has the determination and patience can benefit greatly from this knowledge. I am so sold on the idea that I have made it my sole goal and purpose to spread the word about Expert Success. As a matter of fact, this is what my company Expert Success and its Expert Success Academy is all about – I want to make this as big as I can. And the movement is growing.

The goal is quite simple: to help anyone from any background become a respected, well paid authority in their chosen market or field. The prize? Independence, freedom and purpose. The price? Read on to learn from real life experts and their journeys.

IF YOU ARE SCEPTICAL OR CYNICAL – I GET IT – AND HERE IS WHY

I am not naive. I get that you will be sceptical about what you are about to discover. We have all been disappointed and I've had my fair share of unfulfilled promises. I understand that you may be cynical because of all the blind alleys you have already walked down and all the bad advice you have already followed (if this is not you, then congratulations – you are either very young or very special). I know that life sucks at times. But you've got to carry on. You've got to believe. I would ask you to open your mind once more – to ascertain the possibility that this can happen for you. It is happening as we speak to people all around the world. A silent revolution of people achieving their dreams. This is why this book can inspire you. Because you'll read their stories to success and you will start to see yourself being next.

YOU DON'T HAVE TO PROMISE ME ANYTHING

I won't ask you to promise me anything – I'm not your coach (yet). You are not accountable to me, but from one human to another I would ask you to be kind to yourself. If you should find that what you are about to discover stirs a desire in you – wakes a quiet voice inside – I would ask that you act upon it. Follow your instinct: it's there for a reason. Trust your gut.

Explore the new possibilities of a world so different to the one we're accustomed to. Let go of a world view of doom and gloom, of a disappointing J-O-B and underpaid work, the one of fear and recession. You'll look back at your old life in disbelief and wonder why it took you so long!

I BOUGHT THE WRONG PLAN AND DIDN'T EVEN KNOW IT!

You see, I've been working hard all my life, but most of the years were wasted working for someone else. I didn't feel appreciated and I didn't feel well rewarded (emotionally or financially). I am not ashamed to admit that I was broke, and worse, in debt for most of my working life. Why? Because I was buying the wrong plan. Someone showed me a plan and I bought it. It seems like there was no alternative. Well that's just not true. There is a better way, and you'll find out all about it in this book.

THERE IS A BETTER WAY

The principles I discovered that lead me to found Expert Success changed my life. Its teachings were instrumental in changing many fortunes. The premise of the principle is that human beings are looking for answers and solutions to their questions and problems. Let me give you the executive summary of the three core Expert Success principles I'm talking about.

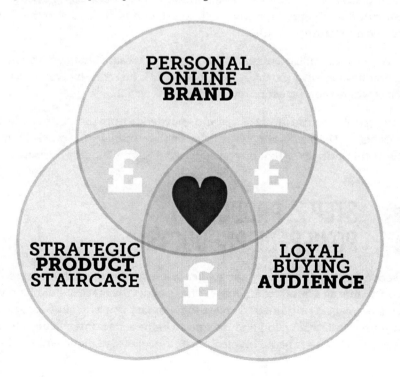

1 STEP 1: ESTABLISH A PERSONAL ONLINE BRAND

Being the 'go-to' person means that you will effortlessly attract the people who are looking for help, as long as you make yourself visible. That is where Step 1: Establish a Personal Online Brand comes into its own. My team and I have helped build nearly 200 brands over the last 24 months and the results have been nothing short of mind-blowing. You see, people are looking for advice and guidance – and they don't trust the big companies any more. So we little guys suddenly have the upper hand – as long as we are prepared to step up to the plate.

A friend of mine told me about a meeting he had in Singapore with a big blue chip company. They asked him about the future and who he thought, in his opinion, would threaten them and take their market share. To their surprise my friend answered that it won't be another big player or company they need to fear, but the solo-preneur and local expert who is diminishing their market share one little crumb at a time.

You can join us in redistributing market share and wealth. But to get a share of the cake, you have to sit at the table! Expert Success is just that. It gives you a seat at the table where the new economy distributes its wealth.

I'm sure you'll pick up a range of tips and knowledge from the stories in the book. But just before I let you get on with exploring the stories, let me quickly highlight the two other principles that drive a successful Expert Success business.

2 STEP 2: PRODUCING POWERFUL PRODUCTS

The second principle is to have a strategically-created set of products and services - I refer to this as a 'Product Staircase'. The Product Staircase should help you to develop a prospect or client and create the ultimate win-win situation; to create maximum client satisfaction and maximum lifetime customer value. Literally all our success stories are based on creating a strategic set of digital and/or physical products and a set of services. So if you are currently in a job or selling your time for money as a coach, trainer, speaker or consultant then the power of the Product Staircase will change your future and fortune forever.

3 STEP 3: CULTIVATING A BUYING AUDIENCE

The third principle is all about people. It's the skill and knowledge to 'Cultivate a Tribe'. We all have an urge and a need to belong, and it has never been easier to create and nurture a community than it is today. It has also never been more important to create new places for people to come together – online and offline. So become a 'tribe' leader and have a mission. I'll show you how – even if at this stage you have no mission to lead.

WILL YOU JOIN THE MOVEMENT?

So there you have it. A new way of making money, a new way of living your life and a new way of making sure your time on this planet has more meaning! Let's get this show on the road. I can see the vision of this new trend sweeping the nations. It will create a better world; that much I'm sure of. Because I've seen what it did for me and hundreds of people around me. This is just the beginning.

THE 2020 VISION – IT'S BIG

My vision is that by 2020 I will have helped to create 20,000 Expert businesses, influenced 20 million people and created a combined wealth of £20 billion. I had better get on with it!

DREAM BIG, START SMALL AND KEEP GOING!

Please get in touch if you have any questions or want any help. Simply find us online or on Facebook. Search for 'Expert Success'.

Here's to your Expert Success.

Daniel Wagner

Daniel Wagner

WHAT IS THE EXPERT SUCCESS ACADEMY?

Throughout the book people will refer to the Expert Success Academy, the Online Brand Masterclass and to my business partner, James Watson. So I thought it would be a good idea to tell you a little bit about each of them.

THE EXPERT SUCCESS ACADEMY

The Expert Success Academy is a fast-growing group of budding and established entrepreneurs and small business owners, who support each other to grow their businesses and help each other to become recognised experts in their respective fields.

A UNIQUE AND PROVEN FRAMEWORK IN THREE PARTS

The Expert Success Academy teaches the unique and proven framework of the Expert Success Formula, which shows anyone how they can become a recognised and well paid expert and authority in the market or industry of their choice.

As described earlier, the three key parts of the tried and tested Expert Success Formula are to Establish a Personal Online Brand, to Produce Powerful Products, and using advanced marketing and sales automation strategies to Cultivate a Buying Audience – in other words building a loyal and lasting tribe.

TOOLS, SUPPORT AND TRAINING

The Academy offers an array of tools, support and training to achieve the goal of making more money, having more time and living a life of purpose doing what you love and creating a resilient and future-proof micro-economy.

The members of the Expert Success Academy learn and implement powerful and life-changing information to fast-track their success. This includes concise teaching and coaching in all areas of: marketing, expert positioning, product creation, tribe building, and of course the very important areas of sales and marketing automation.

WHY KNOWLEDGE IS OFTEN NOT ENOUGH

When I wrote *Expert Success* back in 2011/2012, I literally packed seven years of experience in the Expert Industry into a book, but I quickly became aware of the fact that although people could easily understand the powerful concepts of Expert Success, most struggled to implement the ideas in their business, depriving them of the benefits.

A CURRICULUM-BASED 'EXPERIENCE' — NOT JUST A COACHING PROGRAMME

The Expert Success Academy was created in 2012 as a curriculum-based coaching programme, which over the course of a year covers all nine areas of the Expert Success Formula. It has a rolling intake, which means businesses can start their journey to Expert Success at any time.

The Academy is a multitier programme, allowing individuals and businesses to choose their level of involvement and investment based on their needs. The sole purpose of the Expert Success Academy is to transfer the knowledge of The Expert Success Formula to your business and situation to create a better life for you and your customers.

CHOOSE THE LEVEL THAT IS RIGHT FOR YOU AND YOUR BUSINESS

From the Silver and Gold Level all the way to Platinum and Diamond and the invitation-only Mastermind, all levels of the Expert Success Academy produce transformational results. This book is just a small example of the power of the implementation of its teachings.

If you want to find out more about how the Expert Success Academy can help you and your business, then get in touch. Simply shoot us an email to office@ expertsuccess.com and one of our Expert Success Coaches will touch base and see how we can help and serve you best.

ABOUT JAMES WATSON

James Watson is my business partner and co-founder of Expert Success LLP. Since 2009 James has transitioned from a successful corporate career in sales and marketing to joining me to generate over £1m in sales in multiple businesses.

Prior to working with me James started a small cafe/delicatessen with his wife in their hometown of Bath. Winner of the Best Business Website of The Year Award in 2008, James used his web marketing skills to position his wife as an expert in her industry; appearing in national newspapers, food magazines and as a guest expert on a national TV celebrity chef program.

James is an extensive researcher and analyst with a passion for all areas of marketing, and fully credits Dan Kennedy as a major inspiration. He also has years of experience as a marketing mentor himself, having coached hundreds of business owners. James speaks regularly at Expert Success' events and is the lead coach on the *Expert Success Academy Diamond Program*.

You can find his personal blog at http://james-watson.com and he welcomes all connections via the one Social Media channel he actually likes, LinkedIn http://uk.linkedin.com/in/jamesawatson

WHAT IS THE ONLINE BRAND MASTERCLASS?

The other reference you'll come across in the book is the Online Brand Masterclass. It is our signature three-day workshop, which has helped hundreds of people and businesses get their online presence sorted.

WHY SHOULD YOU ATTEND THE ONLINE BRAND MASTERCLASS?

The three-day Online Brand Masterclass is the UK's only hands-on brand-building workshop conducted by leading Personal Online Brand Expert, Daniel Wagner.

In today's economy it is paramount to have a professional and functional online presence, yet most individuals and businesses fail miserably to comply with the high demands of a modern online brand. This is costing UK businesses millions in lost revenue.

Sadly most current websites fail to achieve their primary objective: to create qualified leads for their business. This is where Daniel Wagner's knowledge comes to the rescue. For the last seven years Daniel has helped hundreds of individuals not just build powerful online brands, but also use the latest marketing strategies to guarantee the best results possible for their business.

The well-structured workshop will guide you through proven processes to produce all the key ingredients to have your online brand created. This includes a session with award-winning portrait photographer John Cassidy as part of the workshop.

The workshops are conducted in small groups to ensure a high level of interactivity and coaching from Daniel Wagner and his team. Meticulously planned exercises throughout the workshop engage delegates at a deep level of emotional thinking and bring to fruition breakthroughs regarding their business, direction and purpose.

The peer-to-peer support in exercises like strapline creation and choosing your banner photograph are invaluable. From the feedback collected, delegates have unanimously agreed that the breakthroughs during the course could have not been achieved without the support of the group and guidance of the team.

WHAT YOU WILL ACHIEVE

At the end of the course, after just three short and entertaining days, you will hold in your hands all the information to create a powerful online brand. This will enable you to finally launch your successful online presence. Here are some of the highlights of what you will walk away with:

A PROFESSIONAL PHOTOGRAPH

Taken by award-winning photographer John Cassidy, the photo is specifically taken to work with your Personal Online Brand Website, and is chosen by the group to guarantee maximum congruence with your message.

A POWERFUL STRAPLINE — YOUR 'PROMISE'

Following a proven four-step process, that includes all three components of the Expert Success Formula, we encapsulate your business within twelve words or fewer. This breakthrough exercise alone will give you a newfound clarity and focus worth multiple times your investment.

YOUR PERFECT DOMAIN CHOICE

Many people have registered one or multiple domains without considering its strategic value and purpose. You will have the right domain registered on the day and if you already own your perfect domain we will give you guidance on how to exploit this valuable online property.

A COMPELLING AND STRATEGIC 'ABOUT ME' PAGE

Research has shown that visitors spend more time on the 'About Me' page than any other. This is why it's paramount you have your 'About Me' page completed to our tested formula. What to share and what not to share will become crystal clear in this exercise.

A SHORT AND POWERFUL 'EARN THE RIGHT'

You will follow our proven formula, successfully tested by hundreds of students in the Expert Success Academy. The process is so natural yet so powerful that you will have a convincing way to influence people in just 30 seconds. Prepare to be amazed.

YOUR OWN 'AUTHORITY HOME PAGE'

Home pages have been misused since their arrival on the internet. At Expert Success we have come up with a process that will not just convince people of your expertise, but also draw them into your page making them want to know more about you. It is distinctly different from the 'About Me' page - an important difference most people don't understand.

AN OPTIMISED TWITTER PROFILE

Twitter is one of the social media heavyweights and it is shocking to see how many people carelessly waste this goldmine of an opportunity. Using the essence of the previously created strapline combined with some valuable additions from your authority home page you will create a Twitter profile that will bring you results – namely targeted followers.

THE RIGHT WEBSITE TEMPLATE FOR YOUR BUSINESS

The look and feel of your website is the first and most important gateway. If your site fails this first test, your visitor is gone – often forever – only to fulfil his need by buying from your competition! This is why it's crucial you choose the right colours, typefaces and template to fit your business and purpose. Armed with your photo, strapline and other content we will easily identify the right template with you.

YOUR OWN 'FREE REPORT' OUTLINE

One of the key lessons of being online is that we need to share value without spending our time. This is what the 'Free Report' has been able to achieve for many years and it is, to this day, one of the best ways to create authority. This exercise will help you create a laser sharp outline and headline for your report that will be the envy of your competitors.

MEET
THE EXPERTS

KEVIN BERMINGHAM PUBLISHING, PROMOTION AND PRODUCTISING EXPERT

Helping Business Owners, Entrepreneurs and Specialists to Become Published Authors

Founder of 90-Day Books and the Successful Author Academy

www.thesuccessfulauthor.com
www.kevinbermingham.com
kevin@kevinbermingham.com
07803 179452

Over 20 years Kevin has planned and managed multimillion pound projects. He's already authored three books and founded a publishing company that published 23 books in the last 12 months alone. Kevin is an author's mentor and has devised a well-proven writing system that's guaranteed to get your first book out of your head and into your hands within 30 days. Kevin helps business owners, entrepreneurs and specialists to become published authors - fast! He helps them publish, promote, and productise their expertise so they achieve more clarity, credibility, and collateral. He previously worked for blue chip corporations as a Business Analyst, IT Manager and Project Manager, then became an independent Project Management Consultant.

- **Qualifications:** Masters Degree in Business Administration. Certified Management Consultant. Certified PRINCE2 Project Management Practitioner. NLP Master Practitioner.

- **Credibility:** Kevin has planned and managed multimillion pound projects for large UK corporates. He once had more letters after his name than within it (MBA, BSc, DipM, CMC, MIMC, MBCS, MIMgt, MIBPR) and it took him five years; now he completely fills the first 10 pages of Google. He has written three books of his own and successfully published 23 books in 12 months for his mentored authors.

- **Personal Lifetime Achievements:** Kevin retired at age 49, never having to work again. He ran a four-hour marathon in 2011.

PUBLICATIONS

Change Your Limiting Beliefs: Three Steps to Achieve Meaningful Goals, 90-Day Books, 2010

The Seven Secrets of Successful Authors: How to Avoid the Dumb Mistakes That Cause Frustration, Heartache and Years of Failure, 90-Day Books, 2012

The Succesful Author Blueprint, 90-Day Books, 2013

❝❝ I GUARANTEE TO GET YOUR BOOK OUT OF YOUR HEAD AND INTO YOUR HAND, FAST!

INTRODUCTION BY DANIEL WAGNER

I met Kevin Bermingham only a few months ago. He attended one of our excellent discovery days in our head office in Wokingham and he stood out from the crowd by persistently asking detailed questions.

I quickly learned that Kevin had been successful in many areas of his life, which is great, because I believe that if you have managed to achieve success in one field, you possess the qualities and mindset to become successful in other areas too.

When Kevin told me that he helps aspiring authors become successful using a formula, I was delighted. It is one of the key pieces of the puzzle to help experts achieve public recognition, and I really wanted him to become part of the Expert Success Academy.

Kevin bought into my vision and came to our flagship three-day workshop the Online Brand Masterclass, which helps people to build and create their authentic Personal Online Brand.

The workshop includes a 'done for you' service, which means that after producing the content together in a supportive coaching environment, the Expert Success web team produces and takes care of all the technical aspects of your online brand.

Kevin then joined the Expert Success Academy and we decided to embark on our first project, the Expert Success Stories book. What you're holding in your hands today is largely a result of Kevin's dedication and ability to help people to achieve results, fast!

I know that Kevin will help many of our members to improve their self-belief and enhance their credibility in the marketplace through his author's mentoring and publishing services.

His generous contributions and support for the Expert Success Academy family makes him a much loved and appreciated member.

I have found Kevin to be trustworthy, responsible and extremely efficient in his ability to get things done.

Daniel Wagner

AN INTERVIEW WITH KEVIN BERMINGHAM

KEVIN, WHAT DID YOU DO AT UNIVERSITY?

I didn't at first. I left school and went to college at sixteen to train as a sea-going Radio Officer, then worked for Shell Tankers for nine months until I got bored sitting by myself in a little radio room on an oil tanker, sending Morse Code all day. So it wasn't until I was 35 that I took a degree in computing as a mature student. Later, I funded myself through an MBA course at age 43, because I wanted to enhance my professional status by moving from project manager to become an independent project management consultant. Eventually those qualifications, and past project management experience, qualified me for membership of the Institute of Management Consultants as a Certified Management Consultant.

HOW DID YOU FIRST GET INTO PROJECT MANAGEMENT?

At heart I'm a systems analyst; a logical thinker and one of life's natural planners. I love to build upon what I already know and then look ahead to build a 'mental picture' of how things will turn out - then I just make it happen. I do it all the time; in fact, I can't ever stop doing it. My dad was a fireman, so very early on I learned about risk avoidance and to always have a Plan A, Plan B and even a Plan C! With that attitude, it was no accident that I was headhunted from my role as a business system analyst and fast-tracked into the project management industry. My first major project management job was to plan a multimillion pound investment programme for the UK's National Air-Traffic Services, then to manage a £4million work package within it. Each project I planned or managed was always successful. So in 1996, I finally decided to set up my own independent company and became a project management consultant.

SO WHAT SORT OF EXPERT WOULD YOU SAY YOU ARE?

As an author's mentor and publisher, I help business owners, entrepreneurs and specialists to publish, promote and productise their expertise so they achieve more clarity, credibility and collateral. After 20 years in project management, my core expertise is obviously in getting stuff done on time. I still manage projects, but these days I specialise in mentoring aspiring experts to write and publish their book fast!

WHY/HOW DID YOU WRITE YOUR FIRST BOOK?

I had a lot of knowledge and knew a load of useful coaching techniques that I was using to help others, but was limited by the number of hours in the day. I decided to publish some of the more essential techniques for anyone to read and use by themselves – and of course I wanted to leave a legacy for when I'd gone. Like a lot of aspiring experts, I'd wanted to write my book for years – yet somehow I never found the time or motivation. Year after year, I'd make New Year resolutions to do it, but they all came to nothing. Then in 2010 I got clever and hired a coach to keep me accountable and was immediately challenged to start my first book. Having made a commitment to start, I just sat down to write and publish it in a month – I didn't know it was supposed to take longer!

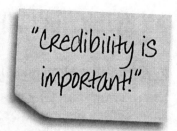

"Credibility is important!"

WHAT WAS YOUR GOAL FOR LAST YEAR?

My main goal last year was to prototype and launch my author's mentoring business and publishing company. That meant publishing a good-sized catalogue of titles, while simultaneously ironing out the mentoring and publishing processes.

WHY SET UP TWO BUSINESSES?

Well, it's more like two services than two businesses. After I'd published my own book in 2010, I started mentoring other aspiring authors to do the same in 2011. My unique proposition was that I had devised a foolproof project plan that could help aspiring authors complete their book incredibly quickly – in eight weeks or less. I'd simply discovered a demand, so I set up a business to satisfy it. However, when I'd finished my first group, it was impossible for them to follow-through into print quickly – because of the production delays imposed by traditional publishers. However, I'd already worked out all the processes and regulations for publishing a book quickly when I did it for my own book, so it made sense to set up another project and a create publishing service too.

THAT'S FASCINATING. WHAT TYPE OF BOOKS DO YOU PUBLISH, AND WHY?

I've published 23 titles in the last 12 months alone. I only publish non-fiction; anything from *Fire Your Webmaster: Create Your Own WordPress Website and Save Yourself a Fortune*, which was a technical book through to *Tune In To Your Baby: Because Babies Don't Come with an Instruction Manual*, written by an award-winning midwife. My last title was more general, *Seven Steps to Creating an Heir-Tight Will*. You can download a free chapter from any book at www.thesuccessfulauthor.com

WHAT TYPE OF AUTHORS DO YOU PUBLISH?

I believe that everyone on earth has skill, knowledge or experience that someone else needs to know about and would pay to learn. In fact, never in the whole of human history has it been easier for ordinary people to write and publish a book about what they know. From my experience, almost anyone can become a published author because – whether they know it or not – they're already an expert in some topic and so any book they write on that topic enhances their credibility and also leaves a lasting legacy, stored in The British Library, for future generations.

As an entrepreneur and author myself, I'm very selective about the types of authors I mentor and publish. When I'm mentoring an aspiring author, I make a big contribution to the concept planning, design and production of their book, so I choose to work with authors that will value my ability as a mentor and my skill as a project manager.

That means I only work with successful business owners, entrepreneurs and specialists that already know their stuff and want to enhance their credibility as an expert in their field – they want to use their book as an *industrial-strength* business card.

"An industrial-strength business card!"

You see, I have no intention of competing with the large publishing houses. Most authors don't know that publishing has become a cut-throat business. Money is tight and the large publishers are enslaving authors, tying them in for years, keeping the digital rights to their book, and requiring authors to do most of their own marketing – that is, unless they've bet on the author becoming the next Paul McKenna or J.K. Rowling.

So I work with ordinary authors with an important message; authors who don't want to spend all their time promoting their book, but simply want their book to promote them.

SO WHAT'S SPECIAL ABOUT THE WAY YOU MENTOR YOUR AUTHORS?

Well, I looked at the areas where I'd had difficulty myself, then devised a simple step-by-step system to overcome these problems in advance. So that's how I designed my writing system the way I did. I wanted it to be well-planned and structured to dramatically reduce the time needed to write a book, while ensuring I included proven project management techniques that prevented authors from procrastinating, becoming overwhelmed or suffering from the dreaded writer's block. As a result, some of my authors have been able to publish more than one book in the same year!

My authors feel elated when they first hold their book in their hand and burst with pride whenever someone buys a copy.

WERE THERE ANY PROBLEMS OR CHALLENGES?

My business is set up to offer a very simple promise: I'll get your book out of your head and into your hands in less than 90 days, or you'll get your money back. Achieving that was quite a challenge. All my authors were published within 90 days – so I always needed to find more clients to succeed them. Apart from a few who were more prolific than others, most authors had no need to come back for another book. Later I found my system could be compressed so authors could write a slightly smaller book in a week, then I would publish it in just 30 days – exactly as I'd done with my first book. In fact, because I know my own system so well I was able to get my second book out of my head and into my hands – written, edited, published, printed, and delivered – in just one week. So the problem was that I couldn't see how to win repeat business from authors as I couldn't legitimately extend their book-writing process.

WHAT DID YOU DO ABOUT IT?

The only reason I'd successfully published my first book after years of procrastination, was because I'd hired a coach who held me accountable to achieve my goal. I thought I'd do the same again – so I went on a few business mentoring programmes. Whilst these programmes were all well designed, there was a real problem: they all focused on explaining the *Why* and teaching the *What* but they were never really practical enough to deliver the *How*!

WHAT IMPACT DID THIS HAVE ON YOU?

Well, I just wanted to find a way to extend my client's journey with me, so I could provide even more value. But I obviously didn't want to lengthen the time taken to write a single book – after all, speed was my USP. So I was going round and round in circles – coming up with idea after idea and wasting time and money planning and trying to put what I'd learned into practice. I clearly had no real idea how to devise an ongoing service that would keep my authors engaged for longer so I could deliver more value.

SO NOTHING HAD WORKED?

Well, of course some things did. I'd designed a strategic set of book formats because authors all wanted to use different formats of books for different marketing and credibility purposes. And I had created *The Successful Author* weekend workshop plus two types of book format already, each with a different function. I had a 30-day process to produce a *Credibility Book* along with a 90-day process to expand it into a larger *Authority Book*. I've recently extended *The Successful Author* workshop by adding a third day, so now authors write and publish a Kindle book before they go home on the last day. But my problem is that my writing system means that they can do it all too fast – depending on their book's size, authors are completely done and dusted in either 30 days or 90 days – then they're gone!

HOW DID YOU MEET DANIEL WAGNER?

I've known of Daniel Wagner for many years and although a number of friends have worked with him, we hadn't met until earlier this year - after I'd read his book *Expert Success*.

WHAT DID YOU LEARN FROM THE EXPERT SUCCESS BOOK?

Well, first of all, I was impressed by the practicality of the book. It doesn't just explain the Why and the What, but gets right down to teaching the How. His book was structured around the three components of his Expert

Success Formula. And within the book I found a clear illustration of a business structure that I could model and build upon. Like me, Daniel is clearly a practical person, so I came to meet him at one of his Expert Success seminars, and then went on to attend his Online Brand Masterclass.

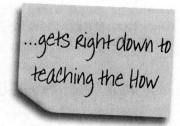

...gets Right down to teaching the How

YOU CREATED A PERSONAL BRAND?

Yes, my online identity was all over the place! That's a key component that was missing from other programmes I'd been on. Being a technical person, I knew what to do to centralise things, but I never actually got around to it. The Expert Success team actually built all the technical elements of my brand for me – even building the website and photographing me for online banners. Daniel Wagner and his business partner, James Watson, didn't just explain why I should have one or simply describe what to do – they actually did it. That was refreshing. Then I was invited to attend a day on The Expert Success Academy's mentoring programme.

WHAT ATTRACTED YOU TO THE EXPERT SUCCESS ACADEMY?

I was intrigued by Daniel's description of The Expert Success Academy. You see, he'd worked out that he couldn't get people to put everything into practice simply by reading a book, or even by coming along to a single Masterclass. So he created an Academy, with an ongoing monthly membership programme that expands on the very same topics that he covers in his book, going further into the practicality of the How.

WHAT HAS CHANGED SINCE YOU JOINED THE EXPERT SUCCESS ACADEMY?

Well, each month we learn more about the topics in the Expert Success formula. And, in addition, the day is well-structured and addresses a lot of peripheral issues that stand in the way to putting things into practice. I found that very valuable.

As a result of attending the Academy, I've redesigned my own mentoring and publishing services along the same lines as Daniel's integration of Formula and Academy. I've now created a framework within which I can build an Academy of my own; one that will continue delivering value even after my authors have published their first book. I'm very excited about that.

WHICH MEANS?

It means that I can now take a business owner, entrepreneur, or specialist and help them build their personal credibility to a much higher level. Over 12 months they'll progress through a step-by-step integrated programme – with each step building on the one previous – so it's a continuous value chain. I'm a project manager and I've always loved creating elegant programmes. I'm very proud of this one!

WHAT ARE YOUR GOALS FOR THIS YEAR?

This year I will work to enhance my personal brand and to implement my Successful Author Academy. Specifically, I plan to consolidate my three existing products into a 12-month fully-integrated mentoring programme, i.e. The Successful Author's 'Write a Book in a Weekend' workshop, my 30-Day Book programme, and my 90-Day Book programme - plus I've included some exciting new products. The Successful Author Academy's extended programme now encompasses: Publishing Your Book, Promoting Your Message and Productising Your Expertise – exactly what my type of clients need. I firmly believe that over the next 12 months I will deliver my promise of: More Clarity, More Credibility, and More Collateral.

HOW WILL THE EXPERT SUCCESS ACADEMY HELP WITH THAT?

Well, I already get great value and advice from the monthly Academy meetings and webinars. And in addition, the Academy members are all experts in their own right, so that's an untapped pool of help and support I intend to follow up.

WHAT ADVICE WOULD YOU GIVE TO READERS?

If readers are tired of the hyped-up sales techniques and huge promises that are so common in the personal development and training industry, they should have a look at the Expert Success Academy – because it's nothing like that. I've found it to be very down-to-earth, giving very practical advice, with scope to follow up and overcome any issues. I don't regret joining the Academy: it turned out better than I'd expected.

WHAT WOULD BE A GOOD FIRST STEP?

Well, first off, I'd suggest people get hold of a copy of *Expert Success*. Then they can take further steps if they wish. The book's great value, and if they're like me, they'll know if Daniel's approach is for them within the first few chapters.

KEY LEARNINGS

- To be an expert, you must stick to what you know.

- To be a truly credible expert, you need to do three things: publish a book, promote your message, and productise your expertise.

- Create physical products: tangible items are easier to plan, measure and value than intangibles.

- Start with the end in mind: don't start until the end is clear.

- Avoid overwhelm: divide your goals into smaller tasks.

- Keep focused: create a rigid plan and follow it.

- Don't reinvent the wheel: if someone has a proven process, use it.

ANNE MCALLISTER
BUSINESS COACHING EXPERT

Helping Business Owners Get the Business They Really Want

The Business Success Academy

www.annemca.com
anne@annemca.com
07815 132429

Anne is a business coach and author of *The Profitable Networking Formula*. She has been training and coaching individuals and business owners for 12 years. In that time she has worked with over 2000 people to help them develop personally and professionally. She founded the Business Success Academy coaching and mentoring group. Prior to this she spent twenty years as a social worker, manager and trainer in the Health Service in Northern Ireland.

- **Qualifications:** Masters in Professional Development. Master Practitioner NLP. Certified Performance Consultant.

- **Personal Achievements:** Having the courage to leave my career after 20 years to pursue my passions of personal and business development. Being a proud Granny to my beautiful granddaughter Miley.

- **Smartest Move:** Finally learning to be an instant-action taker and implementer of what I learn.

PUBLICATIONS

The Profitable Networking Formula: The Business Success Principles, Jackdaw Publications, 2013 (with Alan Leckey)

" MY GOAL IS TO ADD A ZERO TO MY PROFITS THIS YEAR AND HELP 100 BUSINESS OWNERS TO DO THE SAME.

INTRODUCTION BY DANIEL WAGNER

When I first met Anne I was immediately struck by her high level of alertness and her ability to quickly translate teachings into action.

Based in Ireland, she has positioned herself as the go-to business coaching expert in her region.

The fact that she flies into London from Ireland every month to attend our Expert Success Academy meetings shows me her determination and dedication to personal and business growth.

With over a hundred members it's not always easy for me to know about each one's progress and journey, but because of the level of Anne's activity I quickly took notice when she joined the Expert Success Academy.

Many new members tell me of all the plans they have and all the things they will do, but what really counts is what gets done. Anne is a great example of someone who gets things done.

I especially love her attitude to simply taking in what she learns at our meetings and pretty much immediately translating and adopting it for her needs in the field. I do encourage all our members to do that but I have seen Anne excel in using my knowledge and making it work for herself.

I have no doubt in my mind that in the next 6 to 12 months Anne will become one of the most widely known coaches in Ireland and she will lead the way for hundreds more to come.

Her confidence and presence has grown tremendously over the past few months and as success breeds success I know that she will achieve whatever she sets out to.

She is a tremendous inspiration for other women. I believe entrepreneurship is an important trend and Anne should be supported and applauded.

Daniel Wagner

AN INTERVIEW WITH ANNE MCALLISTER

ANNE, WHAT DID YOU STUDY AT UNIVERSITY?

I was offered a place at university to study social work when I left school at 18 but decided instead to go to work and earn some money. I started my career in retail and within two years I was managing a store for a high street fashion retailer. It nearly broke my father's heart as he had high hopes that I would go to university.

I ended up studying social work as a mature student a number of years later when my daughter was born. I knew from the start that I would be a single mum and that I would need a stable career to support us both financially.

It was a rewarding career and as a trainer I learned how to stand up and deliver presentations to diverse groups of people, which is a key skill in my business life now.

However, I knew I couldn't work like that until retirement and I was really concerned about how I would survive financially on an NHS pension so I left and developed my skills as a business coach.

WHAT SORT OF EXPERT ARE YOU?

My expertise is helping business owners to adopt a success mindset and structure their business into something more profitable and rewarding than trading their time for money. I meet many business owners who, like me for a long time, have great skills and expertise but have not got a business model which will support the lifestyle they want to create.

The other common issue I come across is a lack of confidence or willingness to really step up and make it big. Living in Northern Ireland that does not surprise me as we are conditioned from an early age to not 'get ahead of ourselves' and another favourite: 'don't forget the bowl you were baked in'.

Fear of stepping out and achieving success is common.

So fear of stepping out and achieving success is common.

WHAT QUALIFICATIONS DID YOU NEED?

I discovered through attending the Expert Success Academy that I didn't actually need any formal qualifications! That is not why people hire me to be their business coach. However, I trained as a business coach and performance consultant and learned NLP, which is a very valuable skill to have.

WHAT DID YOU HATE ABOUT IT?

I don't really like having to deal with a lot of the technology needed to run the online side of my business so I recently took on a business partner who does. Aside from that I love what I do.

HAVE YOU MADE MISTAKES ALONG THE WAY?

Oh my goodness I think that answer might fill a whole book, not just a chapter. The main one looking back is failing to stand still and really grow one stable steady business. A close second would be in the past failing to fully implement what I was learning.

Again, I see that commonly as an issue for other business owners and those involved in personal development. The term 'shelf development' was coined for a reason.

WHAT DOES THE FUTURE HOLD FOR YOU?

I am excited about the future like never before. I know success is assured and I know what to do to achieve my plan. Tenacity is a skill I have and now I am applying that in the right direction, doing the right things, building my business one brick at a time. One of the things that I am looking forward to is the time and capacity to travel in my downtime.

HOW DID YOU MEET DANIEL WAGNER?

I met Daniel when I was crewing at an event on internet marketing in 2009. I didn't even know what internet marketing was back then, I just agreed to crew to help out because they were stuck.

I will never forget Daniel's presentation. He actually made me cry as his story was so moving, which was a little awkward at the time as I was supposed to be looking after the other attendees!

As I listened to the speakers that weekend I became curious about internet marketing and signed up to a training course from Daniel Wagner and his business partner James Watson. Needless to say I didn't make it big as an internet marketer but I am lucky to have a good grasp of the concepts of internet marketing. Most of them apply to building the online side of any business nowadays. So although I don't want to be very hands on with the technology myself it is important to know how it works in my business.

WHAT ATTRACTED YOU TO THE EXPERT SUCCESS ACADEMY?

I saw Daniel speak again last February at a friend's event. I liked what he said and bought his book as a result. As I said I have learned to implement what I learn so I studiously read the book and tried to the best of my capacity to apply what I had learned. It only really clicked fully for me when I attended the Expert Success Summit and had three days of the formula being presented by Daniel from the stage. I knew from day one that I wanted to join the Academy.

DID YOU ATTEND ANY OTHER TRAINING PROGRAMMES?

I have done a lot of seminars and courses over the last five years, both in person and online with other experts. I have invested in my own education quite heavily. I got a lot of good quality information but never really applied it in a consistent or strategic way. Some of it I didn't apply at all!

WHY/HOW DID YOU WRITE YOUR BOOK?

I actually published a short guide on Kindle about six months before the new book. I just wanted to test how easy it would be to self-publish.

The Profitable Networking Formula was a direct result of being a member of the Academy. I heard Daniel say enough times that writing a book was a great way to position yourself as an expert in your field so I added it to my list, made it a major goal and got it done. I chose the topic as it was one I knew a lot about and it was relevant to the Women's Business Network I founded in Belfast.

To actually make it happen I scheduled in an hour a day, six days a week and began writing. I actually discovered that I like to write. I also worked with a good publisher who knew about Kindle publishing.

I followed Daniel's directions and developed a framework of what each chapter would look like and contain. That made writing it so much easier. I just wrote to the heading of the day.

Because I picked a subject I knew well and had been trained in I didn't need to do a lot of research so that really speeded up the process as well.

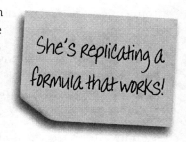

She developed a framework.

I knew from the start that I wanted to publish this book on Kindle and test a marketing strategy I had learned so that meant it was to be a short book, really more of a long report. So again, that made it easier.

The next stage is to write and electronically publish a series of business development books which will go on to become a physical book on Amazon. The planning phase is done and I am giving myself six months to a year to complete this task.

HAS YOUR BUSINESS STARTED TO MAKE PROFIT YET?

Yes it has. I have been slavishly following the Expert Success Formula and 'modelling' what I see other Academy members doing.

There is no equivalent to this programme in Northern Ireland, which is why I invest the time and money to fly to London every month to attend the meetings. James and Daniel give us real information which actually works. What I am in the process of doing is recreating a similar Academy back home. I want business owners in Northern Ireland to be able to access the high quality information which I have had to travel to the UK and Europe to get.

She's replicating a formula that works!

DO YOU HAVE ANY OTHER BUSINESSES?

I was involved in another company but I have stopped giving that any attention at the moment. I am totally focused on getting my Academy up and running and helping local business owners.

ANNE, WHAT IS YOUR GOAL THIS YEAR?

My goal is to add a zero to my profits this year and help 100 business owners to do the same.

HOW WILL THE EXPERT SUCCESS ACADEMY HELP WITH THAT?

The Academy has given me invaluable teaching about setting up a leveraged business model and a loyal tribe. What I love especially about this model is that it fits exactly with one of my core drivers, which is to help others succeed. This way I get to spend at least a year with a group of business owners and make sure they implement what they need to in their business. I am so looking forward to celebrating their successes in 12 months' time.

One of the things I really value about the Academy is having one day a month to work *on* rather than *in* the business. The Academy gives me that time. It also allows me to benchmark my progress from month to month and make sure I achieve the goals I set for myself.

Another important aspect of the Academy is the monthly webinars which give me access to James as well as Daniel. And I get to ask my burning questions and get directly coached on the answers.

Spends one day a month to work on rather than in the business.

The peer group is also invaluable. Having access to feedback on what I am doing from outside educated eyes is such a great resource. I also benefit from the coaching other academy members get as well.

It is an investment which will really give you a return, not just financially but also in how you think, act and conduct your business.

APART FROM THE ACADEMY, DO YOU GO TO ANY OTHER NETWORKING EVENTS?

Yes I am a member of BNI and attend weekly breakfast meetings there. I am the founder of a women's business network in Belfast and recently helped to found a local business networking group in my own town.

HAVE YOU DONE ANY JOINT VENTURES? DID THE EXPERT SUCCESS ACADEMY HELP?

I have taken on a business partner to help set up my equivalent of the Academy. I was looking for someone with complementary interests and values to me but with a different skill set. I also partner with another organisation from time to time and this has been mutually beneficial.

The Academy really taught me to be strategic in all that I do. I have a clear vision of where I am going now and the Academy has helped cure my shiny object syndrome. I evaluate opportunities now in relation to that vision. I ask myself 'are they taking me closer or further away from that vision?'

The answer to that question dictates my response.

 **KEY LEARNINGS**

- Find good mentors.

- Get clear on what kind of a business you want.

- Get a supportive peer group and use them to help you when times get tough.

- Be strategic.

- Finish what you start before you move on to the next thing.

ALLAN FORBES
DIRECT SALES EXPERT

Increasing Direct Sales for Business Owners and Individuals

Quantas Marketing Limited
(Trading as Allan Forbes Coaching)

allanforbes.com
allan@allanforbes.com
07540 885515

Over 25 years Allan has created financial wealth for many individuals and businesses, some of these in excess of eight figures. In the last 12 months he has created a multimillion pound business in Berkshire for a small renewable energy company. Over the last 10 years he has devised a simple, proven three-step formula for increasing money in any business due to be published later this year. He is a sales and marketing entrepreneur, increasing sales revenues and profits for business owners and self-employed individuals, putting real tangible money into their businesses. Allan worked for many blue chip companies in their sales and marketing functions before realising the opportunity to independently supply managed sales and marketing functions as consultant/coach.

- **Qualifications:** HNC Electrical and Mechanical Engineering (Inverness 1983). Fundamentals of Psychology (Glasgow 2001). Fellow Chartered Management Institute (FCMI).

- **Credibility:** Has created many multimillion-pound businesses which were sold and still trade healthily today.

- **Personal Lifetime Achievements:** To have bounced back from adversity stronger, more determined and more focused to help others realise their true potential.

❝ I SPENT 27 YEARS IN SALES AND MARKETING.

INTRODUCTION BY DANIEL WAGNER

Allan Forbes is one of the more recent members of the Expert Success Academy. It is clearly not the length of time that counts, but the level of contribution and dedication that makes a difference.

He made an immediate impact when we first met at our Online Brand Masterclass workshop, and I knew I had a raw diamond in the room. I knew that I could help Allan, but also knew that Allan would bring skills into the Academy that all the members would benefit from.

His burning desire to excel and push himself, his skill to inspire and lead people, and his unflinching enthusiasm, no matter what obstacles life throws at him, make him an impressive and inspirational asset to the group.

Allan immediately joined us at the coveted diamond level of the Expert Success Academy and has already achieved tremendous results in a few short months. When I founded the Academy, one of the objectives and goals was to create a community of experts that can help each other and support each other in their business and personal growth.

I feel that with Allan's direct sales and telesales skills we have found an important missing piece for the group. I have personally experienced how important it is to learn the skill of sales, but many people simply hope that their product or service will sell itself.

The fact is that every success story is a story of mastering sales and marketing. If done well and correctly, sales can be a wonderful opportunity to solve people's problems and leave both parties satisfied and happy.

I would go as far as stating that if you believe that your product or service can help transform people's lives, you have a responsibility and a duty to learn selling to get your message to as many people as possible.

This is what Allan Forbes brings to the table. And it is not just me and the Expert Success Academy members that benefit, I want to make sure that his knowledge and skills reach the widest possible audience to help as many businesses as possible.

Daniel Wagner

AN INTERVIEW WITH ALLAN FORBES

ALLAN, TELL ME ABOUT YOUR EDUCATION?

That for me is the part which probably makes me smile more than any. When at school in the 70s and early 80s there seemed to be a segregation process and for whatever reason I was labelled as one of those not destined for great academic success. I never felt included or stimulated by school, much preferring to chase my dreams. I was excluded and told that I would never amount to very much. My later education came from my own desire to learn about specific subjects.

I know now that my non-education experience shaped my future and I would not change it. Being told you are no good is a great driver in life!

HOW DID YOU GET INTO SALES AND MARKETING?

After a short stint in the Armed Forces I returned to my home town of Inverness, desperate to follow my desire to be a disc jockey. I needed a car and the only way I could possibly get one was to get a job that gave you a car as part of the deal. I knew that if I could get a sales job the chances were high that I would also get a car and then I could chase my dream.

And that is exactly what happened. I got a job selling photocopiers and facsimile machines for a business in Inverness and I have been in sales and marketing ever since. Incidentally, this experience gave birth to my first business which still trades 27 years later.

WHAT KINDS OF BUSINESS HAVE YOU WORKED FOR?

During the last 20 years I have worked across many business sectors including corporates such as Canon Business Machines and Unilever, large UK brands such as Anglian Home Improvements, Space Kitchens, Instock and Luminar Leisure Group.

What I learned on my journey is invaluable. It does not matter what the product or service is or which category of industry it is. The principles of sales and marketing transcend all.

ALLAN, WHY HAVE YOU STAYED IN SALES AND MARKETING ALL THIS TIME?

I have spent 27 years in sales and marketing without really thinking about the time. The privilege afforded to me is the education which I have gained: an education which schools or the general education system in the UK does not or will not deliver. Today I can control not only my own income but the incomes of any individual or business who will adopt a proven process and structure for creating money.

I guess if you were to analyse deeply what motivates me it would be split into two very distinct sections. Firstly, I don't see it as work, it is just something that I do and I am really fortunate to have that mindset. Secondly, well you might call it ego stroking, but I love the reaction! The reaction of creating wealth, money, income, call it what you will. I have had the pleasure of seeing the relief in the faces of business owners who are stuck with no route out of their current cashless situation when they suddenly realise that there is a way. Seeing individuals who are days away from car repossessions and eviction orders, finally understanding how to make real money predictably and consistently is the real reward for what I do.

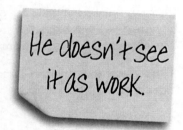

He doesn't see it as work.

Sales and marketing is such a varied job, the title really does not do it justice. I keep saying it but I am fortunate that no two days are the same. I get to meet and help a wide and varied section of people, it's just nice.

WHY SET UP YOUR OWN COACHING BUSINESS?

Setting up my own coaching business was the natural next step for me.

I had created other businesses but none that I would have wanted to run, manage and grow long term. These were more learning projects: rightly or wrongly I believe that if you are going to teach, you personally must have gained hands-on experience. You need to have lived the experiences and understand the stresses of your students, theory is not enough.

The coaching business is a culmination of years of practice and during these years I have made many mistakes. I have been broke, I have taken the wrong route. It has not all been plain sailing but I am a stronger person and professional for those experiences, importantly better placed, skilled and ready to help others make fewer mistakes and make more money.

During the 27-year learning process I was fortunate to discover a formula that when applied to businesses and individuals worked in an extremely high percentage of cases. The coaching business is a vehicle where I can take this formula and apply it to all sorts of businesses and people, helping them to create better outcomes and more money, and at the same time have some certainty that their businesses will survive when they take some time to enjoy the fruits of their labour.

There is one very strong motivator in the decision to make coaching my long term income source and that is access. What I mean by this is having a solution that is both affordable and accessible to the many. I have observed many needy businesses who have failed because the cost of finding a solution has been out of their reach. I want to reverse that trend, making the solution achievable and creating relationships that will have on-going financial benefits for both the teacher and the student.

SO WHAT'S DIFFERENT ABOUT WHAT YOU COACH?

Well, if I was to start a business today from any discipline including accountancy, marketing, sales, product development, etc. which one do I believe would almost certainly guarantee my success? *Sales* of course!

Being an expert in sales and starting a new business would give me an advantage far beyond that of someone else starting the same or similar business. Having that expertise in sales would make me a threat to a similar business with trading experience which was not adept in the sales process. We see examples of this every day; new companies in already matured markets outperforming companies who have been trading in that sector for years and unfortunately the consequences are usually terminal.

My coaching programme focuses the business owner or individual on what is important and for many businesses that means sales. In a recent university study of seven-figure business owners, only 23% had a formalised plan for the sales of their products and services, the other 77% had no plan for establishing or growing sales in their business.

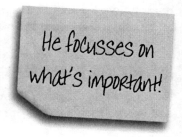

He focusses on what's important!

This is an all too common story, however if you were to ask the 77% in the study if they had enough free cash in their business a large number would answer no. Ask all those canvassed in the study if they could do with more money in their business and the percentage that answer *yes* would certainly be in the high 90s.

My first conversation with any prospective client is around their current sales: the volume of units sold, the cost to create each sale, the profit from each sale, the cost of operating the business, the point at which breakeven is achieved. Even if a client was to progress no further than this point with me I know that the clarity I give them in this highly strategic consultation will have them leave with a true evaluation of their real business picture.

My coaching is different because my clients very quickly 'get me'. They get that I am genuinely interested in them and finding a solution to their problems. I give an extraordinary amount of upfront value in every strategic consultation without any future commitment from a client and I believe it is this giving with zero expectation which quickly builds trust and rapport. The client is free to take the consultation and find another solution provider or to ignore the advice, no strings, and no expectations.

WHAT WERE YOUR CHALLENGES?

The main challenges for me were self-belief: was I good enough to teach others and how I was going to create a product at a price point which would transfer affordably to those I wanted to help.

WHAT DID YOU DO ABOUT THESE CHALLENGES?

I started looking around some two years ago for a solution that would allow me to present myself as the go-to guy for sales and marketing. I knew that in some guise I needed to harness the information age; the internet needed to be part of my solution. I researched many articles on product creation, online marketing and internet marketing, spending around £10,000 on various products.

HOW MUCH OF THIS WORKED?

Nothing worked. I soon found out that the internet was full of people ready and willing to relieve me of my hard-earned cash for little or no reward. I say nothing worked but I did get a crash course on internet marketing and found out a huge amount of things to avoid, I guess you could say that I quickly went from being streetwise to being internet-wise!

HOW DID YOU MEET DANIEL WAGNER?

I was aware of Daniel from one of the few truly valuable resources I had come across on the internet which was teaching about internet marketing. I didn't actually meet him until I attended his Online Brand Masterclass in February 2013, which was part of the earlier learning programme I mentioned.

SO YOU'VE CREATED A PERSONAL BRAND?

Yes, I had no online identity and was told that if I were going to make money from selling my coaching programme I would have to have some sort of authority online. I really didn't know where to start and thanks to the three-day Online Brand Masterclass delivered by Daniel Wagner and James Watson I have an online avatar completely done for me by the team at the Expert Success Academy that works across my website, Facebook, Twitter and LinkedIn. More than this the experience during the three days made me realise that I was good enough to be the go-to guy for sales and marketing; that there was a real value in everything I had learned and achieved. In fact, it was so real and valuable that what I didn't know was that I was already an expert; I just hadn't claimed the space.

Daniel Wagner gave me the confidence to step up to the line and call myself an expert in sales and marketing and to put that expertise to work in the community I was familiar with and to help others achieve freedom from their sales and marketing issues.

I have since joined the Expert Success Academy and teamed up with Daniel and James as my personal business coaches. I am now looking forward to the future knowing that my business is fully supported.

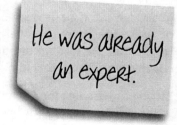

He was already an expert.

WHAT HAS CHANGED SINCE JOINING THE ACADEMY?

Since joining the Academy I have a clear sense of purpose and a fully developed plan for rolling out my business. I have overcome the challenge of developing my knowledge into a product that can be affordably consumed by many, thus fulfilling my dream of helping those who most need it.

I also have a mentor and coach who forces me to look at my business objectively, separating the wood from the trees. Directly as a result of the partnerships I have formed with the Expert Success Academy and following the processes as taught in the *Expert Success* book I have gained new paying clients ready to harness my skills and expertise to strengthen their own businesses.

I strongly believe that had I not done the Online Brand Masterclass and joined the Expert Success Academy my business would not be as complete as it is today. I also know that I have a circle of associates each with their own professional business: a powerful group of like-minded individuals happy to constructively critique my future plans. This alone is a valuable resource!

WHAT ARE YOUR GOALS FOR THIS YEAR?

This year I want to establish my personal brand as the expert in direct sales and marketing. I want to publish my book, *The Expert Sales Formula* and create The Berkshire Business Sales Academy.

HOW WILL THE EXPERT SUCCESS ACADEMY HELP WITH THIS?

As part of the Expert Success Academy I get real value from the weekly coaching calls hosted by James Watson. Like so many things goals can often be relegated in the hierarchy of importance by the perception of other things that seem more important. The weekly coaching call keeps this in check.

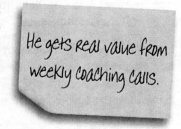

He gets real value from weekly coaching calls.

Setting timeframes for delivery is a very strong element of focus in the Academy and I for one don't want to arrive at a coaching call with my peers with excuses as to why I have not delivered what I said I would.

I know that that I will deliver on time what I said I would, because I have publicly declared it. This accountability is exactly what I need to ensure I achieve my goals.

Also knowing the huge positive difference that each of my goals lend to the business is a massive motivator.

Sometimes, being in business can be a very lonely place and nobody other than people who experience what you feel will ever understand truly what that is like. The community of peers within the Expert Success Academy give a unique tribal affiliation of understanding amongst similar people experiencing the same things as me. I know I am not alone!

WHAT ADVICE WOULD YOU GIVE PEOPLE?

My advice to anyone who is thinking of starting a business or who already has a business is simple. The world has changed and although the principles and fundamentals of business remain the same, the age of industry has morphed to that of technology almost silently. There are many new mediums that your business must adopt if you are to grow, prosper and be successful. The Expert Success Academy understands and teaches many of the key issues surrounding trading successfully in the information age and I would heartily recommend having a close look at how doing this could transform your business. The first step I would recommend is getting a copy of Daniel Wagner's book *Expert Success*. This book is a refreshing twist on the over-hyped personal and business transformation stuff promoted vigorously in today's world. Secondly, I would book a very inexpensive day in the company of the man himself and then make a conscious decision based on your due diligence.

KEY LEARNINGS

- Don't try and do everything yourself; some stuff is better outsourced. My time is better spent doing the stuff that maximises output and profits.

- Having a mentor is critical for separating the wood from the trees; having a second or third pair of eyes strategically evaluating your plans is very grounding.

- Knowing that I am not the only one who experiences trials and tribulations, and being part of a like-minded group exposes you to others who have similar challenges and opportunities.

- I am good enough. What I mean is that I never felt that I was. Being part of the Academy, having exposure to Daniel and James has given me the confidence and belief to ignore the sceptics and follow my instincts.

- Having a plan that is evaluated weekly, monthly and quarterly is an incredible tool which focuses you on doing what you committed to, in the time that you said you would do it. Goodbye procrastination!

JEREMY BALL PETROCHEMICAL PROCUREMENT EXPERT

Inspiring Change Through Innovative Solutions

MasterVendorList.com

www.jeremy-ball.com
www.mastervendorlist.com
jeremy@jeremy-ball.com
0795 7376661

With 24+ years' experience Jeremy is an expert in his field. He has a unique ability to adapt and respond to challenging environments by finding simple solutions to complex issues through his creative and innovative approach. More important though, is his love of people. His philosophy of 'people first' has allowed him to inspire and motivate people all over the world, creating highly effective and motivated teams. Jeremy is the CEO and founder of MasterVendorList.com, an online vendor-sourcing tool designed specifically for the Oil & Gas and Petrochemical industries. He has worked for major oil companies and engineering, procurement and construction (EPC) contractors for almost 25 years, specialising in supply chain management (SCM) both upstream and downstream and in onshore and offshore environments.

- **Qualifications:** I am an avid scholar having successfully completed numerous courses including six business and marketing courses, three on health, six on personal development, seven on wealth strategies including property, and I have an Advanced Diploma in International Procurement and Supply Chain Management.

- **Credibility:** In 2003 I negotiated an $820,000 reduction in project storage costs. In 2005 I saved over $500,000 on a single order. On a 2006 project I saved $980,000 in an eight-month period. I also placed the largest ever single order with Siemens compressor division with a value of over $71million.

- **Personal Achievements:** During 2009 I established the MasterVendorList. com, an online vendor-sourcing tool for the Global Oil & Gas Petrochemical Industries, which, in the four years since its launch, has attracted users from over 100 reputable Oil & Gas companies in over 120 countries. In 2011/12 I transferred a dysfunctional SCM department into the top-performing department in the company in a 22-month period.

❝ I NEGOTIATED AN $820,000 REDUCTION IN PROJECT STORAGE COSTS.

INTRODUCTION BY DANIEL WAGNER

Jeremy Ball is not just a member of the Academy; he has over the years become a good friend of mine. Apart from our passion for business we also share many interests, one of them being nutrition and health.

I met Jeremy at an event in 2009, where I shared a stage with UK billionaires James Caan and Duncan Bannatyne amongst others. Jeremy invested in one of my courses and I immediately recognised his creative and entrepreneurial talent.

He had many great ideas, and I was able to help him to select the Master Vendor List as the one project with the largest scope and potential, while still helping Jeremy fulfil his ideal lifestyle.

Jeremy recently re-joined the Expert Success Academy and has made a tremendous impact on the group. His knowledge, enthusiasm and willingness to help stand out and has enabled much progress.

Although the Master Vendor List is still in its infancy, the potential and the wealth that can be created from it are absolutely huge.

But it is important to point out that even the best idea is worth nothing unless implemented properly. This is exactly why Jeremy has sought the support of the Expert Success Academy and its members.

What I love about the business model that Jeremy has proposed is that it is very scalable, needs very little involvement from Jeremy or other team members, and is highly profitable.

It is rare that I look at a member's business model and think that it is even better than my own but Jeremy's Master Vendor List for the Oil and Gas industry is one of thoe rare exceptions.

I am extremely excited for Jeremy and his project and I can't wait for him to make his first million and report this progress in the Expert Success Academy.

Daniel Wagner

AN INTERVIEW WITH JEREMY BALL

JEREMY, WHAT MADE YOU GET IN TO OIL & GAS?

I kind of fell in to it really. I didn't have the greatest time at school due to my inquisitive mind. I grew up in South Africa during the extremely conservative apartheid era and the schools were very disciplined. While I had no problem with discipline, I asked way too many controversial questions and I was made out to be a disturbing influence. I was made to feel that my inquisitive mind was a bad thing and I left school with very low self-esteem and no desire to do any further education.

My father was a warehouse manager on the construction of the SASOL 2 and 3 refineries in Secunda, South Africa at the time so when I left school he organised a job for me on the refinery. That was what got me into Oil & Gas.

HAVE YOU ALWAYS BEEN IN SUPPLY CHAIN MANAGEMENT?

No. As I only had a high school diploma when I joined the industry I started out as an apprentice boilermaker. While it was not my ideal job, I learnt a vast amount from it and it gave me a real appreciation for what the construction side of the industry was all about. And this was the final step in the life of an EPC project.

After my time on the tools I also gained experience in human resources and engineering. My time in human resources allowed me to appreciate the human side of the business and I learnt the value of people. In engineering I learnt a lot about design and got an insight into how companies establish their material requirements for a project.

WHAT WAS YOUR MAIN GOAL FOR LAST YEAR?

In 2010 I accepted a position with a subsea company to head up their procurement department in Angola. It was a very challenging assignment as shortly after joining the company they merged with one of their competitors in January 2011. My role changed significantly and I was not only responsible for setting up one department but also managing the integration of both companies into a single building. My goal for last year was to leave behind a completely integrated and self-motivated department capable of supporting high profile projects.

Not only did I achieve my goal but, I made a positive impact on every team member's personal life – something I am extremely proud of.

WHAT SORT OF EXPERT ARE YOU?

After 25 years of being in the industry I am an expert in efficiency within SCM. My unusual upbringing and career path has given me a unique understanding of the overall supply chain which allows me to see a wider spectrum of potential bottlenecks when implementing procedures. I make a point of considering any/all potential interfaces and through collaboration find workable, easy to implement systems that benefit everyone concerned.

I also consider myself to be an expert in developing teams. By motivating and inspiring people to live fuller and more passionate lives, they not only learn to value their own lives but also those of their colleagues. They learn the value of the team over the individual and that creates strong, collaborative teams with vastly improved performance.

Developing teams is an important skill.

WHAT MADE YOU CREATE MASTERVENDORLIST.COM?

The problem of unmaintained databases filled with out of date vendor information had been a constant frustration throughout my career. I encountered the same problem on every project I ever worked on. Regardless of whether I was working for Oil & Gas companies or for an EPC contractor I constantly wasted thousands of hours sourcing vendors and vendor contact information.

It all came to a head in 2009 while working on a $20billion project. We had a team of about eight people who spent over six months searching the internet and trawling through outdated vendor lists to source vendors for our project bidders list, only to find that 38% of the vendors we had found could not be contacted because the email addresses we had were incorrect.

After many discussions with my colleagues about the need for a centralised database, one of them said, 'Jeremy. You know no one is going to go through all the effort of doing this so you'll have to do it.' And that started me off.

WHAT QUALIFICATIONS DID YOU NEED?

Rather than qualifications, what was needed was two very different skillsets. The first was an in-depth understanding of the procurement process, in particular the bid process including vendor sourcing. The second was an understanding of material management systems and automation, a skill I had from being systems administrator for two material management systems and an SAP expert.

HAVE YOU MADE MISTAKES ALONG THE WAY?

Yes of course. This was my first ever venture on my own so I was bound to make mistakes. I was only just learning about internet technologies and how best to implement my idea. While I was very sure of how the software would work, I knew very little about the IT side of it and I learnt some very hard lessons. But they benefited MasterVendorList.com as now it is a far superior product than it was when it first launched.

I also learnt about the value of having expert status because although people who knew me were well aware of my ability and my trustworthy character, others didn't and this had a detrimental effect on my ability to sell MasterVendorList. com. While the concept and benefits were obvious, the prospects wanted to know who was behind it. They wanted to know:

1. Could I deliver? Did I have the necessary experience and ability?

2. Would I deliver? Would I follow through?

3. What was my reputation like? What were past colleagues and peers saying about me? Could I be trusted?

I had not considered any of these and they cost me dearly.

HOW DID YOU MEET DANIEL WAGNER?

I met Daniel in January 2009 at a wealth conference and annual dinner in London that had Duncan Bannatyne and James Caan as speakers. I attended the dinner with a view to talking to Duncan as I had a lottery idea I was very keen to talk to him about. Unfortunately due to a bizarre series of events I didn't get to speak to Duncan, but I was very glad I attended.

Daniel was also a speaker at that event and on the second day of the conference he delivered a talk on internet marketing and I was blown away. He was obviously very nervous but who wouldn't be sharing a stage with Duncan Bannatyne and James Caan? His vulnerability and openness made him an extremely compelling speaker.

Having heard his story I connected with him as we had a lot in common and I was so inspired by his talk that I signed up for his three-day workshop.

WHAT ATTRACTED YOU TO THE EXPERT SUCCESS ACADEMY?

As mentioned previously, one of the mistakes I made during the early days of MasterVendorList.com was not displaying credibility. While people loved the concept they doubted its credibility because they didn't trust it. It (and I) was an unknown. All though MasterVendorList.com is not a new concept as such, it is a completely new way of delivering the solution. And, as with any new venture, people need convincing. I had not even considered this as being a problem but it proved extremely detrimental.

I had done numerous internet marketing courses with Daniel since 2009 and we had developed a friendship along the way. When I returned from Africa in December 2012 and heard about the Expert Success Academy, it was exactly what I needed for my venture.

HOW WILL THE EXPERT SUCCESS ACADEMY HELP WITH THAT?

I have two clear objectives for the coming year. The first is to continue to grow MasterVendorList.com as the only global vendor-sourcing tool for the Oil & Gas and Petrochemical industries and the second is to build my own personal brand.

The Expert Success Academy is a key part of that strategy. The wealth of information and experience that Daniel and his business partner James Watson have accumulated is extremely valuable. They are continuously finding, testing and applying the very latest sales and marketing techniques to their own business. As a member of the Expert Success Academy I am able to tap straight in to that knowledge and apply their proven strategies to grow MasterVendorList.com which saves me valuable time and resources.

As well as the Expert Success Academy, their Online Brand Masterclass was the perfect solution for my second objective: developing my personal brand. With my personal website as the main hub, I now have a structured, consistent brand stretching across various social media platforms including Twitter, Facebook and LinkedIn. This strategic branding allows me to establish myself as an expert in my field and increases my credibility and, therefore, the credibility of MasterVendorList.com.

Experts need to display credibility.

IF YOU COULD GO BACK AND DO IT ALL AGAIN, WHAT WOULD YOU DO DIFFERENTLY ON MASTERVENDORLIST.COM?

Everything! Only kidding. I definitely could and probably should have done things very differently but having said that I did what I thought was best at the time. I don't see making mistakes as a bad thing and I would rather do something and make mistakes, than not do anything just to avoid making them.

KEY LEARNINGS

- Don't be afraid to make mistakes. If you do you'll be too afraid to try something that might make a massive improvement.

- Believe in yourself. You are unique and no one else has had the exact experiences you have had.

- Friends and family don't want you to get hurt so they may try to dissuade you from putting yourself out there. Find people who will support you. Find like-minded people you can learn from and who inspire you

- It will take longer and cost far more than you originally imagine but don't give up. Sometimes you just have to take the setback, learn the lessons and keep moving forward.

MARIE REYNOLDS HEALTH AND WELLNESS EXPERT

Helping People Find a Balance in their Lives

TRANSFORM

mariebreynolds@gmail.com
07970 905839

Marie is a health and wellness coach. She has worked in the health, nutrition and weight management industry for over 15 years. Marie has inspired, motivated and encouraged thousands of clients to achieve their own health and weight management goals. Her passion is combining her expert knowledge of health and wellness with personal development to help people transform their lives. She previously spent 20+ years in the hotel and catering industry.

- **Qualifications:** Certified Coach for Dr Sear's LEAN (Lifestyle, Exercise, Attitude, Nutrition) Health Programmes. Certified Health and Wellness Coach with The Health Coaching Training Company USA. Style and Image Consultant. Member of Tony Robbins Leadership Academy.

- **Personal Achievement:** Established and was Chairperson of the Tony Robbins Powerteam in Northern Ireland.

❝ MY BIGGEST CHALLENGE WAS STEPPING OUTSIDE OF MY COMFORT ZONE.

INTRODUCTION BY DANIEL WAGNER

My first memory of Marie is when I noticed her at our Expert Success Summit in September 2012 during one of the many hands-on exercises, where I urged the attendees to work on their 'Earn the Right'.

The 'Earn the Right' is in essence a short paragraph or sound bite that allows your prospects or counterparts to quickly understand that you indeed have the right to speak on a specific subject matter.

Marie bravely volunteered to get some life coaching from me in the room, and I was able to demonstrate how easily and quickly we can create the perception of more expertise which in turn creates more authority.

She must have enjoyed the experience because shortly afterwards she volunteered again to get coaching on how to double or triple turnover to create a six- and multi-six-figure business.

I believe it was at that moment when Marie realised that she could benefit from joining the Expert Success Academy. Marie flies in every month from Ireland to join us as a Platinum Member of the Expert Success Academy.

I also distinctly recall a three-hour coaching session where Marie and her husband flew in to work on her business model. She would certainly testify that the breakthroughs, clarity and focus helped tremendously in creating the change that she desired.

What is fascinating about Marie's story is that she already was an expert in her field of weight loss and nutrition, but as part of Weight Watchers she was part of a company that did not reward her according to her expertise and authority.

There are thousands of people like Marie who have expertise and skill, but who are not paid as much as they should be. The only way to get paid what you deserve is to actually start to write your own cheques – or in other words start your own business and follow the Expert Success Formula.

Daniel Wagner

AN INTERVIEW WITH MARIE REYNOLDS

MARIE, TELL ME ABOUT THE EARLY DAYS.

On leaving school I began my career in the hospitality and catering industry. From an early age I knew I enjoyed meeting and dealing with people so at age 21, and following the death of my father, I went to work in a large hotel in San Mateo, USA. I gained invaluable experience there and on my return to Northern Ireland I continued with my career in the hospitality and tourism sector. In the years that followed I went on to manage a number of very prestigious hotels across Northern Ireland. In 1996 I was approached by a Belfast-based training company to join their team. I was very excited at the prospect of being headhunted but unfortunately the role did not meet with my expectations. I was not at all happy in the new role and I resigned. Little did I know it then but that was to become a life-changing decision. I found myself unemployed for the first time in my career and in the following months my self-esteem plummeted. I found comfort in food and before long I was piling on the pounds. My body weight increased rapidly and substantially. I found myself in that 'pain and pleasure' cycle: feel bad; eat comfort food; regret; feel bad again; eat more comfort food. Is this sounding familiar?

WHAT HAPPENED FROM THERE?

I knew I had to break the cycle. A friend of mine invited me to go along to the local Weight Watchers class with her. Talk about a light-bulb moment! I loved it. The camaraderie, the information around health and proper nutrition, and the motivational after-class talks. I was soon back in control, losing weight and restoring my confidence. Following my weight loss success I was afforded the opportunity to become a Weight Watchers' franchisee. 'As one door closes another door opens,' as the saying goes. I had found my new niche. For the first time I understood 'health is wealth'. As a result of my rollercoaster of emotions journey I was now passionate about my health and wanted to share the message with others. For the following 15 years I went on to educate, motivate, inspire and encourage thousands of people (of all ages and from all walks of life) to achieve their health and weight management and lifestyle goals. Losing any amount of weight is considered a success. However, two of my male clients during that time lost 17 stone and 14 stone respectively. Life changing stuff!

HAVE YOU DONE ANY OTHER TRAINING PROGRAMMES?

It's great that my husband Stephen and I are equally passionate about the world of personal and professional development. Over the last 15 years we have attended and crewed for Tony Robbins (considered the world's leading motivational speaker) at locations around the world. We are members of The Tony Robbins Leadership Academy. We have walked on fire and participated in 'The Leap of Faith'. I have also attended various leadership and training seminars and invested in my own knowledge of nutrition, health, life balance and general wellbeing.

HOW DID YOU MEET DANIEL WAGNER?

Another girlfriend – another invite! She invited me to accompany her to Daniel Wagner's Expert Success Summit in London. By now I was already considering stepping away from Weight Watchers to launch my own new health and wellness business.

I spent three days with Daniel Wagner and his business partner James Watson and by the end of that weekend I was convinced.

WHAT ATTRACTED YOU TO THE ACADEMY?

Jack Canfield (the motivational speaker and author) would ask 'How do you get from where you are to where you want to go?' That's what attracted me to the Academy, because I didn't have a clear strategy on how to move forward with my business. I believed that Tony Robbins had armed me with the tools and the skillset required in launching my new business. Now

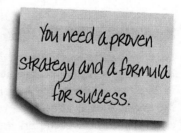
You need a proven strategy and a formula for success.

Daniel Wagner's Expert Success Academy was providing me with a proven strategy and a formula for success for that same new business.

WHAT QUALIFICATIONS DID YOU NEED?

That is a great question! My husband Stephen would say I excel in this arena. Why? Because I always believed I couldn't do things because I did not have the relevant qualification or certificate. Another important message I got from the Academy is *'claim your expert status'*. People want to know that you care – not care what you know. By now I had 15 years hands-on experience of health and wellness.

APART FROM THE ACADEMY DO YOU GO TO ANY OTHER NETWORKING EVENTS?

Yes I have recently joined a local Business Networking Group in my area. I have found this to be a great way to meet and network with other business people.

I am also a member of a number of Women's Networking Groups across Northern Ireland.

DO YOU HAVE ANY OTHER BUSINESSES?

My husband and I are passionate about our health. In 2010 we travelled to the USA to research a company called NSA Juice Plus+. As a result we now own a franchise in Northern Ireland and consider Juice Plus+ to be the world's leading wholefood nutritional supplement.

For the past 23 years we have owned and operated *The Front Page*, a town centre public house situated in our hometown of Ballymena. We were recently awarded Northern Ireland's *Community Pub of the Year* award and over the years we have raised tens of thousands of pounds for local charities. The award was in recognition of the pub's on-going contribution to the local economy and the community of the borough.

If you ever find yourself in the locality please call in – we would love to see you. The Front Page is well known for a great pint of Guinness so it's ironic that I don't drink alcohol and it is always a great topic of conversation: I come from Ireland, I don't drink but I own a pub!

WHERE ARE YOU NOW?

I'm on the journey of establishing my own health and wellness coaching business. My time at the Expert Success Academy is keeping me focused on how to advance my business.

HAVE YOU HAD ANY CHALLENGES?

Yes, lots of challenges. The biggest challenge was stepping outside of my comfort zone: making the decision to leave Weight Watchers to go out on my own. I pondered that one for quite some time. One day it would be yes go for it and the next day it would be no, wait a while longer. The Expert Success Summit helped me to make that decision.

Step outside your comfort zone.

WHAT DOES THE FUTURE HOLD?

I will establish my own coaching business that educates, motivates, inspires and encourages people to make the necessary changes in their lifestyle. I will have an online membership site offering webinars, group coaching and motivational help to my clients.

KEY LEARNINGS

- Believe in yourself. It can be easy to have self-doubt and not see the great person you really are.

- Keep focused. 'Energy flows where focus goes', so always focus on what you want, not what you don't want.

- Action speaks louder than words. Sometimes we know what to do but don't do what we know. Decide. Commit. Take action.

- Never Give Up. Forget all the reasons why it won't work and believe all the reasons why it will.

KEVIN MCDONNELL
PROPERTY
INVESTMENT EXPERT

Helping You Create Wealth Through Professional Property Investment

www.kevinmcdonnell.co.uk
kevin@kevinmcdonnell.co.uk
07787 965902

Since 2007, Kevin has created a property portfolio worth more than £1million, with a four-figure monthly positive cash flow from a starting point of £135k of debt having initially made the mistake of investing in overseas property without any education in property investing. He has created his own unique Five-Step Formula to Successful Property Investing which he now uses to teach others how they too can build a successful property business. Kevin studied Engineering and Quality Management and after finishing university he left Ireland to begin a career in Quality Management for one of the largest construction companies in the UK.

- **Qualifications:** BSc in Quality Management.

- **Credibility:** I have spent over £30k since 2007 to be mentored by some of the top property investors in the UK and have used this learning to build a £1million property portfolio with a four-figure monthly positive cash flow and all from a starting point of £135k of debt.

- **Personal Lifetime Achievements:** Going from £135k of debt to earning more from property every month than the average UK salary in six years. I have represented the Republic of Ireland at the World and European Pool Championships.

PUBLICATIONS

The 7 Biggest Mistakes When Starting Out in Property and How to Avoid Them, self-published.

❝ I CREATED A PROPERTY PORTFOLIO WORTH MORE THAN £1MILLION.

INTRODUCTION BY DANIEL WAGNER

Kevin is one of the many property investors that have found me and my work through my strategic partners Progressive Property. Kevin is one of the quiet ones but you know what they say about still waters – they do run deep!

One of the great features of our unique Online Brand Masterclass workshop is that we work with one of the UK's top portrait photographers John Cassidy. John is well known in the industry for taking amazing photographs of people who hate having their photograph taken – which is, in essence, pretty much everyone!

John makes everybody laugh and it is my strong belief that as a rule people look best when they smile. But I also know that rules are there to be broken, and when it came to choosing Kevin's photograph at the end of the workshop we all agreed that the picture you see in this book was the one that stood out.

When Kevin shared his personal story over the weekend of the workshop, people were touched and moved. One of the special features of the OBM workshop and the Academy is that we are in a safe environment that allows us to share our true vision and goals.

Kevin totally trusted the process and it was wonderful to see how quickly he moved towards achieving the results he aspired to.

There are thousands of people who invest in property in the UK and many of them are looking for financing, deals or joint venture partners. It is simply wise to create an online presence that works for you 24/7 to qualify your prospects.

The two big questions about branding are 'who are you' and 'why should people care'. And it is those two key questions that Kevin answers with his personal brand site.

Kevin has shown initiative, resilience and vision and I'm looking forward to seeing him achieve his dreams and goals with the support of the Expert Success Academy.

Daniel Wagner

AN INTERVIEW WITH KEVIN MCDONNELL

KEVIN, HOW DID YOU GET INTO PROPERTY?

For as long as I can remember I have always had this burning ambition to achieve great things. I remember finishing school and not really knowing how I would set about achieving these ambitions so I began my journey by going to university – more because my family wanted me to do something and I didn't really have any other options. While at university I rented a room in a shared house with other students. Our landlord used to call around every week and collect the rent. I found out he had a few houses in the area all let out and I started to think what a great life this was and how much freedom he had.

After finishing university I moved to London in 2002. One of the guys I shared a house with was from South Africa and he was investing in property in Johannesburg. We would regularly talk about investing and my interest really started to grow. In 2004, we attended a free three-hour property education seminar in London and during the presentation we decided that the cost of training was too expensive and we were smart enough to do it on our own. I mean, how difficult could it be? Well it actually turned out to be very difficult and it cost me years of time and £135k.

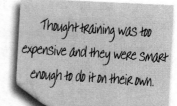

Thought training was too expensive and they were smart enough to do it on their own.

HAVE YOU MADE MISTAKES ALONG THE WAY?

Yes, I've made many mistakes. Making the decision to start investing without any training was a massive mistake. After attending the free property seminar in London in 2004, I set about building my portfolio with no property education and decided that the best method was to invest in cheap properties in Eastern Europe that would give me good capital growth. A friend was investing abroad in South Africa so I naively thought this was the best strategy. Over the next three years I bought myself three foreign properties at an outlay of £135k all of which turned out to be toxic debt. To this day one has never even been built and another is in an apartment complex that has never opened. I learnt an important lesson that cheap does not always mean valuable and there is no guarantee of capital appreciation. Cash flow is King! Staring at financial ruin, I had two options:

1.   Give up.

2.   Lick my wounds, get educated and move forward.

Thankfully I choose option two.

The key thing I have learned is not to worry about making mistakes. Everybody makes mistakes. The important thing is to learn from them and keep moving forward. You will make more good decisions than bad and the more you practice, the better you get.

Don't worry, everyone makes mistakes.

HOW DID YOU MEET DANIEL WAGNER?

I had been receiving emails from Daniel since 2007 and used to read them but never got in touch with him as he wasn't directly involved in property and this was where my focus was. Then in 2012 I received an email from him regarding his new book Expert Success. I was at the point where I had cleared my debts and was looking to help other people who found themselves in a similar place to where I was. I decided to buy the book and attend one of his seminars to see how he may be able to help me. From the moment I met him at that seminar I was sold on what he was teaching. It was the missing ingredient that I was looking for to build my business. I would urge anyone who is looking to make a change in their life to get a copy of Expert Success.

WHAT ATTRACTED YOU TO THE EXPERT SUCCESS ACADEMY?

Having met Daniel and his business partner, James Watson, at one of their one-day seminars and getting more insight into the Expert Success Formula, I knew I needed to have them working with me to take my business to the next level. I love their straight-talking, honest approach and the fact they always have time to spend with you and guide you. The benefit of being part of a group of experts from various different business sectors really is priceless.

DID YOU ATTEND ANY OTHER TRAINING PROGRAMMES?

Yes, since 2007 I have spent over £30k being educated on property investing by some of the UK's top property investors. Without this education I would not have cleared my debts and built my passive income to its current level. Unlike the Expert Success Academy, all my previous training programmes have focused directly around property investment education. The Expert Success Academy really is unique and without it I would not have been able to build my personal brand or have the online presence that I now enjoy. I now have people contacting me looking to invest in my projects and I have also set up a mentorship programme where I teach other people how to build their own property portfolios.

WHAT ADVICE WOULD YOU GIVE TO OTHERS?

Just get started but your first step needs to be getting educated. You will still make some mistakes but not as many or as costly as those you will make without education. You wouldn't be allowed to operate on someone without being a qualified surgeon so why should you think you can do other jobs without education? Don't worry about making mistakes. I made lots of mistakes but if I worried about making mistakes I would never have got started and would not be where I am today.

People contact him to invest in his projects.

Remember: The cost of inaction is far greater than the cost of making a mistake.

WHAT ARE YOUR GOALS FOR THIS YEAR?

- Continue to build my online brand www.kevinmcdonnell.co.uk.

- Personally mentor three people to build their property investment knowledge and portfolios.

- Purchase five properties for my own portfolio. Remember it's not the quantity of properties you buy that's important; it's what each property gives you as a return on your investment.

- Be interviewed on Irish radio as a property expert.

WHERE DO YOU PUT YOUR ENERGY?

That's a great question! Every person has the same amount of time in their day; it's what you do with that time that sets you apart from the masses. I used to waste countless hours surfing the internet looking at properties and looking at articles on forums, reading the wrong information. When I found a property to buy I would carry out the refurbishment work myself, which inevitably took longer and was not done to the standard a professional renovation expert would do it to.

Being part of the Expert Success Academy has helped me to focus on what actually adds value to my business. I now understand the true meaning of leverage and use this to fit so much more into my days. I focus on what I'm good at, which is finding great investment deals, and let others do the refurbishment. My time spent on the internet is more focused on my brand and not on other people. The Expert Success Academy helped me to concentrate on my own brand and businesses and stop spending most of my time and energy looking at other people's businesses.

He'll concentrate on his own brand and businesses.

WHAT DOES THE FUTURE HOLD FOR YOU?

The future is really exciting. Since joining the Expert Success Academy I have realised that I can achieve anything that I set out to achieve. I will continue to build my personal property portfolio and build other property related businesses alongside this. I'm currently starting a portfolio building service to buy and manage properties for people who wish to own property investments but don't have the skill or time to achieve this. I also plan to grow my property education business to offer a unique service that teaches people the various strategies they can use to invest but also to make them aware of all the pitfalls that they could face along the way.

One of my other ambitions is to open a lettings agency that all properties will be managed through, so there are some really exciting times ahead.

HOW WILL THE EXPERT SUCCESS ACADEMY HELP WITH THAT?

It has already helped me in numerous ways, from giving me clarity on where

I am heading, building of my online brand and giving me the confidence and belief to take my business to the next level. The advice and support you get from the group is amazing. I can't think of another place where you have so many experts working together to support each other to achieve their goals and aspirations. It really does drive you forward and I couldn't even start to put a value on what I have gained from being a part of the Academy.

 **KEY LEARNINGS**

- Clearly define what you want to achieve.

- Do something you enjoy. There will be difficult times and it's the love of what you do that will get you through them.

- Harness the power of leverage. Other people's time, money and experience will take you further than you ever thought possible.

- Don't try to do everything on your own. It will slow you down and cost you more.

- Get Educated. There is no better saying than 'You don't know what you don't know'.

- Get a coach and join a group of like-minded people. Working alone can be really difficult and having a group of like-minded people to call upon when you need support is invaluable.

ANTHONY CHADWICK (BVSc Cert VD) ONLINE CPD EXPERT

Revolutionising Online Learning for Vets and Pet Owners

The Webinar Vet

www.thewebinarvet.com
anthony@thewebinarvet.com
07540 173462

Anthony Chadwick qualified as a vet in 1990 from Liverpool University. He has a special interest in veterinary dermatology and education. In 2010 he set up The Webinar Vet to make veterinary education easier for his fellow professionals.

- **Qualifications:** The Royal College Certificate in Veterinary Dermatology.

- **Credibility:** World leader in veterinary education using webinars, with over 16,000 vets and nurses on our database. We have over 1,000 members who pay a monthly or yearly amount to access our webinars.

- **Personal Achievements:** Won *The Frank Beattie Travel Scholarship*, 1997.

INTRODUCTION BY DANIEL WAGNER

I met Anthony Chadwick about three years ago at one of my internet marketing events. He stood out to me straight away, not just because he is 6'3", but because of the calm and collected way he was asking questions.

Anthony was one of two people who signed up for my course back then, which was simply based on online marketing techniques. He had just completed a course with Steven Essa, a webinar expert from Australia. He was excited and determined to use webinars to deliver training to his peer group: vets.

What started out as a slightly crazy idea has turned him into one of the most successful information marketers in the UK. Having already built a multi-six-figure (I'm sure it will hit seven figures this year) business, that he runs very part-time!

There are very few people who personify what the Expert Success Formula stands for more than Anthony. He has indeed become a micro-celebrity in his market niche, and he is now known all over the world as the webinar vet.

Anthony is also a fantastic example of having a big vision but taking small consistent steps towards it. From his first members paying him just £10-£20, he has built a multitier membership site with over a thousand members, producing enviable passive recurring income while helping vets improve their work-life balance.

Only a year ago Anthony was finally able to sell his vet practice to fully concentrate on his information marketing empire. Anthony has become a good friend of mine, sharing his valuable experience in the Mastermind group for the third year running.

Like many creative entrepreneurs Anthony has benefited from the Expert Success Academy. From having our coaches watch for his 'blind spots' and from the Academy members' feedback and second opinions. This has helped generate hundreds of thousands of pounds in extra revenue and also avoided some possibly dangerous pitfalls and wrong turns.

I feel privileged to have been part of Anthony's great success but I admit jokingly that he would still have become successful even if I had tried to stop him!

Daniel Wagner

AN INTERVIEW WITH ANTHONY CHADWICK

ANTHONY, WHY DID YOU DECIDE TO BECOME A VET?

I have always wanted to be a vet. I must have only been about eight when I first decided that veterinary medicine was the thing for me. I became an addict of James Herriot books and I remember a friend inadvertently stepping on a baby bird in the playground at school and thinking that had I been a vet I may have been able to save it.

WHAT QUALIFICATIONS DID YOU NEED?

Other ideas came and went but the idea of becoming a vet stayed firm and, although I was unable to get my A-levels first time I managed to pass them the second time, and in 1985 I began my veterinary education at my home town university in Liverpool. In 1990 I duly qualified and worked at a mixed practice in Wales for two years developing small animal and large animal skills. After about two years I gravitated back to Liverpool where I developed a special interest in dermatology and I began to study for the Royal College Certificate in Veterinary Dermatology. This gave me the dubious honour of being able to put Cert VD after my name! In 1997 I won the Frank Beattie Travel Scholarship which was awarded at the British Small Animal Veterinary Conference: this allowed me to travel to America to Cornell University for a period of study.

WHERE DID YOU DECIDE TO PRACTICE?

At the end of 1997 I opened my own practice in Croxteth Park, Liverpool and stayed there for about 12 years until 2009 when I moved my practice from there to a better and more central position in Liverpool.

WAS IT PLAIN SAILING?

I moved the practice at the height of the credit crunch; the banker promised to give me money but in the end didn't give me all the money they had promised and I had to take other loans out at high interest levels to manage to complete the building. This made life quite difficult and over the 12 years that I had run the practice I began to realise that although I loved to be a vet, I did not really care to be a manager of a practice.

SO WHAT DID YOU DO ABOUT IT?

At the end of 2009 I began to look at other ways that I could supplement my income. I was fascinated by the internet. I felt that this was a massive resource, a huge infrastructure that we had to pay very little to be a part of, and so in early 2010 I went to an internet conference in London which was being hosted by Mark Anastasi. I was fascinated by the different energies in the room compared with veterinary congresses; this event was very lively, with music playing and people pitching from the front. In the end I decided to spend some money with a man called Steven Essa, an Australian, who was talking about webinars. I was fascinated by his presentation and I realised that there was a perfect opportunity here to use webinars to help to educate vets.

HOW COULD THE INTERNET HELP VETS?

As vets we have to do 35 hours per annum of continuing professional development (CPD) as stipulated by the Royal College of Veterinary Surgeons. Often we have to travel long distances to find relevant training, and my idea was that we could bring the training into people's houses in the form of a webinar. Very soon The Webinar Vet was born and from the very early days it proved to be very successful: people loved the concept; they came on the webinars and we began to make money selling webinars to vets.

WHEN DID YOU FIRST MEET DANIEL WAGNER?

I first met Daniel Wagner in March 2010 about three months after I'd started my Webinar Vet business. I was still running my practice in Liverpool and having met him I decided that I would join his Platinum mentoring group that met once a month in London. Within six months I decided to join his Mastermind group along with nine other businesses and I have never really looked back from this.

HOW DID DANIEL HELP YOU?

I am not an internet tech person but I knew what I wanted to achieve with the internet and have got the right people in my team. Daniel has often helped me in suggesting the ideal piece of software I might need. Our regular monthly meetings have kept me accountable to him, James Watson and the rest of the Mastermind group. I always want to be progressing my business and moving closer to the fulfilment of my mission of making veterinary education affordable and accessible to vets worldwide. It is good when you are the sole owner of a business to have advisors that you can go to and chat about ideas that you have. I have always found Daniel to be a good listener in these situations. I could have built this business without outside help but mentors help you to do things quicker. Daniel is a very positive individual and this rubs off when you work with him. I also feel very positive about my business's direction.

I am a huge believer in the value of mentorship, I think that Daniel has brought me the ability to sound ideas off against him; he's introduced me to new pieces of software, new ideas, new ways of doing things and many of the things that we now do have certainly been shaped and helped by some of the suggestions that Daniel has made.

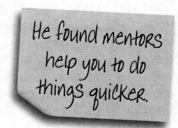

He found mentors help you to do things quicker.

I continue to work with Daniel after three years. I think the three main areas that he has helped me in are:

- Accountability

- Technology

- Mindset

AND WHAT WAS THE BENEFIT OF JOINING THE EXPERT SUCCESS ACADEMY?

As well as the great value and mentorship there is also a similar value in the new connections that I have made over the last three years. Many of the people that I have met in Daniel's Mastermind group have become friends and we work together on projects.

He works together on projects with other Mastermind group members.

COULD YOU GIVE US AN EXAMPLE OF HOW THAT WORKS?

Well, for example Alan Robinson and I are both vets. We knew each other before I met Daniel and I encouraged him to join the Mastermind group with me. We present monthly webinars on practice management for vets to better manage their practice. Gillian Fox writes copy for me for my website and for my emails, Richard Hill did some search engine optimisation on my site, Keith Watson helped to build my site in the early stages, and more recently Sophia James and Nigel Hedge have helped to build some websites for vets who are in my own Platinum membership group on the Webinar Vet.

WHAT EFFECT HAS THIS HAD ON YOUR BUSINESS?

When I met Daniel I had a small, fledgling business with a great idea and lots of potential, but to turn that potential into actual results was always going to be difficult. Over the last three years we've grown to be a world leader in veterinary education in the format of webinars. Many people have begun to copy our approach, which is of course a great form of flattery. We have over 1,000 members who pay a monthly or yearly amount to access our webinars. We hold the webinars three to four times a week and there is great value in the membership. All of the webinars are recorded and our site now has several hundreds of hours of veterinary education on it, a huge resource for the veterinary profession. We have over 16,000 vets and nurses on our database, but this is a relatively small percentage so we still have lots of work to do.

WHERE DO YOU SEE YOUR BUSINESS GOING?

My mission very early on was to make veterinary education affordable and accessible to vets worldwide and in January 2013 we ran a Virtual Congress all day one Saturday. We had 350 vets register from 27 different nations. This was thrilling to me because it proved that we were getting closer to our mission all the time. The quality of our training is fantastic.

He had a mission.

We have vet trainers from North America, Australia and Europe, as well as the UK. Many of my vets now do much more CPD than they need to. This makes them better vets.

HAVE YOU THOUGHT OF DIVERSIFYING?

Since we set up the Webinar Vet we have also set up other Webinar services for suitably qualified persons (SQPs). These are people who are able to dispense and sell certain drugs in pet shops and in farm merchant stores. We also have a site which is called www.petwebinars.co.uk and that is there to help educate pet owners because I am passionate about animal welfare. I am committed to getting ideas across to make people better pet owners.

WHAT EFFECT DID THESE NEW BUSINESSES HAVE ON YOUR VET PRACTICE?

In 2011, 12 months after starting The Webinar Vet, I was able to sell my practice to two friends so that I could concentrate more on the Webinar Vet, and on my great love which is dermatology. In the last year I have spoken to vets in Iceland, the south of France and in the UK and I am able to build my reputation as a veterinary dermatologist off the back of the things that I've been able to do with the Webinar Vet. I have presented many hours of dermatology on the webinars and the flexibility it offers has allowed me to spend more time to care for my mum and dad who both, unfortunately, have dementia.

WHAT HAVE YOU LEARNED PERSONALLY, SINCE JOINING THE EXPERT SUCCESS ACADEMY?

One of my key learnings over the last couple of years was the idea of do what you love and be in flow. If you're in flow then work is very easy, and in fact I don't feel that I work anymore – I have a hobby, which is called The Webinar Vet. I learnt about being in flow at a Mastermind retreat a couple of years ago when a speaker called John Williams (the author of *Screw Work Let's Play*) introduced the concept of wealth dynamics, which had been founded by Roger Hamilton, an entrepreneur based in Bali. Through studying his profiles and his spectrums I realised that I was a star creator: I love to create things. I'm not necessarily great at finishing jobs off but I'm one of those unusual people who would actually like to give the oration rather than lie in the coffin at a funeral. It's said that people's greatest fear in life is speaking in public and their second is dying. My first fear is definitely not speaking in public and by being able to put myself in that position more often I am in flow because I am doing what I love.

WHAT ARE THE BENEFITS OF BEING IN FLOW?

When you are in flow, there is a dynamism and energy that attracts people towards you. On many occasions over the last few years I have had people approaching me who want to work with me. I have not had to approach them.

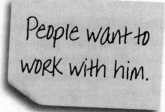

People want to work with him.

HAVE YOU FORMED ANY SPECIFIC JOINT VENTURES?

Over the last three years we have built up very powerful partnerships with the British Veterinary Association and with the Royal College of Veterinary Surgeons, and I think that all of these things have helped me to grow the business into the successful place that it is in today.

SO WHAT DOES THE FUTURE HOLD FOR YOU?

I have learnt to be much more focused and goal-orientated in the last three years. I write my goals down each year. Although I don't reach them all I do a lot better than when I did not have goals. I am very positive about life: I do what I want when I want. I can work anywhere in the world and I am providing a really valuable service for my fellow vets. I don't know what the future holds but I am blessed in that I enjoy what I do!

KEY LEARNINGS

- Do what you love and be in flow.

- I do a lot better when I have goals.

- Mentors help you to do things quicker.

GORDON ROBINSON
DIGITAL BUSINESS EXPERT

Helping Businesses Succeed In The Digital Economy

Online Expert Solutions

www.gordonrobinson.org
www.onlineexpertsolutions.com
gordon@workwithgordon.com
07786 432013

Gordon Robinson is the owner and founder of Online Expert Solutions, a company created to help businesses succeed in the Digital Economy. Gordon has 20 years business experience, which helped him formulate his Five-Step Formula to Business Success. Gordon is also a passionate family man and a keen sportsman, having completed 13 marathons and an Ironman triathlon. Gordon currently operates as an IT consultant and is in the process of establishing his Online Expert Solutions business. His end game is to help small businesses establish themselves with a better online presence through the five-step formula he has created. Gordon has worked for blue chip corporations as a business analyst and project manager for the past 14 years.

INTRODUCTION BY DANIEL WAGNER

By all accounts and measure of the western world, Gordon Robinson had it made. High paid job in the city, beautiful wife and kids, money and time to spare.

Yet something was eating away at him as he cruised for years from one uninspiring assignment to another, drifting towards middle-age. And like so many men in this situation, he started questioning what he was doing and why he was doing it.

The simple truth is that in his heart of hearts Gordon is an entrepreneur and wants to write the rules of his life. It isn't about the money, it isn't just about having more time and spending it as one sees fit, it's about fulfilment and purpose and doing something that is worthwhile.

Gordon started to look online for how he could equip himself with new skills to change his fortunes, and stumbled across one of my friends' websites.

What I found fascinating about Gordon's journey is that he was very passionate about wanting to change his life, yet he had no idea how to do that. This proves to me again that the Why is more important than the What and the How. I've heard it said that 'when the Why is clear, the How will be easy'.

I first met Gordon at one of our discovery days, and I saw that he was hanging on every word I said. It seems like he had found what he was looking for.

The next steps were predetermined. Gordon signed up for our Online Brand Masterclass three-day workshop and then decided to join the Expert Success Academy at the Diamond level.

Although Gordon has not yet made the transition to full-time entrepreneur he now has a plan and direction, which makes the journey easy.

One of the big breakthroughs with Gordon was to understand that he had unconscious competence and skills that people out there would be willing to pay for.

This is all anyone needs to start the journey to becoming a well-paid expert and start exploiting the lucrative expert industry.

Daniel Wagner

AN INTERVIEW WITH GORDON ROBINSON

GORDON, WHAT WAS YOUR MAIN GOAL FOR LAST YEAR?

That was my biggest problem. I had a pretty general goal of getting out of the corporate rat race and starting my own business but I actually had no idea of what I specifically wanted to do. I knew it had to be something online as I have this absolute belief that the internet will become the biggest phenomenon we have ever known and I wanted to make sure I was part of it.

> Only had a general goal of getting out of the corporate rat race and starting a business.

HOW DID YOU GET STARTED WITH THE IDEA OF ONLINE EXPERT SOLUTIONS?

Online Expert Solutions is a fairly new concept. About a year ago I started seriously exploring opportunities online and thought I could make easy money through a number of online businesses. I made a lot of mistakes but the learning curve was immense. It eventually led me to Daniel Wagner which is in truth where the penny dropped for me. The internet offers a huge amount of opportunities but you need guidance and that is now the cornerstone for my business.

YOU SAY YOU MADE MISTAKES ALONG THE WAY, CARE TO ELABORATE?

I think it happens when you are searching for something but are not sure what exactly. I have to admit it's easy to get caught out by clever marketers and there were times when I thought the easy online money schemes where my destiny. Luckily I have always had a solid income from consulting so while I did make mistakes and lose money, the process I went through was absolutely essential to getting me to where I am now.

WHEN DID YOU LEAVE YOUR JOB?

Strictly speaking I have not left my corporate IT consulting job (yet), although Online Expert Solutions is starting to play a bigger role.

HOW DID YOU MEET DANIEL WAGNER?

Part of the journey of exploration led me to join The Six Figure Mentors, a company co-founded by Daniel. Unfortunately for me, Daniel had moved on by the time I joined, but after watching several of his training videos I decided to buy his book, *Expert Success*. When I purchased the book I was given a ticket to one of his events and that is where I met him for the first time.

WHAT ATTRACTED YOU TO THE EXPERT SUCCESS ACADEMY?

Again, this is where I have to say that there was some sort of destiny about my journey. As an extension of The Six Figure Mentors I also became a Platinum Member of The Digital Experts Academy, a membership programme designed to teach you everything there is to know about being a digital entrepreneur. Part of the Platinum Membership is that you get to attend Daniel Wagner's Online Brand Masterclass. The irony is that I did not know that the Online Brand Masterclass was included in the Digital Experts Academy programme and was about to sign up independently: to me it was a sure sign I was heading down the right path.

DID YOU ATTEND ANY OTHER TRAINING PROGRAMMES?

Yes, as mentioned I am a member of The Six Figure Mentors and The Digital Experts Academy. Both offer excellent online mentoring and, along with many years practical experience, have allowed me to position myself as an expert in my field.

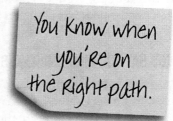
You know when you're on the right path.

WHAT HAPPENED NEXT?

Well this is where my journey gets really interesting. A few months ago I attended the Online Brand Masterclass and this is where the penny dropped for me. At the start of the course I openly admitted that I only had a general idea for a business but was not sure exactly what it was. During the three-day course I started to get real clarity on a number of things and through probing questions and a number of exercises Daniel helped me create Online Expert Solutions. The amazing thing for me was that there were people on that course that already had established businesses and yet the Masterclass catered for everyone.

WHAT DID YOU DO NEXT?

There is nothing like seeing a plan coming together. I now have a very clear action plan and am busy putting the final touches to my Five-Step Formula that will help me help other businesses succeed in the digital economy. I know there is a massive market for what I want to do and I have already started helping businesses create the online presence that will bring them more customers which equates to more revenue.

HAVE YOU HAD ANY CHALLENGES?

There are many challenges. For one I have three small children and one large mortgage and I am the sole income provider, so I need to make sure that money is coming in from my consultancy work. This unfortunately leaves me having to find extra time to fit it all in but I manage by working on the train and usually get some work done in the early and late hours of the day. Time is a challenge but not a showstopper. The other challenge that I am starting to deal with a lot better is managing the learning curve. I am taking so much in these days that it's easy to get ahead of myself and miss something important. I now try to slow the learning down so that I can fully understand and absorb the new information. And the last challenge is my own demons of stepping into the unknown. I am extremely excited about what I am doing and can see small victories every day but it's still an unknown experience for me. What I can say though is that life is too short and there is nothing like making things happen: action speaks louder than words!

WHAT ADVICE WOULD YOU GIVE TO OTHERS?

Get a mentor and don't be afraid to pay for expert advice. A few years back I would never have dreamed of paying someone else to teach me something new but now I cannot value my education highly enough. I would also say that you should never be afraid to fail, but try to fail forward. Also learn from your mistakes and never give up.

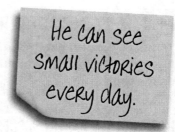

He can see small victories every day.

ANY TIPS YOU'D LIKE TO SHARE?

Yes, listen to Daniel Wagner and when you've finished doing that come and see me. In all honesty I would say that if you see something working then why reinvent the wheel? I also would say that you have to be authentic. Do not try and 'fake it till you make it' – it's my honest belief that there is an opportunity for all of us in this world but if you are not honest and authentic it will come back to bite you later. Don't risk losing it all for the sake of short-term gain: you should be looking to create long-term sustainable wealth with a reputable brand.

WOULD YOU EVER CONSIDER WRITING A BOOK?

I have already decided that I am going to write a book. In fact it's one of the key lessons I learnt from Daniel in that it is a superb method of showcasing my expert status. It's hugely powerful and I am completely convinced it will take my business and my expert status to another level. Imagine meeting someone at a networking event and they give you their card and you hand them your book: who has more expert status and who will remember who?

DO YOU HAVE ANY OTHER BUSINESSES?

I do, but the second one is more to run some personal affiliate programmes that I promote. If I am teaching people how to market themselves and get a bigger online presence I feel I need to be actively walking the walk in order to talk the talk. The internet changes all the time and through the second business I can stay up to speed with the best strategies and techniques that are crucial to my core business.

WHAT ARE YOUR GOALS FOR THIS YEAR?

Without a doubt to get Online Expert Solutions well established, write my book, fine tune my Five-Step Formula for Success and solidify my expert status in the online community.

HOW WILL THE EXPERT SUCCESS ACADEMY HELP WITH THAT?

I think what I said above in my goals for this year is a perfect definition of what the Expert Success Academy can offer me. I like and trust Daniel Wagner and really get a sense that he cares. Sure, he is building a business for himself but the community he is creating is so dynamic and I am very proud and privileged to be a part of it. Watch this space is all I can say, the next twelve months with the Expert Success Academy is going to be huge.

WHAT DID YOU LEARN ON THE ONLINE BRAND MASTERCLASS? WHAT IMPACT DID IT HAVE ON YOU?

As I mentioned before, the Online Brand Masterclass was the turning point for me. The clarity and direction that I now have is directly linked to the Online Brand Masterclass. When I went into the course I only had a basic idea of what I was trying to create. I left with a business plan and the tools to get me started. I also made some great friends and gained a huge amount of confidence in my abilities.

WHAT DID YOU LEARN FROM THE EXPERT SUCCESS BOOK? WHAT IMPACT DID IT HAVE ON YOU?

To be honest it's been a few months since I read it but the one thing that I remember and have come to understand is the Expert Success Matrix and becoming an authority. It's such a simple concept: the higher you are on the matrix, the more money you make. It was a one of those light-bulb moments when I first read this.

KEY LEARNINGS

- Get yourself a mentor. The moment I opened my eyes to the concept of mentorship things started to change for me.

- Never be afraid to fail. If you don't try you will never know.

- Keep things simple.

- Never give up. Have a positive attitude and make sure you keep trying to complete what you set out to create.

- Be authentic in your actions.

- Create a great brand that has a long-term sustainable ethos.

PHIL WALTERS
PROPERTY
INVESTMENT EXPERT

Proven deal engineer for high net worth investors

Phil-Walters.com

www.phil-walters.com
phil@phil-walters.com
07912 039738 or 01603 340270

Phil qualified as a Geological Engineer in 1983, worked offshore for 20 years and simultaneously built up a considerable property portfolio. Property runs in the family with his mother an ex-estate agent and his younger brother also a full-time property investor. Between them they have 127 property units and rising. Phil is a full-time property investor and trusted advisor. His area of excellence is engineering profitable big deals. He bought his first investment property in 1986 and is a well-respected member of the ethical property investment world.

Phil uses the current economic climate to dramatically increase the wealth of his clients, JV partners and himself.

- **Achievements:** Speaker at *East of England Buy to Let Expo* with 180 attendees within a week of completing the Online Brand Masterclass. Leveraged my business so I no longer work in it but on it. Developed my core business areas of excellence.

PUBLICATIONS

Successful Ethical Joint Ventures, self-published, 2012.
Shareslide account Phil Walters, Norwich btl expo nov 2012 v02 (1)

Choosing a Reliable Trustworthy Letting Agent, self-published.
Available via Eastern Landlords Association members-only site.

Profession: Landlord Phil Walters, self-published.
www.edp24.co.uk/lifestyle/landlord_1_1078944

Multimillionaire Joint Venture Bible, self-published.
Available to private clients and JV partners only.

❝❝ I WORK ON MY BUSINESS NOW, NOT IN IT!

INTRODUCTION BY DANIEL WAGNER

When I met Phil, he was already successful. I have observed over the years that successful people are always driving to become more successful and better leveraged.

So I believe that anyone, no matter how successful and wealthy they already are, can improve how they do things by applying new distinctions to their business.

It doesn't really matter what market or niche you're operating in, to be perceived as the go-to authority can only help to enhance your profile – resulting in higher prices and better results for your clients.

Some of my students are easy to work with as they already have all the components in place. All I have to do is put them in the right sequence and order and then let people discover what we have created.

That is in essence what our authentic branding process is. We extract the most important information from people's previous successes and key moments of their life story and put this information into an easy to navigate and understand format.

Once that is achieved, we simply put their message out there and let the website do all the heavy lifting, prequalifying prospects.

When I spoke to Phil in person for the first time, it was at our yearly Expert Success Summit shortly after handing out the high achiever awards. Phil looked me deep in the eye and promised me that next year he would be on that stage collecting the award.

Whether he will or not I don't yet know, but I do know for sure that his determination and goal-setting is guaranteed to help him achieve more. And the public commitment he made on the day creates an even stronger magnet in the future to make his goals come true.

You will have heard many times, that mindset is the most important part of success. I do need to point out though, that you need a simple formula or process to apply that mindset too.

Looking at Phil's success I can see that I am one of many mentors and teachers that he has used to refine his vision. And that is a common trait of successful people!

Daniel Wagner

AN INTERVIEW WITH PHIL WALTERS

WHAT DID YOU DO AT UNIVERSITY?

I left home at the age of 15 and lived in a bedsit whilst I studied for my A Levels in Cardiff. I discovered a passion for geology and went on to university to gain an excellent Honours degree in Engineering Geology with a postgraduate computing qualification.

WHAT DID YOU DO AFTERWARDS?

I began a career in the oilfield and through hard work and a passion for my work I was fortunate enough to become one of the most experienced members in a team of highly specialised oilfield engineers. I travelled around the world as a solo specialist engineer until I retired from the oilfield at the age of 40.

WHEN DID YOU LEAVE YOUR JOB?

I had been an oilfield engineer for almost 20 years earning a six-figure salary. I was fortunate enough to retire from the oilfield almost 10 years ago and I have been far happier and far more profitable with the resultant continuity of my life.

WHAT SORT OF EXPERT ARE YOU?

I have been an expert in property investment for a long time (even if I didn't know it). People are now saying I am an authority on big deal structuring which is very kind of them.

Sometimes people don't know they're an expert.

HOW DID YOU GET INTO PROPERTY INVESTMENT?

My mother was an estate agent back in the 1960s and she has always instilled a strong work ethic and integrity in all we strived to do. I have worked from a very early age to make my own money. The generous oilfield wage allowed me to concentrate on building a leveraged property portfolio that enabled me to become financially free. It also paid for my divorce and left me with more than enough money to live financially free.

WHAT QUALIFICATIONS DID YOU NEED FOR PROPERTY INVESTING?

Qualifications are not essential but experience is a major advantage. However, my academic qualifications are a benefit in the way I do due diligence and apply logic to property investment. People tell me I'm different; that my mind works like a flow chart and I have been blessed with common sense and an exceptional memory. The fact that I am an insomniac and have a strong work ethic is a bonus as well.

HAVE YOU MADE MISTAKES ALONG THE WAY?

Of course I've made hundreds of mistakes. If you haven't made mistakes you aren't trying hard enough. I have held myself back in the past for fear of making mistakes and I've actually found that certain situations that didn't work out as I planned have led to far better opportunities as a consequence. If I make a mistake I always try to ensure I learn from it.

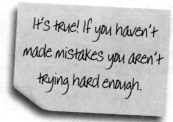

It's true! If you haven't made mistakes you aren't trying hard enough.

WHAT DOES THE FUTURE HOLD FOR YOU?

Whatever I wish for. I have big ambitions and already several of my projects are well on the way to producing great results.

HOW DID YOU MEET DANIEL WAGNER?

I saw him on a YouTube site and thought 'Well if he can make them a greater success, then why not me?'

WHAT ATTRACTED YOU TO THE EXPERT SUCCESS ACADEMY?

Daniel's drive, common sense approach and integrity. I appreciate James's role as the skeleton within the body of the Expert Success Academy and apply that role to several key members of my businesses.

DID YOU ATTEND ANY OTHER TRAINING PROGRAMMES?

I did a property mentor course and the first mentor said to me, 'Phil you are on the wrong side of the table, you should be a mentor not a student.' However, it gave me accountability and I met a couple of experienced people whose opinion I respect. Now I mentor several people myself, but solely on a non-fee paying basis.

I also did a three-day residential property investment course. Lots of people questioned why I was there with the depth of knowledge in property investment that I already had but I feel I learnt more about the world of property investment than anyone over those three days!

I also took along a friend who has great ethical values like myself as a free guest. He was living on his Dad's sofa whilst going through a very expensive divorce. He has helped me immensely.

I was fortunate to be sought out by my first joint venture partner that asked to invest with me having gone there with the intention of investing with the guy that was running the course. She has £750,000 to invest.

That was just the beginning.

HOW DID YOU RAISE FINANCE?

I restructured my portfolio, found excellent opportunities and achieved a very large facility running into the millions with joint venture partners and commercial and conventional financial institutions.

WHAT HAPPENED NEXT?

Opportunities have appeared on an almost daily basis. I now joke to my business associates, 'Today's opportunity of a lifetime is...'

HAVE YOU HAD ANY CHALLENGES?

If it was easy anyone could do it. I have the same challenges as everyone else I'm just fortunate enough to have broken many of

Opportunities can appear on a daily basis.

my own glass ceilings and sought out the people that I respect and wish to work with. Fortunately they have all been kind enough and have agreed to work with or advise me.

WHAT DID YOUR BOSS/FAMILY/PARENTS SAY?

I am blessed to have a supportive wife that has helped me immensely. She is successful in her own right having completed her PhD in Creative Writing.

My family are proud of my achievements and I have several joint venture projects with them.

HOW ARE YOU FINANCING YOUR LEARNING WITH THE EXPERT SUCCESS ACADEMY?

With the increased revenues that result from what I learn.

WHAT ADVICE WOULD YOU GIVE TO OTHERS?

Educate yourself, find people you trust and keep your integrity. Also don't chase the transaction, try to realise an opportunity's true potential.

ANY TIPS YOU'D LIKE TO SHARE?

It's not about the money, it's about the people. Get the people and the ethos right and the money will come as a by-product.

WHERE DO YOU PUT YOUR ENERGY?

Before I joined the Expert Success Academy I used to be caught in the landlord trap thinking I was saving money doing all the jobs myself. I learnt a long time ago that the macro decisions are the critical ones. I work on my business now not in it! I have leveraged other professionals with experience and integrity to maintain my businesses while I develop other more rewarding opportunities.

HOW MANY JOINT VENTURE PARTNERSHIPS DO YOU HAVE?

Nine at present and rising.

WHY/HOW DID YOU WRITE YOUR BOOK?

I have written a property investment manual. However it is not for general release and I provide sections of it to my joint venture partners to maximise our businesses' profitability.

HAS YOUR BUSINESS STARTED TO MAKE PROFIT YET?

My business has always made a profit. Recently that profit has grown considerably by engineering leveraged solutions and efficiently structuring several different joint ventures.

DO YOU HAVE ANY OTHER BUSINESSES?

Yes, they are all property based but independent and generate as large and as passive an income as possible.

WHAT ARE YOUR GOALS FOR THIS YEAR?

To create leverage.

HOW WILL THE EXPERT SUCCESS ACADEMY HELP WITH THAT?

I could get them to do the leveraging for me! The Expert Success Academy will give me accountability, clarity and structure.

APART FROM THE ACADEMY, DO YOU GO TO ANY OTHER NETWORKING EVENTS?

I networked exhaustively for the first couple of months, finding people with integrity, experience and the same aligned ethical values as me. I now tend to aim for high net worth investors as I have been told that is my area of excellence. I'm more about quality than quantity now and tend to stay under the radar more.

WHAT DID YOU LEARN ON THE ONLINE BRAND MASTERCLASS? WHAT IMPACT DID IT HAVE ON YOU?

I cannot overestimate the impact the Online Brand Masterclass has had on me. It was an epiphany and a revelation rolled into one. As I have been involved in property from an early age and we are fortunate to have a very substantial amount of property in our family portfolio I had a wealth of experience already. My experience as a director of the Eastern Landlords Association and being the chairman of the Norwich branch meant, that unknown to me, I was an expert already. I'm now doing deal clinics for property investment networks across the East of England, engineering some massive deals in the South East and London. All I needed to do was go out and claim my expert status. Next I am aiming to be recognised as an authority in the world of high finance property investment.

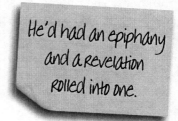

He'd had an epiphany and a revelation rolled into one.

WHAT DID YOU LEARN FROM THE EXPERT SUCCESS BOOK? WHAT IMPACT DID IT HAVE ON YOU?

I was on a cross-country mountain bike ride across mid Wales when I read *Expert Success* from cover to cover in one day after a 50-mile bike ride across some of the toughest terrain in the UK. We were in a bunkhouse in the middle of nowhere and I just couldn't put the book down. It explained so much about marketing from both sides of the equation. I have since bought about 10 copies and given them away to each one of my joint venture partners.

DID THE EXPERT SUCCESS ACADEMY HELP WITH JOINT VENTURES?

Yes, I have done and I am doing several joint ventures. I am in the process of doing nine joint ventures projects at the moment:

- Two creative property deals.

- One exciting lettings venture which we intend to franchise.

- A joint venture with a guy who has cancer where I have provided all my knowledge for free and also put £30k of my own money up front to stop him getting repossessed and his wife and child being evicted.

- One exciting joint venture that will be the pinnacle of my property investing career to date when it comes to fruition.

- A portfolio buying joint venture.

- A development project joint venture.

ANY PLANS TO DO ANY MORE JOINT VENTURES?

Hundreds. The opportunities are out there, you simply need the experience, mindset and ability to realise them.

 **KEY LEARNINGS**

- Believe in yourself but don't be afraid to listen to good advice.

- Act now, get perfect later.

- Focus.

- Glass ceilings are there to be shattered.

- You are blessed to be you. Appreciate it!

SOPHIE MAHIR
BUSINESS
STARTUP EXPERT

Setting Your Business Free

www.sophiemahir.com
sophie@sophiemahir.com
01273 840534

Sophie has worked for over 10 years with business startups, both as women's ambassador and then with her own business, coaching and training over 300 people to build profitable businesses. She has created her own formula: The Five Simple Steps for Business Success, which combines all her skills. She is a business coach, trainer and speaker. She helps people who have the mindset and practical abilities to create a successful business. Sophie has previously worked as an art teacher, been a professional artist, and worked on a one-year Women's Business Startup Programme via SEEDA.

- **Qualifications:** Steiner Art Teacher, Life Coach, Results Coach, NLP & Hypnosis Practitioner and Performance Consultant.

- **Credibility:** Coached and trained over 300 people to build profitable businesses.

- **Personal Achievements:** Selected as an ambassador for women's enterprise. Raising two incredible daughters on my own whilst building up my business.

PUBLICATIONS

How to Create Your Successful Artists' Open House, eBook, self-published.

> **❝ I TRAINED OVER 300 PEOPLE TO BUILD PROFITABLE BUSINESSES.**

INTRODUCTION BY DANIEL WAGNER

I knew Sophie casually for many years before she joined one of my meetings and ultimately became a member of the Expert Success Academy.

That is something I have seen over and over again. This is why it is important that any entrepreneur or business owner exercises patience and consistency in spreading their word or message.

It might be many months or even years before a prospect that is already aware of your products and services is ready to take advantage of them.

As they say, a prospect is ready to buy when they are ready to buy, not when you are ready to sell!

One of my early memories of meeting Sophie was at a local property event, where I was immediately enthralled by her passion and excitement. I felt aligned and akin with her values and energy, and somehow I knew that it would only be a matter of time until we would work together.

Sophie has worked as a coach helping people get started in business for quite some time, but never specialised in any specific market segment. And like so many solo-preneurs, she juggled many balls, including being a single mum and running her business.

So many people struggle when it comes to what to put on their website, and most coaches make the mistake of trying to appear corporate, when in reality is their personality and humanity that is the most unique selling point of their offering.

Now Sophie has found her flow, has a web presence that represents what she stands for, and started to get her division aligned with her values.

Sophie recently upgraded from her Platinum to a Diamond membership of the Expert Success Academy, which is always a good sign. It shows me that she has just upped the stakes and increased her commitment. And more commitment naturally leads to more results!

Daniel Wagner

AN INTERVIEW WITH SOPHIE MAHIR

SOPHIE, WHEN DID YOU START OUT IN BUSINESS?

I fell into business at the tender age of 17. I spent a lot of my spare time knitting and created jumpers for myself (very often during school hours too, when I should have been studying for exams...). My friends liked what I made and asked for something similar. That's how 'S.W. Knitwear' was born – I left school and after a year had five ladies knitting up my designs. At that time you couldn't buy quality hand-knitted jumpers in the high street stores; I had a window of opportunity. It lasted about three years. As I knew nothing about running or growing a business, after that time I (happily) went bust!

WHAT HAPPENED NEXT?

I was living on the campus of Tobias School of Arts (a Rudolf Steiner Art Therapy/Education School in Sussex), where my mother was a tutor. Very soon I realised I wanted to join, and three years later I had completed a specialist Steiner Art Teacher course. I had also met my husband and soon after became pregnant with my first child. The next few years were some of the toughest of my life. I ended up divorced, on the benefit system, a single parent of two gorgeous children, living in a town where I knew no one, and totally alone. I waited out those next few years till I could apply for an art teacher position at the Brighton Steiner School and when I was finally successful I worked hard to learn the craft of teaching and become a respected expert in the Steiner Art Teaching field.

Without business education, she went bust.

WHEN DID YOU LEAVE YOUR JOB?

In a moment of clarity in the summer of 2004, I realised there must be something better out there for me and my girls. I wanted more control over my life, more money and to be able to paint and sell my own art. So I left and started out as a professional artist. I had a fairly successful career, exhibiting and selling regularly at open houses, art fairs, solo gallery shows and via my agent. I also started up The Newhaven Art Trail where I lived and associated support group Newhaven Arts.

HOW DID YOU GET STARTED AS A COACH?

I found that what I loved more than the painting was helping other artists to set up their open houses as viable business concerns. I wrote (what I now know as an ebook) How to Create Your *Successful Artists' Open House*, and then somebody suggested I was really good at all this and should train as a coach. It was 2007, and I had no idea what that was but after a bit of investigation I felt this was the right thing to do, so I made a quick decision and a week later was on a plane to Amsterdam to start my life coach training. I got my first clients during the three-month training programme and haven't looked back since.

WHAT SORT OF EXPERT ARE YOU?

I would definitely say that after all these years I am great at putting a plan together and getting started up quickly. So, I would say I'm an expert business startup coach.

During my career as an artist, I not only got a lot of business help and advice myself from a Business Link advisor, but I then got asked to work on a one-year Women's Business Startup Programme through SEEDA (South East Enterprise Development Agency) and then became an ambassador for them before funding was eventually pulled.

I love helping people get clarity around what they really would love to do, then find out how that could work as a business, and finally get them set up and making money fast.

DO YOU MISS YOUR ART CAREER AT ALL?

Not specifically, as my passion for making a difference to people's lives, inspiring them to do better, to make the changes they really want, and to create and build the life of their dreams, is what lights me up every day (and sometimes keeps me awake at night with excitement!). I still have studio facilities and paint occasionally for pleasure.

Interestingly enough, this year I realised more than ever that I needed to tap into the true authentic person I am, with all my past 'lives', and so I am finding ways to bring my spiritual background, artistic experience and practical business skills together. Now I am stepping into a new name: *The Unconventional Coach* and I'm very excited about the future and how this will unfold.

DID YOU NEED ANY SPECIAL QUALIFICATIONS?

One of the beliefs that I used to hold was that you needed to come from the 'right' art college, with the 'right' art degree. This was the primary reason why I didn't progress my painting career as fast and as far as I could I think. Thank goodness I know better now! What a limitation!

She's become excited about the future.

I believe that all the qualifications in the world won't make you brilliant at what you do. Experience is what really counts, and real world results. So, I have nine certificates in my office, but nobody ever wants to look at them.

HAVE YOU MADE MANY MISTAKES ALONG YOUR PATH?

Absolutely! And I'm so grateful for each and every one of them, for they have made me the person I am now.

COULD YOU SHARE THE BIGGEST ONES?

I suppose I would say that my number one mistake is thinking I could build a big business on my own. I thought I didn't need to invest in any coaching or mentoring help; that I could learn it all myself.

Similarly, I thought I didn't need to bring anyone into the business, because they would never do things as well as I could (I had noticed the drop in quality when I outsourced my knitting at age 18-19). I wanted to be in control of it all. Or so I thought. But as time went by I could see I kept getting the same old results rather than the growth and improvements I was looking for. 'Maybe next year when I've made more money...' I kept telling myself.

My second mistake was allowing myself to get distracted too quickly with other business opportunities, and what they call 'shiny pennies'. I often started other projects as sidelines to my business, but actually I just caused confusion. Now I am really happy to say 'no'.

I would say my third mistake was thinking that I'd be happy once I'm wealthy. Actually I am wealthy now, and more importantly I believe the money only comes once you are happy and have found that state of 'freedom' within yourself, so don't wait!

Sometimes it's good to say no!

DID YOU INVEST IN ANY OTHER TRAINING PROGRAMMES?

In 2008 I changed my life thanks to a ticket to Christopher Howard's Breakthrough to Success seminar, which arrived out of the blue through the post, although I needed the ticket to arrive three times before I actually booked and went! I finally realised I needed to get out of my comfort zone, change the limited way I was thinking, and that I needed all the help I could get. So bit by bit I bought onto their fast-track series of personal development courses and made dramatic changes to my confidence and mindset. This enabled me to finally charge what I was worth and feel fantastic about it. Not only that, I realised that investing in yourself is the best investment you can make.

WHAT IS YOUR MAIN GOAL NOW FOR THIS YEAR?

The main focus for me right now is to move more into working one-to-many rather than one-to-one and create my monthly membership learning programme for business startups: *The Sophie Mahir Business Freedom Academy*. Of course this will be unconventional and will involve artistic creative learning with fun exercises as well as some easy practical steps to get people started up.

COULD YOU EVER HAVE IMAGINED DOING SOMETHING LIKE THIS?

Not in a million years as my daughters used to say! This is a dream come true and has only come into fruition since I started working with Daniel Wagner and The Expert Success Academy.

HOW DID YOU MEET DANIEL WAGNER?

Daniel made a massive impression when I saw him tell his story some years ago at a weekend seminar on wealth creation. I always knew that one day I would work with him, and I know now that he is one of the main reasons I have a thriving growing business today. Of course I work consistently every day to grow and improve and implement.

WHAT DID YOU LEARN ON THE ONLINE BRAND MASTERCLASS? WHAT IMPACT DID IT HAVE ON YOU?

Before I went on this course I had an incredibly confusing online presence, with multiple homemade sites (another moment when I thought I could do things alone) and unclear messages, with – need I say it – very few leads from the web. During the weekend I found clarity in what I was offering, and I was delighted that I left with a long list of exactly what I was going to get rid of. Now I have one clear, clean and professional site that brings me regular clients and speaking opportunities.

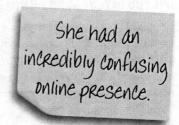
She had an incredibly confusing online presence.

WHAT ATTRACTED YOU TO THE EXPERT SUCCESS ACADEMY?

Throughout my life I have felt I didn't really fit in, and have been drawn to various 'tribes'. Once I found I could just be myself in the Expert Success Academy it was a relief. The fabulous welcome, warmness of the team and incredible knowledge and generosity from Daniel and James are what makes this the massive success it is.

HOW ARE YOU FINANCING THIS?

Having spent so many recent years without support, a regular mentor or professional business help, I now know that it's as important as the food I eat! This is my number one business expense – so how do I finance it? Well, by implementing everything I have learned my business grows every month. Having started on the Platinum level, after just a few months I was able to upgrade to the Diamond level. I can't afford not to do it!

WHAT HAS CHANGED SINCE YOU JOINED?

The first thing of course was my online presence, then the refocus on what I was offering which led to my name The Unconventional Coach. Then came the new coaching programmes (Free your Business, Gold, Diamond and Platinum), my Five-Steps to Business Success formula, the Business Freedom Academy monthly programme and the draft of my first book. I now have systems in place, have taken on a PA (a major dream for the last few years) and love every minute of my life!

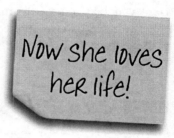

Now she loves her life!

WHERE DO YOU PUT MOST OF YOUR ENERGY?

I would say I focus mainly on feeling great and being happy every day (lots of meditation and visualisation and an appetite for learning new things), which means I attract the clients I want to work with. I enjoy helping them change and grow and make running my business a thing of enormous pleasure!

WHAT WILL THIS MEAN FOR YOUR FUTURE?

I can create my life exactly the way I want to – and most importantly I can inspire and assist others to do exactly the same.

WHAT OTHER GOALS DO YOU HAVE?

I want to write a couple of books, and become an international speaker, inspiring and motivating others to make change and get creative to design their ideal life. I plan to have a physical centre where I will provide a crossover between art and business.

HOW DO YOU SEE THE EXPERT SUCCESS ACADEMY HELPING YOU?

Every step of the way – right up to the cutting of the red ribbon on my centre's opening day and beyond!

WHAT ADVICE WOULD YOU GIVE TO OTHERS?

Don't wait till you have the money to get high quality coaching and mentoring - commit and believe and it will come to you. Sometimes you are so stuck in your business that you can't look out, and you need someone from the outside looking in to help you.

HOW COULD THEY BEST GET STARTED?

I would suggest reading *Expert Success first*, then booking on an Expert Success Formula (Live) day where you can see Daniel and James in action.

 KEY LEARNINGS

- Don't try and go it alone.

- Stay open and enjoy the journey.

- Do something to move you forward every day.

- Your mindset determines everything.

- Have one core message and base everything around this.

PENNY LOWE
BUSINESS FINANCE EXPERT

Enjoy Accounts and
Grow Your Business

Wellington Consulting Ltd

www.pennylowe.com
www.wcon.co.uk
penny@wcon.co.uk
0870 766 4982

Penny is an unusual accountant who trains business owners to understand and make use of their figures and take control of their business. She originally trained as an accountant working in practice and industry before becoming a trainer of accountants. Penny has also had roles as project manager and marketing manager so has not spent all her life buried in figures. She now runs her own accountancy practice and specialises in educating business owners as well as preparing accounts and tax calculations for a few lucky clients. Previously, she provided accountancy services and offered classroom style training.

- **Qualifications:** AAT accounting qualification and practice licence, PGCE teaching qualification, PRINCE2 Project Management qualification and an MBA gained through the Open University.

PUBLICATIONS

Understanding Your Accounts for the UK Business Owner,
Anoma Press Ltd, 2013.

❝I PREFER PEOPLE TO PAPER.

INTRODUCTION BY DANIEL WAGNER

I met Penny when I spoke at a friend's event about personal online branding. Penny is an accountant with a passion for teaching and is determined to help entrepreneurs make accounting fun!

Penny is an absolute joy to work with, as she accepts my coaching but is always ready to defend her own point of view! One of our recent successes includes her book being published, which was a big undertaking and massive breakthrough for Penny.

One of my favourite aspects of the Expert Success Academy is that people start collaborating and working together. There are many aspects to running a successful business, and it is a pleasure to see that businesses source their talent within the community.

The way I see it is that many business owners look at me and my team as their marketing and business coaching experts in their company.

So you won't be surprised to hear that I call on Penny's expertise to help my company with financial processes and accounting procedures. I have to admit that I'm still a little bit away from fully 'enjoying my accounts' but I have to say that I'm far more confident about numbers in my business, which is an absolute survival skill for any entrepreneur.

Penny is another great example that the Expert Success Formula and its principles can be transferred to any service-based professional with ease.

We could all do with more time, but as we cannot create more time, we have to use the time available more wisely. Going to workshops, choosing and working with mentors and coaches, having people do stuff for you that you are not an expert in – all these count as using your time more wisely.

And to grow your business you have to leverage other people's expertise. Success is a team sport!

Penny's knowledge and expertise will help hundreds of businesses in the UK increase their profits and help many others from going broke. And if you ask me, that is a very important message indeed.

Daniel Wagner

AN INTERVIEW WITH PENNY LOWE

PENNY, WHAT IS YOUR MAIN, CURRENT GOAL?

For several years I have wanted to spread the word that accounts are not really as bad as people think they are. Many business owners' impression of accountants is that they may be good with numbers, but are poor at communication. As a result, business owners do not bother to ask for explanations, as they are scared they may not understand the answer. Also, it may cost them more money if the accountant takes time to explain or educate them. As a result, they sign on the dotted line and pay the tax without asking questions.

What the business owner is missing is that the accounts hold a wealth of information that can help them run their business, make it more profitable and allow growth, sale or change of focus depending on what they require in the long term.

My goal is, by offering structured programmes, to help business owners feel comfortable with the figures and make use of them to grow their profits.

WHAT SORT OF EXPERT ARE YOU?

I trained as an accountant in the late 70s and over the years have had roles in practice and in industry. In addition I enjoy sharing knowledge so have taught in both the private sector and at colleges and universities. I even taught motorcycling when in my twenties. I set up my own accountancy practice in 2003, which I still run and combine with offering training over a variety of media.

Although I have worked for international as well as local firms, my love is the small- and medium-sized business. For many staff and owners, their first experience of accounts is when someone says 'can I have a budget please'. Whether it is the bank wanting a business plan when you go to open an account for your new business, or if you have become department head and your senior suddenly holds you responsible for spending and profits, financial education is one area that is often overlooked.

I prefer people to paper. Although I know that the figures must be done, it is what the figures mean that is more important than how to calculate them. There are lots of accountants and bookkeepers around that can produce them in a format suitable for the authorities. As a business owner, it is important to understand what shape they need to be for you to understand what has gone on and what needs to happen to move forward.

So, in summary, I am an accountant who works with business owners to help them understand their figures and increase their profits.

WHAT MADE YOU CHANGE YOUR APPROACH TO WORKING WITH BUSINESS OWNERS?

Over the years I have had a number of clients who rely too heavily on me as their accountant to produce the figures for the tax office and Companies House, but didn't want to look at them on a continuous basis. I have seen several businesses go under as they have gone ahead and either moved into bigger premises or taken on invoice finance without understanding what they were getting into and working out what the impact would be on their business. They have only told me months after the event.

Informing the accountant at the end of the year allows them to produce accurate accounts, but is often too late to get back on track or unpick what has been done. The impact on the business can be devastating.

I have now trained my clients to talk to me before they act. But I do not want to take over the world. I am not looking for lots more accountancy and tax clients. I prefer to reserve time to work with clients of other accountancy practices. When the accountant realises that I am acting as translator and educator, rather than trying to take over their client, they are happy to work with me as it will make their life easier in future as well as giving them an educated client with a sound business that won't be doing anything silly.

I still have limited time, so writing the book was my first step to getting the message out to as many business owners as possible.

WHAT ARE YOUR PLANS GOING FORWARD?

I will continue with my accountancy practice as this allows me to have hands-on experience of running a business on an ongoing basis. It also means that I keep my skills and experience up to date and know what other accountants are expecting to do for their clients.

In addition, I will be offering assistance to many businesses both on a personal basis and through online programmes. The online programme allows businesses who are not yet ready to commit time and money to personally work with me.

I have also started doing regular blogs and articles so that I can educate in bite-sized chunks. I have received emails from people saying that the content has enabled them to think in more detail before making a decision. It is so much easier and cheaper to review all options and work out implications before committing than trying to unpick or deal with the consequences after the event.

Knowing I am making a difference is what is encourages me to put more effort into reaching out to those I have never met and don't know.

HOW DID YOU MEET DANIEL WAGNER?

As you might imagine, I am a great believer in training. The test of training is how much you actually put into practice. I first met Daniel at a training course early in 2012. He was presenting on the importance of personal branding. What he said made sense, as my business plans were not to expand the size of my accountancy practice, but to promote me and my services to business owners.

I decided then to attend the Online Brand Masterclass weekend as I could see it offered physical output rather than just ideas that I would not have time to implement.

As time is so precious, I did not want to commit unless I knew I could give it sufficient time, so I booked on the course at the end of May 2012. I am really glad I did. The output from the course has given me the basis to go forward as well as clarity as to what I am trying to promote.

WHAT ATTRACTED YOU TO THE EXPERT SUCCESS ACADEMY?

Having attended the course, I really appreciated the hands-on nature and accountability of his style. Other courses have often been just the sharing of information and then what you do or don't do with it is up to you. There is often little follow-up to deal with any confusion or queries.

As Daniel is keen to ensure success, he and his team interact with all the attendees and he is happy to spend his own time during the course answering questions or making suggestions. He is also good at assisting networking by putting people in touch so you can use other services from within the group.

Having attended the Online Brand Masterclass, I had the opportunity to sign up to the Expert Success Academy. Again, I knew I could not commit time straight away so agreed a future date and started on the programme in August 2012.

As a Diamond member, there are weekly coaching sessions as well as meeting up once a month for face-to-face coaching, Although this is done in a group, so many of the issues are similar that you can learn through others' experience and the help they are given.

Although you could refer to it as coaching, it is a lot more than that. Due to the experience of the team at Expert Success Academy, they have been there and done that and can tell you what works and what doesn't. For example, earlier in the year I placed an advert in the magazine for the Federation of Small Business. I was intending just putting an email link for a free report. It was suggested that I also include a phone number, with a pre-recorded message asking them to leave their details. The answer phone message is then emailed to me so I don't have to keep checking whether a message has been left. This all seems logical when you break it down into steps, but to be spoon fed the steps so I knew what I was trying to achieve, made the difference in that I, as a busy person, put the effort in and achieved the result. I was surprised that I got nearly as many messages left as I did requests for information via the internet. As the system is now set up, anybody finding the magazine in their 'to read' pile, or being handed the edition at the annual conference can phone through and I know I will get the message.

I have therefore learnt that if I raise a question, the team, as well as the group can help come up with the answer.

Accountability is another benefit of any type of coaching. The Expert Success Academy makes you accountable to the others in the group as well as the coach. Not only do you therefore think before you commit, but you are more likely to ensure you deliver.

DID YOU ATTEND ANY OTHER TRAINING PROGRAMMES?

I have attended courses run by others in the past to help me fulfil my dream.

They have taught me the skills but I have not felt the buy-in for the ongoing support that the Expert Success Academy gives. I can now see how I can use the skills and some of what I have learnt at previous courses. It all makes more sense.

HOW DID YOU RAISE FINANCE?

My company took out a bank loan to pay for the Expert Success Academy. It means there is no question about being able to claim the interest as a business expense. Although I am the one attending, all my training/mentoring is sold through the company, so there is no question that the company is benefitting.

When it comes to renewal, my company will be paying outright as turnover has increased and there are funds in the business to pay without taking out further loans.

HAVE YOU HAD ANY CHALLENGES?

My biggest challenge is time. As I run my accountancy practice as well as the coaching/training/mentoring, finding time to market my services is my biggest challenge. I keep getting asked to act as accountant for new clients, but as one doesn't like to say no, I have learnt to discuss what is required and then refer them to a friend of mine who also runs his own practice. When I see him, he says, 'no need to ask how you are doing as you keep sending me new clients!' I have known him since he set up in practice and it's good to help others grow their business.

As a business owner, I know it is easy to get buried in the delivery of goods and services rather than standing back and looking longer term. The Expert Success Academy helps me do that. As an ongoing programme with monthly meetings, you can never go on for too long without being reminded that you need to stand back, plan and act.

WHAT ELSE HAVE YOU FOUND HAS HELPED?

Systemising as much as possible has made a tremendous difference. I have moved from my old contact management system to InfusionSoft, which has strong email communication functionality. We are also getting to grips with its sequencing so we can input an enquiry simply into the system setting a series of events in place that includes reminders and to-do lists. As this is cloud based, my team and I can access it when we are not in the office, or working from home.

I have a wonderful PA called Kerry. She helps me stay on track. Although she only works part time, having a second pair of hands and eyes – and brain – means I can work much more effectively. The cloud-based system means she can keep an eye on what is going on and do extra bits of work as needed.

WHAT'S NEXT FOR YOUR BUSINESS?

Using The Expert Success Formula, I have been able to put a repeatable structure on what I offer. Business owners can hire me for a programme of five days spread over several months to work one-to-one on their business. Because the programme is structured, it has made explanation and marketing so much easier, to the extent that one contact offered to promote it for me as he could clearly understand what I was offering and what the benefits to the business owner would be. I have delivered the programme before, but just not given it the clearly defined structure it has now.

In addition to this top end product, I also have the online version where I only had to write it once – and then can add to it at will, and deliver it to many people without using more of my time. This has allowed me to get my message out without running out of available dates to deliver the training.

By having this range of products and services, I have something to offer individuals at all levels of my target audience. From those who want a taster, through to those who have big plans and want personal help implementing them, there is something at each level.

As time goes on, I may start to expand the range of products offered, but for now I will be consolidating and improving those I have – as well as running my accountancy practice.

Since working with Daniel, I have also released my book, which is a good introduction to my style of delivery.

HOW DOES A BOOK HELP?

Business owners that have not met me can glean useful information as well as food for thought. They can learn what benefit they can get from taking an interest in their figures rather than just leaving them to the accountant.

HAS JOINING THE EXPERT SUCCESS ACADEMY MADE A FINANCIAL DIFFERENCE?

Yes. I have seen my turnover increase for both accountancy and training. I have been able to give my PA more hours so she has benefited too. By using systems we both know what is going on and the clients know what to expect. I have applied what I have learnt to both accountancy and training clients and am enjoying the results.

I am not making huge sums from my book but I didn't expect to. I am more than covering costs, but most importantly getting the message out there and introducing myself and my style.

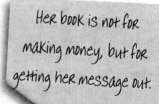

Her book is not for making money, but for getting her message out.

I have also been asked to write various articles which gives me further marketing opportunities at no cost hence keeping costs down as well as increasing turnover.

WHAT WOULD YOU SAY TO OTHERS WHO ARE THINKING OF JOINING THE EXPERT SUCCESS ACADEMY?

As with any learning, the benefit comes when you practise what you have learned. It is your business and things are not going to be magically done for you. What will happen is you will find out what needs doing and how to get things done. This may be outsourcing or doing it yourself. The key is that you still need to be in control and making the decisions. By committing to others, you are more likely to achieve your tasks leading to your goals.

I have found some reliable and good businesses to work with to achieve my goals. Some, such as the virtual reception I use, I have used for years but had not asked the question as to what more they could do. When I had the conversation stating what I wanted, it turned out they offered it, I just hadn't asked. Knowing what you want – and what might be possible – is the first step to getting there. Don't assume you have to go elsewhere, just be clear about what you want and ask.

KEY LEARNINGS

- Clearly define what you offer so that you and your prospects understand.

- Clearly defining your offering keeps the costs down by being repeatable.

- Good systems make you more efficient.

KEITH KRUGER
BUSINESS GROWTH EXPERT

More Focus – More Direction – Better Results

KpK Associates

www.keithkruger.net
www.kpkassociates.co.uk
keith@kpkassociates.co.uk
07801 387790

Keith is a business coach and mentor who aims to bring out the best in people and help them fulfil their true potential. He previously worked for a multinational manufacturing company in different senior management positions in South Africa, USA, France and the UK. Having 21 years corporate employment and also running his own business in developing and leading people in four different countries has given Keith a unique understanding of human behaviour. His experience has been gained first hand and his passion is to help people realise their full potential – be it in their personal or professional lives.

- **Qualifications:** BSc Civil Engineer, from Kwazulu Natal, South Africa. Advanced Management Programme – Insead, Fontainebleau, Paris.

- **Credibility:** I have had the privilege of coaching and training in excess of 1000 people on my Leadership and Management programmes.

- **Personal Lifetime Achievements:** I have been married for 34 years to Mieke and have three beautiful children, Jason, Tarryn and Bradley, all of whom I am very proud. As Chairman of Governors I turned around a local independent school from near bankruptcy into a viable ongoing educational concern.

"MY PERSONAL BRANDED WEBSITE LED TO A 12% INCREASE IN BUSINESS.

INTRODUCTION BY DANIEL WAGNER

Keith was aware that while he was working, the world around him had changed. So he went out and got himself educated. Now that story sounds good so far, but what you don't know at this stage is that not every course and programme out there is created equal.

And Keith is not alone in his experience that you have to kiss a few frogs before one turns into a prince! Characteristically though, Keith wasn't prepared to stop or give up looking, even though his first experiences didn't yield the rewards and results he had expected.

That is the sign of a true entrepreneur. Never give up; always look for better ways. Keith always tells the story of how we helped him even at a point where he couldn't spend much money with my company.

That seems to be the exception rather than the rule in my industry, but I simply look at it as common sense. I believed then and I believe now that if I simply do my best to help people that these acts of kindness will come back to me in other ways that I cannot predict.

Keith is an avid contributor to the Expert Success Academy meetings and I really value and appreciate the corporate and executive coaching expertise that he brings to the table.

Because of the results he was able to achieve since working with me, Keith has also become an advocate and referral partner for the Academy. These Expert Success Partners are rewarded well for spreading the word. Word of mouth is still one of the best ways to get your message out there. So if you too are interested in spreading the word about Expert Success and the Academy Programme, then please get in touch using the contact details at the end of this book. You don't have to be an Academy member to benefit!

I am looking forward to watching Keith's journey and growth over the coming years as I believe he is just getting started. I know that his knowledge and expertise will help hundreds of executives and businesses achieve better results in this difficult economy.

I am also looking forward to having Keith's son Jason join the Academy as he is just transitioning from his job to becoming an entrepreneur. Looks like it runs in the family!

Daniel Wagner

AN INTERVIEW WITH KEITH KRUGER

KEITH, WHY DID YOU GO TO UNIVERSITY?

My father was a train driver on the South African Railways and no male from either side of our family had been to university before so it was a big deal at the time. I wanted to go to university but was unsure what direction to follow. Science and mathematics were my favourite subjects and I had always done very well academically. This led me to engineering and the outdoor life of civil engineering appealed to me.

HOW DID YOU END UP IN THE SOUTH AFRICAN AIR FORCE?

At the time during the late 70s it was still compulsory to do two years' military service in South Africa. At the end of each year of university I had received call up papers to the army but luckily in my final year I was called up to the air force, which was my preference anyway. At university there was a friend of mine who had the same surname and he had written a long letter as to why he wanted to be drafted into the air force but he was called up to the Army. To this day he swears blindly that they got the two of us mixed up!

WHAT MADE YOU GET INTO SALES AND MARKETING?

After completing my compulsory military service I went to work for a civil engineering design office as part of my professional certification. Doing design work behind a drawing board (CAD systems were in their infancy then) and not interacting with people drove me absolutely crazy. At heart I am a people person and I wanted to get into sales and marketing using my engineering qualification in the background. It was at this point that I came across an advert looking for a technical sales engineer. As an added bonus part of the training was to take place in Colmar, France, a picturesque place in the Alsace on the German-Swiss border. I would gladly have paid them to give me the job!

HOW LONG WERE YOU IN THE CORPORATE WORLD?

I was in the corporate world for 21 years and during that time had the good fortune to work and live in various different countries. This gave me a unique insight into people and their respective cultures, which has helped tremendously in my own business. As mentioned, I started in sales and marketing as a technical sales engineer and then worked myself up the corporate ladder to head up the sales and marketing division and then to eventually head up the division as managing director.

HOW WOULD YOU SUMMARISE YOUR CORPORATE EXPERIENCE?

My corporate experience can only be described as brilliant. I travelled the world, met some amazing people and attended some excellent training and development programmes. I was also very fortunate to have an excellent mentor named Kendall Brooke, who sadly is no longer with us. Kendall believed in me and encouraged me to show respect for others while at the same time focusing on and pursuing my goals and ambitions.

HOW DID YOU GET STARTED WITH KPK ASSOCIATES?

My family and I had been transferred from South Africa to the UK by the company I was working for at the time, with the intention of moving me on to the US to potentially take over from one of the vice presidents who was nearing retirement age. My position as Director, European Rail was created for me to learn about the railroad industry in the UK and Europe. Unfortunately or fortunately, whichever way you look at it, the company restructured and the plan did not work out. The end result was that the position that had been created in the UK could not be sustained and after some initial trauma I had an amicable split from the company.

DID YOU FIND THE TRANSITION FROM CORPORATE LIFE TO STARTING YOUR OWN BUSINESS EASY?

The simple answer is no! One of the biggest challenges after you have been in employment for several years and then find yourself in a position to start your own business is deciding what business to start. Eventually, after a lot of soul searching and trying to decide what I'm good at, I realised that I had been coaching and developing people both individually and in teams for most of my time in the corporate environment. So it was simply a case of putting what I was doing subconsciously into practice in a structured format. This is not as easy as it sounds and I speeded up the process by buying into an international training company where I had access to training programmes, marketing materials and years of selling experience and methodology. However, this also has drawbacks, as there is the initial license fee and ongoing royalties. After five years of this relationship I developed my own programmes based on my own practical experiences and knowledge and have never looked back.

WHAT WERE THE MAIN PROBLEMS, OR CHALLENGES, YOU FACED AT THE START?

Starting a new business is a daunting task and one of the first challenges was to find customers. My corporate background did not really help as most of my customers were in Europe and my target customers for my new business were in the Midlands in the UK. Initially, I bought a database of selected customers and then, using that information, made use of a direct mail campaign and followed this up by phoning each of the prospects. This was not easy as it took 7 to 15 calls before managing to speak to the decision maker. Persistence did pay off however and I was able to put my business on a sound financial footing. Once cash flow had improved I made use of a telemarketing service.

SO WHAT SORT OF EXPERT ARE YOU?

I have been running my own coaching/training business, specialising in leadership and management development for the past 11 years. This has made me an expert in improving these skills in people and giving them the confidence and tools to be the best that they can possibly be.

WHAT'S SPECIAL ABOUT YOUR MENTORING AND TRAINING PROGRAMMES?

One of my favourite sayings is, 'Knowing what to do and actually doing it are two completely different things'. Business principles are not that complicated but applying them consistently is another matter altogether. All my clients complete an action plan and these are rigorously followed up by myself or my

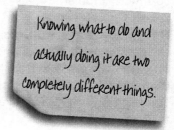

Knowing what to do and actually doing it are two completely different things.

team. It is all about turning those good intentions into action. Plans without action are worthless!

HAVE YOU MADE MISTAKES ALONG THE WAY?

If you haven't made any mistakes you are not pushing yourself hard enough! Mistakes are only mistakes if you make then again – up to this point view them as learning experiences. When you are faced with a difficult decision some good advice I was given when I first started was always think of three possible scenarios:

- What's the best outcome?

- What's the worst outcome?

- What's the most likely outcome?

This always helps me put things into perspective.

HOW DID YOU MEET DANIEL WAGNER?

I met Daniel about three years ago at an internet marketing event. Unfortunately this was after I had spent a considerable amount of money with other marketers who, dare I say it, were more interested in taking my money than in helping me. I stayed in touch with Daniel via email and then attended one of his very first Expert Success Live events.

WHAT ATTRACTED YOU TO THE EXPERT SUCCESS ACADEMY?

The Academy is where you get to meet with like-minded individuals and talk about common problem areas as well as share success stories that keep you motivated. More importantly, you get the opportunity to interact with Daniel and ask for advice on your own projects from all participants – it's invaluable immediate market feedback.

Sharing success stories keeps you motivated

You not only attend live events but also have regular webinars to facilitate further learning and discussion.

WHAT DID YOU LEARN FROM THE EXPERT SUCCESS BOOK?

From my perspective there were two ideas that really made a lot of sense to me.

- The importance of a personal brand.

- Creating a product staircase.

I had my business website under the banner of KpK Associates and although I 'was' the business there was no proper connection between the two. I now have a personal branded website depicting me as the Expert Business Coach which is connected to my business web site.

I also had different product offerings that did not really lead on and support one another. My product offering is now structured in a product staircase that naturally flows from one programme to the next where each one gives added value.

His branded website led to a 12% increase in business.

WHAT IMPACT DID IT HAVE ON YOU?

By having a personal branded website my profile has increased and this has enabled me to attract additional followers, which has led to a 12% increase in business. In addition, when my clients complete one programme there is a natural follow-on via the product staircase that will increase their learning and take them to the next level of personal performance.

WHAT ARE YOUR GOALS FOR THIS YEAR?

I will continue to build my personal brand and work at improving my product staircase by offering a one day sales programme and a three- and six-month leadership programme, followed by group and individual mentoring.

Having recently subscribed to InfusionSoft I want to automate as much of my back office administration as possible and improve my customer service and personal contact by having a sequence of email follow ups, similar to how Daniel remains in contact with all his Academy members. I will also give added value to my clients by introducing monthly webinars that will follow on from my workshops.

HOW WILL THE EXPERT SUCCESS ACADEMY HELP WITH THAT?

The Expert Success Academy keeps me on track by having 90-day business plan reviews and monthly feedback reporting at the live sessions. Being part of a successful crowd of people motivates you and you can call on members for support and encouragement when needed.

WHAT ADVICE WOULD YOU GIVE TO OTHERS?

My advice would be to come along to one of the Expert Success Formula (Live) discovery days. This will give you a good idea what we are all about and give you the chance to see Daniel live. Daniel is passionate about what he does and is sincere in that he really wants to help you and see your business grow and flourish.

I would also suggest reading *Expert Success*, by Daniel Wagner.

WHERE DO YOU PUT YOUR ENERGY?

Into talking less and doing more. And putting my plans into action.

KEY LEARNINGS

- Start with a plan – otherwise how can you hit a target you don't even have?

- Remember – small differences make a big difference!

- Avoid procrastination.

- Don't confuse activity with accomplishments.

- Follow up and follow through on everything you do.

IAN WHITFIELD BESPOKE PERFORMANCE CAR EXPERT

Performance by Design

Whitspeed

www.ian-whitfield.com
www.whitspeed.co.uk
ian.whitfield2@btinternet.com
07881 811979 or 01256 889800

Ian and his son Darren started off restoring classic cars and upgrading road cars and now build custom cars, fast road cars and track day cars for a variety of clients. Ian had a grammar school education and served an engineering apprenticeship with H. J. Heinz (the beans people). He had his own garage business from an early age and has always been involved with modified cars. Ian worked as a motor trader for many years and has personally owned over 1000 vehicles but has only been impressed by a few of them. He lost the sight in one eye in 1994 and was forced to retire. In 1997 his eldest son Wayne started driving and the following year the youngest, Darren, followed. Enforced retirement allowed plenty of time to tinker and in 1998 Ian completely restored a Mk 1 Escort for Wayne. Both sons joined a car club and then other members wanted their cars modified and tuned. So Darren joined Ian in the business during 2001 and Whitspeed was formed. Darren now does all the manual work while Ian runs the business. Darren is a formidable welder and fabricator and nothing scares him. He does have Ian to seek advice from and the experience is not wasted on him.

- **Achievements and Credibility:** In August 2005 we had one of our cars (built for a customer) featured in *Classic Ford* magazine. In January 2006 we, as a company, were featured in *Classic Ford* magazine. From March 2006 to November 2006 we had our own demonstrator vehicle featured in seven issues of *Practical Performance Car* magazine as a continuous story of the build. In February 2011 our completed demonstrator vehicle was featured in *Classic Ford* magazine.

“ WE ARE ALMOST UNIQUE IN OUR FIELD.

INTRODUCTION BY DANIEL WAGNER

Ian's story is typical in many ways and yet very unusual in others. Like many of my current students, Ian found me in the heyday of internet marketing, where I was speaking to large audiences at multi-speaker events.

Ian invested in one of my courses and – like many other students – found the technical aspect of it overwhelming and therefore wasn't able to take advantage of the transformational knowledge.

This part of Ian's story is the typical part. What is unusual about Ian's business though is that he is building high-performance cars from scratch with his son Darren.

So it is clear that an online presence could benefit Ian and Darren, but at the same time their needs are slightly different than the standard information marketers needs. So we decided to build personal online brands for Ian and Darren, helping them to get their profiles out into the marketplace.

Because much of what we offer is a 'done for you' service, it meant that within a few short weeks Ian and Darren had their brands completed, ready to share their message with the world.

Ian loves the community, contributes loads from his past entrepreneurial experience, and is a true asset to our group.

Creating a personal online brand is not just about attracting qualified prospects, it also has hidden, intangible benefits, like increasing the confidence of the business owner. The simple fact that one has a professional-looking online presence creates expert authority and status.

Ian is very creative. For example, I remember he once offered me sponsor space on one of his high performance vehicles in exchange for entry to one of my coaching programs.

Ian and his business are a fantastic example of how universal the principles of the Expert Success Formula are and how the Expert Success Academy can provide a nurturing home for almost anybody.

Who knows, maybe one day Ian will build a high-performance vehicle for me.

Daniel Wagner

AN INTERVIEW WITH IAN WHITFIELD

WHAT WAS YOUR MAIN GOAL FOR LAST YEAR?

We were not always doing the type of work we most enjoy, which is designing and building Custom Cars. We would be bogged down in mundane restoration and 'same old' basic tuning. So our main goal was to do more of the work we like most, like fabrication and chassis building, and less of the boring work like restoration and rust repairs.

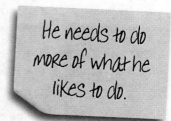

He needs to do more of what he likes to do.

WHAT SORT OF EXPERT ARE YOU?

We are almost unique in our field, inasmuch as we do every part of designing and building custom or bespoke cars. Several companies offer fabrication and welding. Many offer engine tuning and conversions. Bodywork and painting, mechanical and electrical, even upholstery are available if you look for it, but we do it all, and to a very high standard.

HOW DID YOU GET STARTED WITH VEHICLE FABRICATION?

I have always modified my own vehicles. Production cars are a compromise to suit as many customers as possible but I always wanted my cars to be individual, like me. Back in the early 70s when I started driving, cars were a lot more basic so there was much more room for improvement.

WHAT QUALIFICATIONS DID YOU NEED?

My father was an engineer, so I served my apprenticeship as an engineer as well, but my passion was always fast cars. I also read a lot of *Custom Car* magazines and learned by doing the work myself and watching others.

DID YOU DISLIKE ANY OF IT?

No, not really. I soon found that I could not work for a company though. I don't like taking orders from people who know less than I do, so I soon started working for myself and have done for most of my working life.

HAVE YOU MADE MISTAKES ALONG THE WAY?

Probably. Hasn't everyone? I wasn't very good at running a business because I have always done what I liked, not necessarily what made money. I have never been driven by money, and I am still not. Enjoy what you do and live according to your means and the money will be enough. I did an A Level in Business Studies when I was 40 and that has helped.

WHAT DOES THE FUTURE HOLD FOR YOU?

When I reach 65 I promise to grow up!

HOW DID YOU MEET DANIEL WAGNER?

At a property seminar in 2007. He was one of the speakers there and he just made sense to me. I did one of his two-day events as well and he really is so genuine. I like that.

WHAT ATTRACTED YOU TO THE EXPERT SUCCESS ACADEMY?

We had reached a point in the business where I could not see how we could move up a notch and I got a copy of *Expert Success*. What a revelation. So many things that I had never even thought of and some were so easy to implement that I could see improvements straight away.

DID YOU ATTEND ANY OTHER TRAINING PROGRAMMES?

Yes, I did the three-day summit and the Online Brand Masterclass with my son. We both have personal online brands now and Darren loved the event too.

HOW DID YOU RAISE FINANCE?

From business income.

WHAT HAPPENED NEXT?

Almost without trying, the business took off – so much so that we have to control what we do as we were already busy, but now the work is the type of thing we love doing, not just the mundane stuff. There is still so much to do but we have to take tiny steps, otherwise we will be overwhelmed by the extra business.

HAVE YOU HAD ANY CHALLENGES?

Yes. I am a bit of a dinosaur when it comes to Facebook, LinkedIn and Twitter. But I will get there in my own time.

IS SOCIAL MEDIA SOMETHING YOU SAW YOURSELF DOING IN THE PAST?

No, never.

WHAT ADVICE WOULD YOU GIVE TO OTHERS?

Read Daniel's book, get onto the programme and start or boost your business.

ANY TIPS YOU'D LIKE TO SHARE?

If you think this will not help your business, then think again. We had been in business for many years and were doing OK. Now we are reaping the benefits of our expertise. We knew we were experts, we just didn't know how to use our expertise.

WHAT ARE YOUR GOALS FOR THIS YEAR?

To finish writing my book. I have wanted to write a book for many years, but never got around to it. I have now made a start, about 80 pages to date, and it is really quite easy because of the new structure in my life. Time is still an issue as we are so very busy, but I am not complaining.

Writing a book is a perfect goal.

HOW WILL THE EXPERT SUCCESS ACADEMY HELP WITH THAT?

In every way. Structure, focus and commitment. Knowing that I will get published and people will buy my book because of our expert status.

APART FROM THE ACADEMY, DO YOU GO TO ANY OTHER NETWORKING EVENTS?

No, I don't need to, unless Daniel is running it, of course.

WHAT DID YOU LEARN ON THE ONLINE BRAND MASTERCLASS? WHAT IMPACT DID IT HAVE ON YOU?

I learned so much. It had a terrific impact on our business.

WHAT DID YOU LEARN FROM THE EXPERT SUCCESS BOOK? WHAT IMPACT DID IT HAVE ON YOU?

Same again. You don't know what you don't know until someone as good as Daniel shows you the way.

KEY LEARNINGS

- Claim your expert status: nobody will come and give it to you.

- Whatever you do, do it better than the rest. If you do something that most people cannot do, then you are an expert.

- Find your niche and stick to it.

- Writing a book to spread the word will prove that we are the experts.

LIZ BROWN
CREATIVE FLOW EXPERT

Inspiring Change
Through Creativity

www.liz-brown.net
liz@liz-brown.net
07800 551478

Liz previously enjoyed a successful career in financial services then moved into the life coaching industry. She's worked with three global coaching businesses and has now developed her own coaching business. Liz is a member of the Expert Success team, working with Daniel Wagner to achieve his 2020 vision. Her own coaching business combines coaching and creativity to encourage group and individual transformations. Liz has coached hundreds of people as a financial adviser, sales manager, coach, business owner and member of the Expert Success team. Her creative skills have bought delight to those who have experienced her cooking, art and creativity. Liz's clients range from two years old to 81; mostly women but sometimes men. With a subtle, gentle and supportive approach, the clients she interacts with feel inspired and supported enough to step forward and embrace change, just as she has.

- **Personal Achievements:** Completed two long-distance cycle rides in Spain and Vietnam, for the charity CLIC Sargent. Won Bristol & West's Premier Performer Financial Adviser Award.

PUBLICATIONS

Expert Success Newsletter. Monthly, *Expert Success* LLP.

❝I LOVE LEARNING AND I INTEND TO CONTINUE ALL MY LIFE.

INTRODUCTION BY DANIEL WAGNER

T Harv Eker teaches that 'everything is one thing is energy' and when I met Liz Brown I was reminded of this truism.

You will learn more about Liz when you read her story but all I can say is that when she attended our Online Brand Masterclass she had no clear idea of where she was going, but had some deep faith that things would somehow be OK.

Her enthusiasm and energy was so contagious that by the end of the workshop I couldn't help but ask her if she wanted to join my team.

What I love about Liz's business and her situation is that she completely followed her heart and made something seemingly impossible a reality.

She is not after making millions or even the big elusive financial freedom, but she wants to be in flow, helping people find their creative genius and she achieves this through her own unconventional methods and ways.

I know how difficult it can be to back yourself when everyone else around you is against you, but that is what you must do and I can proudly say that the members of the Academy are always supporting each other's dreams.

Let me be clear though here before you go all fuzzy on me: I am a tough-love coach when I don't think a members' plan or strategy will give them what want.

Liz has now been a member of the team for over a year and brings many wonderful qualities to the Academy.

I always say that success is something very personal and subjective and looking at Liz's success story you can see how true that really is.

When you select a mentor or group to support you in your growth, make sure that they are aligned with your values and ideals.

I personally believe that the growth in your business is directly linked to your personal growth and that true life success can only happen when your business and personal growth are aligned.

Daniel Wagner

AN INTERVIEW WITH LIZ BROWN

LIZ, WHAT DID YOU DO AT UNIVERSITY?

I didn't go to university. I left school at 16 and went into financial services. I don't have any regrets – I love learning and I intend to continue all my life.

WHERE DO YOU PUT YOUR ENERGY?

I focus on what I am passionate about and put my energy there. I have a good level of personal motivation and I'm an eternal optimist.

HOW DID YOU GET STARTED IN COACHING?

After a successful career over 34 years in financial services I decided at the age of 50 that if I didn't make the change then I would be stuck on the corporate wheel until retirement! In 2007, as I sat in a hospital bed, I saw an advert for a life coaching qualification – I thought, 'if I've helped people get from A to B with their finances, why not in other areas of their lives?' and so I applied and passed the qualification. The transition had begun.

LIZ, WHAT WAS YOUR MAIN GOAL FOR LAST YEAR?

I had an idea of combining coaching and creativity, and my goal last year was to take that idea and turn it into a business; I had trialled it on family and friends with some amazing results.

WHAT SORT OF EXPERT ARE YOU?

I am a coaching/sales consultant. I've worked with three global coaching businesses, consulting with people worldwide over the phone and face-to-face who are interested in their products and services. Providing connection and support to these potential clients has provided me with opportunity, flexibility and income while also helping the businesses increase their profitability, profile and prospects. However, I knew in my heart that I needed to step up, step out and develop my own coaching business.

HAVE YOU HAD A BUSINESS BEFORE?

When my two daughters were small, I moved to Bristol and didn't know a soul. I loved painting and cooking, and thought if I paint a picture someone may buy one but if I paint it on a cake – they, along with everyone at the party, will eat it and want another. With no business training, but a passion for being creative and a love for cooking I started Lizzie's Cake Kitchen. It was a success: I crafted cakes for two years, having them flown abroad, made for charity, delighting young and old. I learned business acumen and how to promote my business, deliver a product and build a pipeline of orders – skills that have been invaluable since. Over 800 cakes later I found myself needing to support myself and my daughters financially and so returned to financial services, a career I'd started as a 16-year-old.

Sometimes we all need to step up and step out.

HOW DID YOU MEET DANIEL WAGNER?

In August 2011 the role I had with a coaching business finished. I was offered a role back in financial services, but I had outgrown it, and I was really doing it just for the money. I knew in my heart that I wanted to combine coaching with creativity and I believed it could help change lives. In February 2012 I heard Daniel speak at an event. I knew nothing of him or Expert Success prior to that day. But in the time it took for him to make his presentation I knew and believed he was the man that was the nuts and bolts of getting my name and idea out there!

WHAT ATTRACTED YOU TO THE EXPERT SUCCESS ACADEMY?

I trusted my intuition and just asked Daniel Wagner. I had this idea of combining coaching with creativity and asked if he thought the Online Brand Masterclass would help me. Daniel asked me if I had tried out my idea yet. I told him that I'd already had some amazing results. And with that insight, I signed up.

WHAT HAPPENED NEXT?

In April 2012 I was sitting excited but nervous in the first session of the Online

Brand Masterclass. I immediately knew I was with the right people in the right place but I didn't realise just exactly how right!

WHAT DID THE ONLINE BRAND MASTERCLASS TEACH YOU AND WHAT IMPACT DID IT HAVE ON YOU?

It was an awesome, nurtured, supported and inspiring three days with Daniel Wagner and James Watson that enabled me to develop my online presence, position my unique expertise and propel my business forward. I created my content and my strap line and it started to feel very real – and scary! I came away reassured that my website was being created professionally. I joined the Expert Success Academy to support me as I progressed.

I also had the fantastic result of being asked by Daniel if I would consider working with the Expert Success team. Within a month I had left my job in financial services and was working with the Expert Success team, loving the role and the connection.

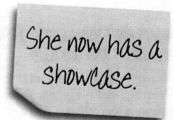
She now has a showcase.

In June 2012 my website went live and at last I had somewhere to showcase my business and the wonderful testimonials from my clients.

WHAT ADVICE WOULD YOU GIVE TO OTHERS?

Find the right mentor, programme and support. Check out what Expert Success offers before you spend your money and time with others.

ANY TIPS YOU'D LIKE TO SHARE?

Buy Daniels *Expert Success* book and get to know the man and his message.

WHAT DID YOU LEARN FROM THE EXPERT SUCCESS BOOK AND WHAT IMPACT DID IT HAVE ON YOU?

The *Expert Success* book has given me direction, education and strategies to follow.

With my online presence in place, the next step to look at was my product staircase. I had only held one-to-one coaching sessions before but Daniel and James encouraged me to look at group coaching. The strategies and the framework of the Expert Success Formula, along with the monthly coaching, meant I gradually expanded my content and belief. That meant that, in November 2012, I could hold my first *Creative Flow – Time For You* workshop. Four wonderful women got creative with beautiful flowers, were pampered with wholesome delicious food, found an oasis of calm in the busyness of their lives and it brought amazing transformation for them in the days after.

I made a profit and donated 10% to Msizi Africa to enable a child to attend school, changing all our lives for sure.

She donated 10% of her profits.

WHAT HAVE YOU LEARNED FROM THE ACADEMY AND DANIEL?

Daniel's authenticity and belief in the Expert Success Formula and his genuine desire to see me succeed as a student of the Academy inspires me. When I couldn't see how I could develop the group coaching with the creativity included, his vision, strategies and framework showed me how.

YOU'VE HAD A SLIGHTLY DIFFERENT ROUTE WITH EXPERT SUCCESS, HOW HAS THAT CHANGED YOUR LIFE?

Working with the Expert Success team is special. I love each and every one of them. The contribution I make comes from my own awareness and belief of what happened when I personally joined Daniel and the Expert Success Academy. I know it can bring fantastic outcomes for anyone if you follow the Expert Success Formula, be mentored by Daniel and James and have the unique business and personal support provided by the Academy.

SO DID YOU GET MORE TIME, MORE MONEY, MORE PURPOSE?

You bet I did, and I know it is unlimited in its possibility.

HAVE YOU DONE ANY JOINT VENTURES?
DID THE EXPERT SUCCESS ACADEMY HELP?

I have just held my first joint venture. I was invited to take my coaching and creativity workshop to Moulton Therapies and I wanted to see if I could hold them at different locations. I listened to other Academy members and their experiences of joint ventures and read the JV content in the *Expert Success* book. My workshop was promoted to a new list of contacts. It was a success.

ANY PLANS TO DO ANY MORE JOINT VENTURES?

Yes, I have another event planned at Moulton Therapies and monthly events locally in North Somerset.

KEY LEARNINGS

- Work with a great mentor.

- If you don't have the know-how or time – get it done for you.

- Believe in your bigger vision.

- Find the expertise to develop your own expertise.

- Create your plan with passion and focus on it with purpose.

- Believe in your own worth and what you can offer.

- Listen to your inner guidance – and Daniel!

IAIN WALLIS
TAX STRATEGY EXPERT

Proven Tax Strategies for High Net Worth Individuals

Iainwallis.com

www.iainwallis.com
Iain@iainwallis.com
0191 206 4080

Iain helps people invest in property to give them the financial freedom to live the life they love and legally pay less tax. Iain qualified as a chartered accountant in 1984, started an accountancy practice in 1992, sold it in 2007 and then started investing in property. He bought his first investment property in 2006. Despite the current economic crisis Iain has purchased, using solid investing techniques, more than 20 properties for family and private investors, all yielding in excess of 10%.

- **Qualifications:** Chartered accountant.

- **Credibility:** Progressive Property Investor of the Year 2011. Invested in more than 20 properties for family and private investors all yielding in excess of 10%. Appeared on Homes Under The Hammer (the television programme).

- **Personal Achievements:** *Expert Success* Academy High Achiever Award Winner 2012.

❝ WITHIN 3 YEARS I WAS ON STAGE AT WEMBLEY STADIUM!

INTRODUCTION BY DANIEL WAGNER

Iain Wallis must be everybody's dream student! Hard working, very coachable, and a keen implementer, he has made tremendous progress and it is an absolute pleasure and joy to work with him.

I feel really honoured and proud to be able to help Iain achieve his vision and his dream lifestyle. Sometimes you do need a little bit of luck and I would say that in Iain's case the timing of building his personal online brand and his appearance on Homes Under The Hammer (the television programme) came hand-in-hand, which allowed us and him to take full advantage of his media exposure.

Iain is part of the Mastermind group, the highest level of our Expert Success Academy, and he has been a passionate contributor and great sounding board. His financial and accounting background is a great addition to the skillset in the group.

What we were able to do for Iain is easily summarised: we honed in and focused on a key market segment, helped him with pricing and structure of his Strategic Product Staircase and helped him become exposed to a wider target audience.

The higher demand on Iain's time naturally pushed up his prices and made him the go-to expert in his market and field. I must say that I was impressed with the speed of his progress once we got the ball rolling, and one of my highlights of the year was seeing Iain present alongside me at the UK's largest property conference in March 2013.

Although extremely successful, Iain has chosen to stay involved with the Expert Success Academy far beyond the 12-month term, as he clearly understands and appreciates the power of ongoing coaching and masterminding.

A beginner looks for new opportunity, a successful person looks for small distinctions to help him adjust his strategy and slightly correct his direction.

It is those small adjustments though that produce the best results for the person who decides to stay the course.

Iain is a great example of how valuable the Academy is and how it helps successful people become even more successful.

Daniel Wagner

AN INTERVIEW WITH IAIN WALLIS

IAIN, WHAT WAS YOUR MAIN GOAL FOR LAST YEAR?

To gain more clients who want to invest in property through me, make use of my property tax advice and also gain access to legal tax saving strategies.

WHAT SORT OF EXPERT ARE YOU?

I trained as a chartered accountant and had my own business, which I sold in 2007.

By that stage I had already started to invest in property but the rules of the game were changing and, indeed, continue to change. So after reinvesting in myself and my property knowledge I felt confident to have a complete career change.

The financial investment analysis was easy for me with my background and, allied with my tax knowledge, they proved the perfect combination.

HOW DID YOU MEET DANIEL WAGNER?

I met Daniel at the Property Super Conference in March 2010 when I began to refresh my property knowledge. He helped me build my first website.

WHAT ATTRACTED YOU TO THE EXPERT SUCCESS ACADEMY?

It was the opportunity to work with two proven business marketers in Daniel and James. By now I had a successful property business and was gaining new property tax clients. So I joined the Expert Success Academy to help me take my business up to the next level to sell high value niche products to my niche market.

DID YOU ATTEND ANY OTHER TRAINING PROGRAMMES?

I've invested with Progressive Property and Unlimited Success to assist with both business and personal development.

IS THIS SOMETHING YOU SAW YOURSELF DOING IN THE PAST?

If you had suggested to me when I first met Daniel in 2010 that within three years I would be presenting on stage at the UK's largest Property Conference at Wembley Stadium I would have thought you were completely mad but that's exactly what I did in 2013.

He appeared on stage at Wembley Stadium.

Yes I had the knowledge but without the mentoring and guidance from Daniel and James I would not have been able to position myself as the go-to property tax expert for high net worth individuals.

Nor would I have received an email like this:

> '*I was referred to you as a leading UK property expert, and I believe our members at SIPP club would love to hear what you have to say. Our members are all high net worth individuals, and we have thousands of other readers too. They're always asking for more property information.*'

The SIPP Club is a members-only group dedicated to helping those with Self-Invested Personal Pensions.

WHAT ADVICE WOULD YOU GIVE TO OTHERS?

Believe in yourself and your product or services. Only you can stop your business succeeding.

Believe in yourself and your product or services.

ANY TIPS YOU'D LIKE TO SHARE?

If it was easy everybody would be doing it.

DO YOU HAVE ANY OTHER BUSINESSES?

Alongside the property investment and tax strategy work I mentor other people in property investment.

WHAT ARE YOUR GOALS FOR THIS YEAR?

To continue to build the existing business by increasing turnover and profitability.

HOW WILL THE EXPERT SUCCESS ACADEMY HELP WITH THAT?

As part of the Mastermind group we are held accountable to our mentors and also our strategic board. This ensures that challenges are swiftly identified and suitable solutions provided and implemented.

APART FROM THE ACADEMY, DO YOU GO TO ANY OTHER NETWORKING EVENTS?

Yes, I'm actively involved with Progressive Property and recently joined BNI.

WHAT DID YOU LEARN ON THE ONLINE BRAND MASTERCLASS? WHAT IMPACT DID IT HAVE ON YOU?

I realised that other, less qualified property investors were perceived as more knowledgeable than me through their branded websites! The OBM helped me clearly define what the business and I stood for. It also helped me identify what my target audience was and the need not to sell to anyone with a pulse and regain that expert status.

I now have a recognised niche which is that of property investor and tax strategist. People now come to me as a recognised expert, often predetermined to buy.

Shortly after attending the OBM, I was featured on a BBC1 television programme as a property investor and, before the programme had ended, I was taking calls from people who had found me through Googling 'Iain Property Tax'.

WHAT DID YOU LEARN FROM THE EXPERT SUCCESS BOOK? WHAT IMPACT DID IT HAVE ON YOU?

The importance of your personal brand and how you can claim your expert status without the fear that someone else can claim it. It also gave me the confidence to know that I was an expert and could charge premium prices from a clear product staircase. Yes there are others who do what I do, but no one delivers it my way and in my unique style.

 **KEY LEARNINGS**

- The importance of a clearly defined pricing structure.

- The importance of a product staircase.

- To create multiple ways for people to buy from you.

- To add value to your services to attract higher prices.

- That people will pay amazing prices for simple things.

- That you must claim your expert status.

KIM AND DANIEL BENNETT BRANDING AND DESIGN EXPERTS

Branding and Design Experts to Grow Your Business

Bennett Design

Kim and Daniel Bennett | www.bennettdesign.co.uk
daniel@bennettdesign.co.uk | 07583 047103

For over 20 years Kim and Daniel Bennett have designed, produced and implemented brands, websites, printed collateral, advertising and exhibitions for over 100 clients. Their focus is to extract your customer value proposition and then design and implement great ideas to draw customers and sales opportunities towards you to grow your business. They design and implement highly effective online and offline marketing tools for businesses by understanding their customer value proposition. They set up Bennett Design in 1990, after working with Daniel's parents in their Lake District hotel. Daniel was managing director of a printing company until 2010.

- **Qualifications:** Kim has a Diploma in Design from Nene College of Art in Northampton. Daniel has a National Diploma in Agriculture.

- **Credibility:** We are proud to have been in business in our own right for over 20 years. Kim worked as a graphic designer for a large national paper merchant.

- **Personal Achievements:** Established and maintained over 100 client relationships. Created and maintained two that have lasted over 20 years: James Cropper plc. and Footpath Holidays.

❝❝ YOU HAVE TO INVEST IN YOURSELF.

INTRODUCTION BY DANIEL WAGNER

I simply love husband and wife businesses! I love the fact that they work together and share a common vision for their business and personal life.

Sadly though, those visions can sometimes turn into nightmares and it is sad to see that many startups and even businesses that operate successfully for many years can get into trouble and the economic circumstances change.

I know that Daniel and Kim love what they do but also know that they should be paid more for their specialist skills and live the life that they deserve and desire.

It is a classic story of a small service-based business that has to compete in ever-tougher market conditions. So I was delighted when Daniel and Kim not only attended my Expert Success Summit, but also after some deliberation decided to join us in the Academy and bring their expertise and skills to the group.

Investing in your education and furthering your marketing and sales knowledge is not an easy decision for solo-preneurs, so I respect and honour everyone who makes those choices.

Daniel and Kim came through the recommendation of one of our other Academy members, Keith Kruger. It is a testament to the experience our members have, that they recommend our products and services to their friends and professional circles.

As with many other service-based professionals, it's not the skills that they have, but the way they are perceived in the marketplace and how they are able to translate their expertise and market these services.

Daniel and Kim have only been part of the Academy for a few short months, but already some of the distinctions of the Expert Success Formula have transformed how they do business.

I am certain that their branding and design skills are a welcome addition to the range of services already available to the Academy members and I've seen a growing trend that members do business with each other in the Expert Success Academy.

Daniel Wagner

AN INTERVIEW WITH KIM AND DANIEL BENNETT

KIM AND DANIEL, WHAT WAS YOUR MAIN GOAL FOR THIS YEAR?

We knew it was time to change our business. Whilst we have managed to maintain a reasonable standard of living from our business over the last 20 or so years, we needed to create more purpose, time and money for ourselves. We needed to find new energy and excitement, and use our experience and knowledge to build new customers. As a result we looked for, and

They rediscovered enjoyment and determination. Now it's fun again!

found, the Expert Success Academy, which gave us the inspiration and knowledge to drive our business forward, rather than letting it control us. Of course financial success is important, but that comes from our rediscovered enjoyment and determination: it's fun once again!

WHAT SORT OF EXPERTS ARE YOU?

Kim and I have different areas of expertise, which reflect our quite different personalities. Kim is quiet and very thoughtful, and her real expertise is listening, learning, and interpreting, then designing wonderful pieces, whether it's branding, websites and online activity or print, packaging or exhibition stands that, to put it simply, work. Kim is highly intuitive, and if you want to know what she is thinking, ask her to draw it, not write it. On the other hand I am rather loud (known by some as Booming Bennett) and boisterous. My energy seems to attract people, at least those I have not scared off, and I build relationships, which enable me to learn about people and their businesses. My expertise is identifying opportunities within our clients' businesses to create value, and then working with Kim to deliver results. Kim likes to say I am the talker and she is the doer. Together, our expertise is creative business development.

HOW DID YOU GET INTO GRAPHIC DESIGN?

Kim has a Diploma in Design from spending four years at Nene College of Art in Northampton and worked as a graphic designer for a large national paper merchant. I had completed a Diploma in Agriculture and was working on a large arable farm operating big tractors and equipment, with my sights set clearly on farm management. We were both ambitious and driven, and we wanted more responsibility, so we took up my parents' suggestion to move to the Lake District to work with them in their hotel. We both retained some involvement in the hotel until 2001 when they retired and sold up, but Kim and I wanted to run our own business, and the obvious route was to use Kim's design skills. The decision was almost as simple as that and then we were in business.

WHAT QUALIFICATIONS DID YOU NEED?

We used Kim's portfolio from her previous graphic design jobs as evidence of capability; her qualification had got her into the position to build her portfolio, but in reality had little bearing on building our business. I had loved my college days, which included quite a lot of farm business management so I had a basic understanding of accounting, planning and business systems which did prove useful, although I wouldn't necessarily advocate a National Diploma in Agriculture as necessary for setting up and running a design company!

HAVE YOU MADE MISTAKES ALONG THE WAY?

Absolutely, but if we hadn't we wouldn't have got anywhere. In business you must try things. OK, you need to assess risk, but you cannot run a business without taking a few. Our biggest mistake was during the mid-90s when we were focused on building turnover. We were on course to reach £0.5million turnover, but then we realised that all revenue was going out on wages, rent and cars! We had to restructure, which was tough on people, and costly, but fixing our mistake of focusing on turnover will stay with us forever.

WHAT DOES THE FUTURE HOLD FOR YOU?

Kim and I have rekindled our enthusiasm and energy, and the future, whilst challenging, is very exciting. Our expert status, based on our knowledge and experience, has given us the confidence to move our relationships with our clients from that of a supplier to business partners. Now when we start working with a prospect, building our understanding and getting to know them as people – their values and drivers – they quickly understand the value of what we do, and the focus we bring to delivering results. To extract a prospect's customer value proposition we ask the question, 'Why should an ideal prospect buy from you, rather than any of your competitors, or not buy at all?' And we don't accept their first answer; we challenge and probe to ensure we all really do see things from their customers' perspective.

HOW DID YOU MEET DANIEL WAGNER?

I was invited to take up an empty seat on one day of Daniel Wagner's Business Success Summit in September 2012. Whilst I was intrigued by what I had read and heard about Daniel, and so accepted the invite, as a fidget I was dreading the thought of having to sit still from 9.30am until 6.00pm on a Friday listening to someone drone on. The day was a revelation, I even managed to sit still, and I wanted more, so I persuaded Kim to attend a Discovery Day with me, so she could meet Daniel and the team.

WHAT ATTRACTED YOU TO THE EXPERT SUCCESS ACADEMY?

Both of us now having tasted the Expert Success Academy, agreed that the content, presentation style and support was what we had been looking for to help us move our business forward. Not only could we use what we learnt to develop our business, we could also deliver our new knowledge to our clients as branding and design experts. Another significant factor in making our choice is the way Daniel uses his own business as a case study, warts and all. Seeing how Daniel builds his audience and client value, using his own product staircase, is a very powerful demonstration of the potential of your own business.

'Expert Success' is a good case study, warts and all.

HAVE YOU HAD ANY CHALLENGES?

Kim and I have faced many challenges. One we get asked about quite often is, 'How have you managed to work with your wife/husband for so long?'

We were both relatively young to start in business; I was 23, and of course I'm not allowed to reveal Kim's age. In the 1990s we both sought perfection, and we would fight our own corner for what we believed was right: surely the other must agree with my point of view, neither of us willing to compromise. This did lead to some heated arguments, and somewhat frosty atmospheres, often lasting for a few days. I'm glad to say we're much better at dealing with differences these days. We both now accept that perfection is not always necessary, and in fact can be a hindrance, and often action is far more important. Now, when we do disagree, the silence doesn't last much more than half an hour, and the offer by one to the other of a cup of tea usually brings about a fresh and constructive discussion and agreement.

WHAT DID YOUR PARENTS SAY?

Both Kim's and my parents have always been totally supportive. The only stories that come to mind are that when Kim first decided to go to art school her father told her she would never be able to make a living doing 'that'. And I remember my father telling me (although he denies it now), that if I didn't knuckle down and do my school work I'd end up a salesman. Both dads are great people and truly loved, I think it just boiled down to how things were viewed at those times.

IS THIS SOMETHING YOU SAW YOURSELF DOING IN THE PAST?

Kim and I both had a desire to do our own thing. Kim's best friend from art college was also called Kim, and they had always talked about running their own business 'Kims' Creative'. This didn't happen, but the other Kim is still in the industry and we're all friends still. I always wanted to run a farming business – and still do – so ending up as a branding specialist didn't come close to my vision, but I am very happy to be doing what I am.

HOW ARE YOU FINANCING YOUR LEARNING WITH THE EXPERT SUCCESS ACADEMY?

You have to invest in yourself. Running a business presents many challenges, and whether you are in business by yourself, or with a partner, you must look after yourself. You need to connect with other people who understand, who can support, cajole and challenge you. Developing your skills is a must, and so financing your learning and personal development should be near the top of your list of priorities. We pay for the Expert Success Academy out of cash flow and it's one of the first items in our budgets.

WHAT ADVICE WOULD YOU GIVE TO OTHERS?

Kim and I have spent the last 12 months deciding who has a positive influence on us, and those who are negative. We refer to them as radiators and drains. You can't always totally ignore the drains, but you can choose to direct your energy to the radiators. In business you will no doubt question yourself and your abilities from time to time: nobody needs a drain around to suck you down, and make you believe your doubts. Believe in yourself and choose your counsel carefully.

You have to invest in yourself.

ANY TIPS YOU'D LIKE TO SHARE?

Have fun. Of course you're not going to enjoy every minute of every day: dealing with insufficient cash can be stressful. But if running your business causes you both heartache and a headache do something about it. Learning more about Daniel Wagner and the Expert Success Academy is a pretty good place to start to make positive changes.

WHERE DO YOU PUT YOUR ENERGY?

The beauty of Kim's and my partnership is that whilst we're opposites, we do balance. Kim directs her energy to creating and learning: happiest and most effective sat at her beloved Mac challenging herself to come up with that idea. Fortunately, unlike many creative people, Kim is highly structured and organised: everything needs to be in its place, and she has to know what is on her schedule. That is until I come along and ask her to 'just do this for me please', to which the response is 'why do you always leave things to the last minute?' and then promptly does it anyway.

My energy is all about people. I love to be out meeting people, learning about them and their businesses, and hoping to identify if Kim and I can add value for them. I do a lot of networking, and have worked hard at becoming a go-to person, someone who others approach for thoughts and advice. That does stroke my ego. When I identify an opportunity I usually bring Kim in so we both learn and build a genuine understanding of the client, otherwise it would be like playing Chinese whispers, a game, we know from experience, seldom leads to a satisfactory result.

HAS YOUR BUSINESS STARTED TO MAKE PROFIT YET?

From 1998 through to 2010 Bennett Design made profit and a reasonable return on the time and money invested. Due to changes in the business environment, and health issues for both of us, our business suffered in the following two years and we incurred losses. Having met Daniel Wagner we chose the Expert Success Academy to help us because we wanted more money, more time and more purpose. Are we there yet? No. Are we on the right path and moving forward? A definite yes.

They're on the right path and moving forward.

DO YOU HAVE ANY OTHER BUSINESSES?

We don't have any other businesses, but we have been involved in others. The Bennett family hotel in the Lake District was a very important part of our lives. Working with my parents was, on the whole, a genuine pleasure, particularly towards the latter years of owning the hotel. The work ethic that my mother and father had was incredible to see, and a great example to follow, although I would like to have seen them less hands on with many of the routine daily tasks. Business aside, there are many great family memories of sitting around a large table to eat together, with multiple conversations and laughter.

In 2004 I was asked to work with a very old printing company. Although I could see problems and wanted to help, the role transpired into 'you're getting involved with things you don't need to, just go and get some sales'. Despite the fact there was over £7,500 of waste work each month, the biggest capital investment in 2005 was two new typewriters, and the average debtor days was 96. I did allow myself a little self-congratulation when I was asked to be managing director a couple of years later but during 2010, having run in to health issues, I felt it necessary to leave the company to allow clarity and space for someone else to drive the business on.

ANY PLANS TO DO ANY/MORE JOINT VENTURES?

We have found it difficult to establish viable, genuine joint ventures in the past, although we are in the process of changing that having learnt from the Expert Success Academy. Now, Kim and I share responsibility in building relationships: either of us can declare if we're not entirely happy, and so we are able to withdraw before over-committing ourselves. When talking with potential partners, whilst of course we want to understand what they want from a relationship, we communicate what we require with greater clarity. If agreement can't be reached, or a detailed contract is required, it is unlikely to work for us. A joint venture is sustainable if all things are equal; inequality will manifest itself in to a problem further down the line. However, we do see greater opportunities for partnering, and in particular we are very excited about a recent new relationship around building online communities around business brands.

 **KEY LEARNINGS**

- We are experts in branding and design.

- The most powerful way to grow your business is to win a space in the hearts and minds of your customers and prospects.

- You must know and understand who your audience is. If you have more than one audience you must understand each audience separately.

- Developing a product staircase is a highly effective means to build value from and for your clients. Each step must give clearly understood added value.

- You must be able to answer the question; 'Why should your ideal prospect buy from you, rather than a competitor, or not buy at all?' otherwise price is your only differentiator.

MEBS MERCHANT
WEALTH CREATION EXPERT

Promoting Financial Freedom Through Wealth Creation Strategies

Armchair Investors Club

www.mebsmerchant.com
www.armchairinvestorsclub.com
mebs@armchairinvestorsclub.com
0208 577 9990

From a humble background, Mebs is now a well-respected personality in the financial and property investment circle. His career includes estate agent, mortgage broker and property investment consultant. Trained in skills of trading the financial markets, Mebs trades stocks and currency markets for a living, as well as teaching selected and unique investment strategies in the financial and property market to individuals who aspire to have financial freedom.

- **Qualifications:** NLP Practitioner Certificate. Certified Life Coach. Financial Trading Institutes courses. *Expert Success* Academy Brand Awareness. LSE Cert. Lifelong Learning. Certified Mentor Institute of Enterprise. Equity Options. Exchange Traded Funds specialist.

- **Credibility:** Over the past 17 years Mebs has helped over 300 individuals create their financial future, collectively worth well over £140 million.

- **Specialties:** financial markets trader and trainer. Real estate project development and investments. Wealth development coach. Business and personal mentor.

❝ MY LIFE HAS CHANGED FOR THE BETTER.

INTRODUCTION BY DANIEL WAGNER

If you ever have the privilege of meeting Mebs Merchant in person, you will immediately notice his genuine warmth and humanity. When Mebs first joined one of my online coaching programs, I wasn't really aware of him as many of our students were online students who I had never met face-to-face.

I first became aware of him when he signed up for the Online Brand Masterclass, our authentic personal branding programme. It is not unusual that people join us at this masterclass without a clear vision of what they would love to do for the rest of their lives, and often there may be two or three ideas in their mind.

The goal of the coaching process over the weekend is to unearth the best option for the attendee, and Mebs and I were able to hone in on a set of skills that he possessed.

If that wasn't breakthrough enough, what I remember much more vividly is that Mebs was burdened with a business that cost him thousands of pounds in losses every month.

Sometimes it's hard to let go, but it is also important not to have unfinished business, which will take up your energy and what I refer to as 'mental RAM'. We all have only a limited amount of time, energy and attention to give, so if we spend it on negative pursuits or activities that lose us money, we will suffer.

In one of our coaching sessions I was able to demonstrate that it would be a better decision for Mebs to sell his business, even at a loss, instead of trying to hang on to it for any length of time.

I can safely say, and Mebs agrees, that this is a decision he would have not taken by himself. Ironically or incidentally, Mebs was actually able to sell his business at a profit in no time and quickly resolve the situation, which allowed him to move on and focus on the new opportunities.

So sometimes the benefits of being part of a tribe or group is not why you initially joined at all, but it could free you from a millstone around your neck.

I'm pleased to see that Mebs is now pursuing his new career and that his health has improved as a result of being able to let go

Daniel Wagner

AN INTERVIEW WITH MEBS MERCHANT

MEBS, WHAT WAS YOUR MAIN GOAL FOR LAST YEAR?

My first main goal was to free myself from running a day-to-day estate agency business! I wanted to be free (mainly due to health reasons) of the day-to-day problems and other unavoidable issues of running an office turning over £1million a year. Selling my ailing estate agency business freed me from all this.

My second goal was to have more time for my family and myself and to have a better quality of life. To do things that I always wanted to or dreamt of today, rather than when I retire.

Like others, he wants more time and a better quality of life.

Today, I am working under 40 hours a week. In the last six months, I have already had three holiday breaks with my family and I have no 9-to-5 syndrome to put up with on a daily basis. I am also learning photography and travel journalism, which has always been my dream.

Being a passionate financial market trader, I always wanted to have this as my main source of income and work from home. I was able to sell the estate agency mainly because I had other skills and was able to replace my income by trading the markets as my main source of income.

My third goal was to use my expertise, knowledge and skills of property investments and financial market trading with others and teach others how to be financially independent by having more than one stream of income: how to become successful investors in properties and profitable traders of the financial market.

WHAT SORT OF EXPERT ARE YOU?

Having spent 17 years owning and running an estate agency as well as investing in a personal property portfolio and advising others on theirs, I have gained an insight into the tips and tricks of being a successful property investor and becoming a portfolio landlord. Having completed various courses and learned from experience, I am in a position to guide others correctly and help them avoid the pitfalls of property investment. I can also help property owners with their property management according to legal obligations and legislation. Through my network of other estate agents, property developers and management companies I can reliably refer any individual seeking such services to the right person in their local area.

My experience of trading the financial market as a currency and stock trader has given me the knowledge and skills to share with others and teach them in few months what took me years to learn.

My knowledge and expertise has enabled me to develop certain unique tried and tested strategies, which give an individual a higher probability of success. I teach and share these on a one-to-one mentorship programme and through the Armchair Investor Club network. I also actively trade my personal account in stocks and currencies on a daily basis.

HOW DID YOU GET STARTED WITH YOUR ARMCHAIR INVESTORS CLUB?

In the recent economic downturn, a large number of property investors, including myself, had to face difficult times and saw our wealth diminishing rapidly. However, I was fortunate because I had the knowledge and skills of trading the financial markets, which I had been doing since 2006. This knowledge of the financial market saved me from financial downfall; it made me realise that one should always diversify one's means of accumulating wealth and aim for multiple streams of income.

After working in the professional and business world for over 30 years, latterly working a 65-hour week most of the time, I ignored my physical restrictions and needs and I had my first reality check in 2006: my first heart attack. This brought me to realise I needed to slow down and instead of just concentrating on money, I should concentrate on what matters to me most – my quality of life with my family.

Your first heart attack is an important wake-up call!

Selling a 17-year-old business has a lot of emotional baggage attached. Even a couple of years later, I saw no change in my stressful business life until, one fine day, the 30th of April 2012, during a weekly online live webinar for Platinum members of the Expert Success Academy, with the help of my newly found and trusted mentors Daniel Wagner, James Watson and other members of the club present on that live-call in, I made my final decision to sell my estate agency business. I decided to do something that would give me far greater satisfaction than just concentrating on the money factor and that was to work smarter and share my knowledge and skills gained in property investments and financial market trading with others who could possibly be in a similar situation.

With the moral support and feedback from my mentors and other members of ESA, I felt confident in taking this major step in my life – a successful step towards a better quality of life.

I eventually sold the estate agency in August 2012 and since then have established an online member's community, The Armchair Investors Club, where all individuals are welcome to share their knowledge, skills and information of the investment markets, for the benefit of the public at large. I have also co-founded a training institution, the London School of Financial Trading, where members are taught the skills of investing in the property and financial markets, through live workshops and live webinars.

WHAT ARE THE CORE SERVICES OFFERED BY ARMCHAIR INVESTORS CLUB?

It is a community where experts and members share their knowledge, skills, information and finances for the benefit of those who desire financial freedom and could do with a helping hand.

No one person possesses all the skills and means required to build a strong financial future and create wealth and a better lifestyle. Some are experts in property investments and some in financial markets; some have legal and professional expertise and some are expert in raising finance. Others require a hand with property management and maintenance. Even experienced investors may require the services and knowledge of these experts.

The club brings all the above expertise under one roof. It also offers members the opportunity to invest in property joint ventures as well as learn about property investments and trading the financial markets alongside their full-time jobs or business activities.

WHICH MEANS?

It means that individuals can secure their financial future by having a second stream of income at a low level of investment, without giving up their main occupation, by using safe, tried and tested strategies and skills.

WHAT QUALIFICATIONS DID YOU NEED?

You need determination and the desire for more knowledge and financial independence.

DID YOU ATTEND ANY OTHER TRAINING PROGRAMMES?

Since leaving college, I have attended numerous courses and training programmes in my earlier chosen careers in travel and tourism, financial services, property investments, personal development, mentorship and financial coaching.

HAVE YOU MADE MISTAKES ALONG THE WAY?

Several! Not having had the privilege to attain a university qualification, I had to embark on a journey of self-educating and learning from experiences. Some of these experiences were very costly but I learnt from my mistakes and made sure every mistake made me stronger and wiser. Today, I can confidently tell my audience that I have walked the talk!

WHAT DOES THE FUTURE HOLD FOR YOU?

An exciting challenge of utilising my expertise for the benefit of a larger community. The future for me is not just about counting my success in light of monetary rewards only; it is more about personal satisfaction and better quality of life for me and my family. It's about stopping to smell the roses.

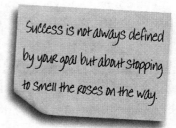

Success is not always defined by your goal but about stopping to smell the roses on the way.

HOW DID YOU MEET DANIEL WAGNER?

I was introduced to Daniel and James, about four years ago, through their online marketing home study course, Internet Buddies. Always having the hunger to increase my knowledge further, I kept in touch with the duo and in February 2012 attended their live workshop at Heathrow, which introduced the participants to Expert Success Blueprint.

WHAT ATTRACTED YOU TO THE EXPERT SUCCESS ACADEMY?

Having attended the Expert Success Blueprint introduction evening and met Daniel and James for the first time in person, I was convinced that this pair had a genuine interest in others at heart and there would be a lot for me to learn and gain as a member of the Academy. I signed up as a Platinum member, which gave me more access to the expertise and benefits. I am very pleased to say my life has changed for the better as a result.

The Academy provided a strong community of like-minded individuals to network and exchange ideas to mutual benefit. Joining the Academy truly showed me the power of networking (with the right people).

WHAT DID YOU LEARN ON THE ONLINE BRAND MASTERCLASS? WHAT IMPACT DID IT HAVE ON YOU?

At first, the cost of attending the Online Brand Masterclass was the major impact. However, after attending the weekend workshop and completing the basics of establishing my personal brand, I can convincingly say that it was a worthwhile investment. Creating my brand has fast-tracked my expertise profile in the public domain and within four months it has given me, or rather my expertise, the status and exposure which would have taken me years to achieve by myself.

WHAT DID YOU LEARN FROM THE EXPERT SUCCESS BOOK AND WHAT IMPACT DID IT HAVE ON YOU?

I consider the book to be my guide to business success. It has created a paradigm shift in my way of looking at marketing and business. It provides simple, yet very effective strategies and facts to confidently position yourself with other prominent leaders of your industry.

Amongst many others, one strategy I am currently utilising in my business promotion is the options for individuals to 'Do It Yourself', 'Do It with Someone' or 'Let Someone Do It for You'! This concept has given me my product staircase for selling my services to individuals on different level of investments.

HOW ARE YOU FINANCING YOUR LEARNING WITH THE EXPERT SUCCESS ACADEMY?

As my new business activities are in their infancy, I am currently utilising my savings, which I consider a wise spend since as with any new business, one needs to invest money and efforts. I am confident of achieving financial returns from my new venture by the summer of 2013, at which time my investment in the Academy would be self-financing.

WHAT ADVICE WOULD YOU GIVE TO OTHERS?

Attend the introductory Expert Success Live one-day event. Meet the mentors and the tribe of like-minded individuals aspiring to success. Ask other current members for their feedback and then decide with sincerity if it is for you or not. The Academy may not be for everyone and it certainly is not a ticket to get rich quick. Whether the membership has any benefit for an individual depends on the person. There are some members who have managed to attain financial results in large numbers and fast and then there are some who are still working on it and may be for some time. How fast and to what extent the Academy benefits an individual is entirely up to that person and their expectations.

ANY TIPS YOU'D LIKE TO SHARE?

Do not let money restrict you from gaining further knowledge and success. Let your determination and motivation lead and money will follow.

HOW MANY JOINT VENTURE PARTNERSHIPS DO YOU HAVE?

I am currently in discussion with other members of the Academy regarding four possible joint ventures. Outside the Academy, I have attracted a small group of individuals desirous of investing as a consortium in a couple of property investment opportunities.

HAS YOUR BUSINESS STARTED TO MAKE PROFIT YET?

No, but in the first four months I have one paid mentee and by summer will be holding a couple of paid workshops and educational webinars, which should contribute further towards becoming profitable.

WHAT ARE YOUR GOALS FOR THIS YEAR?

1. To cultivate the discipline required to make the most from what the Academy has to teach and share.

2. To build on my personal brand as an expert in my field and increase my consortium of investors to 20 individuals by end 2013.

3. To help at least five people this year attain financial freedom.

HOW WILL THE EXPERT SUCCESS ACADEMY HELP WITH THAT?

Regular meetings of the Academy and interaction amongst the network will keep me on track and keep my knowledge and awareness in alignment with my goals.

KEY LEARNINGS

- Aspire high and put into practice the teaching of the Academy.

- Be sincere and genuine and the same will come back to you.

- Aspire that on every day, in every way, you will get better and better.

ALEXANDER KRUNIC BUSINESS DEVELOPMENT EXPERT

Connecting You With World-Class Knowledge for Business and Personal Development

Business Bestseller
VerlagsgmbH, Austria

www.business-bestseller.com
a.krunic@business-bestseller.com
00 43 (0) 512 56 17 40

There are tens of thousands of business books published every year; very few become bestsellers and even those few more often lead to 'shelf-development' rather than self-development. Since he founded the leading business book magazine in the German language in 1989, Alex has reviewed literally thousands of books about personal and business success and has attended, as well as organised, seminars and speeches with some of the world's most respected public speakers. With *Business Bestseller* (eight-page summaries of the best business books) he provides shortcuts and recommendations on what to read and whom to listen to for more than 30,000 subscribers in 17 countries. It's Alex's mission to provide his readers with recommendations and insights on the best knowledge available for business and personal development, no matter whether it's a book, e-book, audio, video or delivered through a motivational speech or seminar.

- **Qualifications:** Studied law at the University of Innsbruck, earning a degree as an export merchant. Attended a general management programme at the Management Centre St. Gallen, Switzerland.

- **Credibility:** His *Business Bestseller* has more than 30,000 subscribers in 17 countries.

❝ I HAVE MORE THAN 30,000 SUBSCRIBERS IN 17 COUNTRIES.

INTRODUCTION BY DANIEL WAGNER

How Alex ended up as part of the Expert Success Academy is a truly wonderful story. We actually went to secondary school together, which means that I've now known Alex for almost 40 years.

That was of course back in Innsbruck in Austria and I had not seen or met him for over 25 years. I didn't know what he did for a living and I can honestly say that from my memory of him I didn't expect him to become an entrepreneur at such an early age.

So you can imagine my surprise when I saw Alex's name crop up in a list of attendees in one of my preview webinars in the middle of 2012.

I was even more surprised to learn that Alex has been ploughing away at becoming the largest publisher of business book summaries in the German-speaking market.

When he contacted me and told me that he had bought Expert Success and judged it to be one of the best business books that he had read and reviewed, I was bowled over.

What many of you won't know is that when I left Austria, back in 1995, I was not just broke but I had no prospect of improving my life and that in almost 30 years had not shown any sign of success or growing up.

So when Alex and I started talking about expanding the reach of Expert Success into the German-speaking market I was delighted and felt it was a chance to return home as a successful entrepreneur.

This is why I embraced the opportunity with both hands and I'm extremely excited about the upcoming speaking engagements and opportunities to share my message with a wider audience.

I've got to know Alex in the last few months as a caring, generous and visionary entrepreneur with an astute awareness of marketing and sales and I'm looking forward to helping us achieve our vision together

I feel honoured and touched that successful entrepreneurs like Alex would fly in from Austria every month to join us for one day at the Expert Success Academy.

Daniel Wagner

AN INTERVIEW WITH ALEXANDER KRUNIC

ALEX, HOW DID YOU COME UP WITH THE IDEA OF FOUNDING A BUSINESS BOOK MAGAZINE?

Actually this wasn't a strategic decision. As long as I can remember I've loved to read books – to dive into them, into new worlds, ideas, concepts, the life of great men and women, the principles of success and of leading a meaningful life. One day in 1988 a friend of mine, who worked at our local bookstore, mentioned to me that book publishers provide journalists with free review copies of all the new books. And so I decided to found this business book magazine – to get all the books I'm interested in for free.

SO THERE WAS NO PROFIT-MAKING IDEA INVOLVED AT THAT STAGE?

Not really. Some friends and I started the magazine with zero budget. The legal entity was a students' club and our only financial goal was to raise enough advertising revenue to publish the magazine we'd like to read. I remember one initial meeting with the treasurer of the club, where he gave us permission to do whatever we like with the magazine, as long as we did not produce a deficit.

WHEN DID YOU TRANSFORM YOUR MAGAZINE INTO A REAL BUSINESS?

That journey took almost 10 years, during which time I published the magazine alongside studying law at the University of Innsbruck, earning a degree as an export merchant, attending a general management programme at the Management Centre St. Gallen, Switzerland, and working for a member of the Austrian parliament for several years. In November 1998 I quit my full-time job as head of a semi-governmental department dedicated to do research on the future of work. This has been one of my best decisions ever. It completely freed me from an 8-to-5 job I would probably have loved if there hadn't been some side-effects like the complete lack of freedom and fun at work.

AND BECOMING AN INDEPENDENT PUBLISHER TURNED OUT TO BE FREEDOM AND FUN?

You bet! Owning your own business is one expression of freedom and fun, even if you have to deal with decisions, situations or facts that sometimes aren't funny at all. Of course you get the freedom of making all the mistakes yourself too. And I've made lots of them.

WOULD YOU MIND SHARING YOUR MISTAKES WITH OUR READERS?

You'll see some important ones if you study my Key Learnings below. But I'd rather like to share some successes here as this is a book about success stories. In summer 2000 we acquired a Hamburg-based publishing company which provided eight-page-summaries of the best business books on a subscription model. A few months later we signed a joint venture with the FAZ-institute, a publishing house related to the renowned German newspaper *Frankfurter Allgemeine Zeitung*. Today we've over 500 of these business bestseller summaries in our archive. Instead of hours of reading, you become acquainted with the main insights and key concepts of a business book in fewer than 20 minutes. Readers in 17 countries rely on *Business Bestseller*'s recommendations on what to read.

BUT YOU ONLY COVER THE GERMAN-SPEAKING MARKETS — HOW DID YOU HEAR OF DANIEL WAGNER AND THE EXPERT SUCCESS ACADEMY?

Actually, I went to school with Daniel, who, as you may know, was born in Innsbruck. But I hadn't seen him for more than 25 years since we left school and he moved to England. It was a crucial coincidence in summer 2012 that made me search for him online, and then one thing quickly led to another. I read *Expert Success* and almost immediately thought of transferring the whole concept behind the book to German-speaking countries. The Expert Success Matrix was a real eye-opener to me and the strategy behind the Expert Success Formula is concise, compelling and extremely powerful. It was a logical first step to publish a German summary of Expert Success, which we did in February 2013. The next steps will be a German edition of the book, the Expert

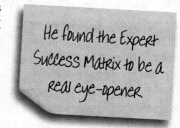

He found the Expert Success Matrix to be a real eye-opener.

Success Newsletter and then the first Online Brand Masterclass to be held in July by Daniel and me in our hometown of Innsbruck.

YOU ATTENDED THE ONLINE BRAND MASTERCLASS AND THEN SIGNED UP FOR THE ACADEMY. WHAT MOTIVATED YOU TO JOIN THE ACADEMY?

First of all, I wanted to gain a personal insight in the strategies – the Why, What and How – that Daniel and James teach. Almost instantly I recognised that the strategy behind the Expert Success Formula is of great value for me and my business too. I have tried to establish my company brand Business Bestseller for almost 24 years so that I can personally take a back seat. Now, after studying Daniel's book and attending the Online Brand Masterclass, I know that establishing my personal brand will be of great value and allow me to exploit my expert status and knowledge for both personal and business growth. It will be crucial for expanding to the English-speaking world too. Unlike in Germany and Austria, where Business Bestseller is well known and relies on a 24-year-long reputation, business partners and prospects in a completely new market definitely want to know from the beginning, who represents Business Bestseller, what this company and its owners stand for and what's their story.

I am convinced that creating a personal online brand is the fastest and most reliable way to establish a trustworthy connection with potential business partners and customers.

SO, YOUR FIRST STEP WAS BUILDING YOUR OWN PERSONAL ONLINE BRAND?

Actually, no. I first focused on redesigning the product staircase. I expect immediate positive results from this measure, as we will implement not only new membership levels, but add some exclusive high-ticket products as well. My personal online brand will have to wait a little while as I regard it mainly as a means to enter the English-speaking markets, which is scheduled for 2014. On the other hand, I think of using my personal online brand site to establish another expert business of my own, providing recommendations for keynote and public speakers.

Creating a product staircase was a logical step.

SO THAT'S WHY YOUR STRAPLINE ISN'T JUST ABOUT BOOKS?

Exactly, and neither is our company brand Business Bestseller. A bestseller need not necessarily be a book, but can be an audio, video or public speaker as well. By the way, it was Daniel who came up with my current strapline during the exercise in the Online Brand Masterclass. He really has a knack for this kind of thing.

DO YOU THINK THE EXPERT SUCCESS FORMULA WILL WORK AS WELL IN GERMANY AND AUSTRIA AS IT DOES HERE IN THE UK?

Definitely! Although it'll be necessary to adjust some details to the local markets (e.g. It is not only the German language that is different, the mentality is as well), the basic principles and concepts apply to the expert industry all over the world. The Expert Success Matrix is quite universal, I think: the higher you are positioned, the more you earn, the fewer competitors you have and the more customers you can attract.

And Daniel's trinity of the Expert Success Formula: Authentic Personal Online Branding, Strategic Product Staircase and Cultivate a Buying Audience is definitely universal too.

KEY LEARNINGS

- You recognise successful people by the size of their library, not their flat screen.

- It's all about context, not content.

- Even if you already have a strong business brand, develop your personal brand, too.

- One of the biggest problems with prices is that they are often too low to attract the right customers.

- You don't need thousands of customers to build a wealthy business; a loyal tribe of one, two or three hundred will do very well.

- Never run out of cash! – The sooner you become self-employed the better, but it's a good idea to keep your (well-) paid job until your business idea begins to produce positive cash flow.

- One usually overestimates what can be achieved in one year, but underestimates what's possible in ten.

SASIE THOMPSON
WEALTH CREATION EXPERT

Unlocking Financial Freedom for Female Entrepreneurs

A Woman's Worth (AWW Network)

www.awwnetwork.com
sasie@sasiethompson.com
0845 052 3924

Sasie Thompson is a woman with many strings to her bow. She worked in HR for a number of years and is also a qualified beauty therapist. She now coaches and mentors females in wealth creation and business. Sasie has over 12 years in property and business and has also been qualified in beauty therapy for over 14 years. Her mission is to help women become wealthy and financially free, something that needs to be understood and achieved with definite intent.

- **Qualifications:** 2:1 in Music and Media Management.

- **Credibility:** Bought first property at age19. Owned seven properties in Bristol and London worth £1.2million by the time she was 26.

❝ I WAS WORTH £1.2MILLION BY THE TIME I WAS 26.

INTRODUCTION BY DANIEL WAGNER

I think that Sasie's work is even more important than mine! The reason I say that is that I sincerely believe that women are discriminated against all over the world.

And although we have generally made progress in treating women equally, there is still a long way to go, especially in the areas of entrepreneurship and the boardroom.

So this is why Sasie's work of empowering women to become entrepreneurs and help them on their journey to financial freedom is so important.

Sasie is able to copy much of my business formula and business model, as she has decided to run regular events and base her business model around one-to-one and group coaching.

This is possibly one of the biggest advantages of being part of the Expert Success Academy, as we can take shortcuts by copying what other successful members already at doing!

Startups are traditionally very fragile and vulnerable to cash flow issues, and Sasie had to learn fast that resilience and vision are paramount to long-term success.

When you read Sasie's story over the next few pages you can immediately see how varied her background is and how everything she has learnt so far is invested into her next venture.

I observed this as a common thread in successful expert businesses: that it is individuals and their experience of success and failure that create unique approaches and frameworks to success for others to follow.

Sasie's contributions to the Academy have transcended from professional to personal, having established friendships beyond business with many of the members.

It is indeed that trusted environment that allows us to openly share even our flaws and weaknesses. And because you don't have to worry about over-protecting yourself and pretending to be something you are not, you make progress much faster.

Daniel Wagner

AN INTERVIEW WITH SASIE THOMPSON

SASIE, WHAT SORT OF EXPERT ARE YOU?

I am a wealth creation expert and my aim is to assist females in becoming financially free. Wealth can mean many different things to different people. But for me it means more than just money, even though financial stability is a large part of it.

wealth can mean different things.

HOW DID YOU GET INTO WEALTH CREATION?

I would say I got obsessed with wealth creation and personal development after I filed for bankruptcy. I started young and bought my first property at 19. I quickly realised I didn't need all three bedrooms, a garage and a driveway to myself so decided to rent part of it out. Being the type of person I am I knew I had to have my own separate living space so I sold my car to pay to convert the garage into a self-contained flat and got a tenant whose rent covered my mortgage payments. About a year or so later the tenant's sister was looking for somewhere to live, and because I got on with them I felt comfortable with renting her one of the spare rooms in my living space. So now I was getting my mortgage paid for, my salary from my job and extra income from the lodger. I thought wow! This is easy money. To cut a long story short I continued to buy properties in Bristol and London and had seven in total by the time I was 26. My portfolio was worth £1.2million at that point but a couple of years later I had nothing! I had to start all over again from scratch. Since then my whole life has been about rebuilding. About creating a foundation based on what I learned from my experiences, good and bad. Having enough money to buy food, clothe yourself and keep the heating on is something that is taken for granted until you aren't able to do it. Basically, my wealth expert formula is largely based on what I've been through and what I've learned throughout my life so far.

WHAT DID YOU DO AT UNIVERSITY?

I went to university as a mature student at the age of 24 and I graduated with a 2:1 in Music and Media Management. The funny thing is, most people assume my degree was a creative and musical one but it was actually a business degree that concentrated on the legal, administrative, management and business side of the music and media industry, and I loved it. Has it benefited me in anyway? Well yes: I'm never one to knock education. I believe it helped to develop my natural 'business head' and has provided me with the discipline of working to deadlines. However, I also believe the education I have received and continue to receive through academies like the Expert Success Academy, seminars, books and personal development benefit me on a much larger, wider scale.

HOW DID YOU MEET DANIEL WAGNER?

I met Daniel at a free three-day seminar, which was not one of his events. He was one of the last speakers to take the stage on the last day. I was exhausted, overwhelmed and brain-dead with all the content I had been exposed to over the three days and fed up with being 'sold to'. But you know what? Daniel managed to revive me. He touched me with his honest overview of his past and he spoke passionately about claiming your position as an expert. He made it clear that no one was going to give it to you. His explanation message was stand up, stand tall and be seen. He was promoting the Online Branding Masterclass and was the only person who admitted that writing a book or producing other products simply doesn't make sense unless they are strategic. This made him stand out to me as there were many other speakers who were only concerned with selling their course. Basically, he touched me with his honesty and, more importantly, made me laugh. Something about him and his story just resonated with me. I met his business partner, James Watson a few months later at the Expert Success Summit.

> *She learned the benefit of education.*

WHAT ATTRACTED YOU TO THE EXPERT SUCCESS ACADEMY?

I went to the Expert Success Summit in September 2012. I was blown away because it was the first time I was exposed to the whole Expert Success Formula and I also got the chance to meet the rest of the team. I felt so relieved that I had found something that I could apply to all the business ideas I had. Daniel's framework works for everything. James was another factor that attracted me. His knowledge, understanding and experience in sales, IT and business are beyond belief. He manages to break things down into simple processes that you can then implement into your own business. I saw the Academy as a one-stop shop and decided from that point on that I was going to stay in touch in some way. As a result I joined the Expert Success Academy at the end of the summit and haven't looked back since. Each month I go to the Platinum meetings I learn way more than what I can actually implement. This is why I see it as value for money, because as my business(es) grow I can always refer back and implement what's required for them at the right time.

She's learned way more than she can actually implement.

WHAT DID YOU LEARN FROM THE EXPERT SUCCESS BOOK?

The *Expert Success* book has taught me the Formula in great detail. It's like having Daniel and James at my every beck and call. I have learnt the importance of having a framework and formulising information in my head that just seems like 'the norm' to me but which is actually my own unique way of doing and seeing things. This is what will attract customers or clients to you because people buy into you as a person first. This is why I am confident with my unique positioning as an expert wealth creator, even though there are many others in this field.

DID YOU ATTEND ANY OTHER TRAINING PROGRAMMES?

Yes and I still do. I have been on many training programmes ranging from very specific topics, like buying properties at auction for example, to more generic ones about business and health etc. These have sometimes been online, long distance, in person, with groups and one-to-one. I will always attend training programmes that will improve my knowledge and understanding in the topics I'm passionate about.

APART FROM THE ACADEMY, DO YOU GO TO ANY OTHER NETWORKING EVENTS?

Of course. I love the Academy because it has an invaluable net worth of knowledge and contacts, plus everyone is an expert in their chosen field. However, I still think you need to network outside of this circle, even if it's only to keep your ear to the ground in your specific industry. I go to other networking events which are not always for business purposes but I normally end up doing some sort of business in one way or another as a result. I also have my own networking event called A Woman's Worth (AWW Network), pronounced 'awe' network. It's a female-only event that I set up with the sole intention to empower women in wealth creation and financial independence. It's a continuous work in progress and has over 90 female entrepreneurs registered to date. You can find us at www.awwnetwork.com

DO YOU HAVE ANY OTHER BUSINESSES?

Yes, I have multiple businesses simply because I believe we should all have multiple streams of income. As well as A Woman's Worth, I have a MLM (multi-level marketing or network marketing) business in the health and well-being sector which is rocketing, and is what I call my pension. I have a property investment business and I'm also about to provide a new business startup product and launch some additional services to coach females in wealth and business – so watch this space.

WHERE DO YOU PUT YOUR ENERGY?

I put a lot of my energy into my businesses and ideas. But more recently I've been concentrating on me, and by that I mean mentally and spiritually. I've always paid attention to myself physically, by trying my best to exercise and eat healthy foods (I do this most of the time – well kind of!) This usually keeps me feeling good but since the beginning of this year (2013) I felt like something was missing. Even when I was able to tick goals off my list I still didn't feel content. This, along with some other factors, forced me to look within. So now I put a large portion of my energy into myself, by being happy with all that I have, by being aware and by taking the time to meditate. By default this means most other parts of my life benefit.

HAVE YOU DONE ANY JOINT VENTURES? DID THE EXPERT SUCCESS ACADEMY HELP?

I'm working on two joint ventures right now and both contacts are Expert Success Academy members so yes, the Academy has definitely

Planning two joint ventures with Expert Success Academy members.

helped. Business is so much easier when the people you're working with are experts in the industry concerned. The fact they know and work to the Expert Success Formula means creating or mixing products and services automatically blend. The synergy is there straight away because everyone is singing from the same hymn sheet. I see the Academy as my extended family: there is always someone to hand to help with advice or support or both.

WHAT ARE YOUR GOALS FOR THIS YEAR?

My goals for the rest of this year are to implement the rest of the Expert Success Formula by working on my online brand (step one) and further developing new and existing strategic products for my businesses (step two). I also plan to work on cultivating my audience (step three) and I most definitely need to automate some aspects of my businesses.

HOW WILL THE EXPERT SUCCESS ACADEMY HELP WITH THAT?

The Expert Success Academy will help me with my goals by being there as a trusted support network and by keeping me updated on the best tools and methods that have been tried and tested in Daniel's and James's own business.

KEY LEARNINGS

- The importance of having a framework.
- That we should all have multiple streams of income.

DR DANNY SCAHILL (DOCTOR OF CHIROPRACTIC) ULTIMATE ENERGY EXPERT

Creating Wealth Through Your Health

Ultimate Performance Formula

www.dannyscahill.com
danny@dannyscahill.com
07828 682694

Dr Danny is a high performance expert and founder of 'Ultimate Performance Formula'. As a chiropractor he has been teaching his patients this material for the best part of a decade now, so he decided to create a business mentoring business owners and entrepreneurs on how to rapidly transform their energy and performance too. He regularly schedules free breakthrough consultations with prospects to see if there's a good match to work together on the client's health transformation. His coaching business is growing steadily due to fast implementation of Daniel and James's advice and coaching. He regularly gets the opportunity to speak to audiences both large and small and train them in how to make better health and lifestyle choices.

- **Qualifications:** BSc (Hons) Chiropractic, Welsh Institute of Chiropractic (WIOC) at Glamorgan University. Wellness Practitioner and NLP Practitioner.

- **Personal Achievements:** Continues to fulfil his purpose by speaking to audiences both large and small.

"IF YOU WANT TO BE TRULY HEALTHY THEN YOU NEED TO EAT WELL, MOVE WELL AND THINK WELL.

INTRODUCTION BY DANIEL WAGNER

I have known Danny now for a good number of years, and what impresses me most about him is that he has tried and failed at a good number of ventures.

And he did that without ever showing the slightest moment of doubt in his ability to ultimately succeed. He understands at a very deep level that success can be achieved by failing forward, by copying from other people, and by staying on course.

And, as with many other experts, in the end it was what he already knew that became the area of his expertise that produces results. As a doctor of chiropractic, Danny's very much aware of how many people are lacking good and full health, and it is his passion to change that.

Danny is an avid contributor on the membership site and the forum and is always helping with his advice in the community. He is also not afraid at times to go it alone and try some more outlandish ideas.

It is his ability to take massive action though, that will ultimately give him the financial freedom he desires.

I know from my own life how demanding a business can be on your health and energy, and therefore I fully endorse Danny's message and his simple strategies for more energy.

Danny is also passionate about sharing his message from the stage and is looking to become a well-known speaker in the health and wellness industry.

The health and wellness market is actually the largest market in the world, underpinned by ageing baby boomers.

Danny has now refined his approach and has tested many different ways to get results for his patients and students. And the way I see it? He is ready to take this message to the widest possible audience.

Becoming an expert in any field is simply based on your confidence in claiming that space and Danny has certainly done that.

Daniel Wagner

AN INTERVIEW WITH DR DANNY SCAHILL

WHAT DID YOU DO AT UNIVERSITY?

I obtained my Chiropractic degree whilst studying for five years at the Welsh Institute of Chiropractic (WIOC) at Glamorgan University. Also prior to Chiropractic College I did three years training at Osteopathic College and then that college closed down just when I could see the finish line in sight!

That's when I went on to study chiropractic, so I completed eight years training in all before I ever adjusted my first Chiropractic patient! I knew what I wanted and there was no way I was going to give up.

DO YOU HAVE ANY OTHER BUSINESSES?

As a doctor of chiropractic, I have run a busy practice for over seven years now.

WHAT SORT OF EXPERT ARE YOU?

I'm an expert in achieving high performance and if you are a business owner or entrepreneur, I can help you 'Create Wealth Through Your Health'.

Typically two types of clients seek me out:

1. Exhausted and looking for a programme to teach them how to turn their health around and boost their energy levels.

2. Pretty healthy with fairly good energy levels but they just want to take their energy and performance to the next level.

HOW DID YOU GET INTO CREATING AND TEACHING THE ULTIMATE PERFORMANCE FORMULA?

I've been in chiropractic practice for close to a decade now and have taught chiropractic health and wellness principles to thousands of patients in that time. Now we've all heard the old adage, 'it's simple but it's not easy' yes? The principles are indeed simple but I still found that not every patient would act on the health knowledge I had given them.

However, those that did take action and implemented my advice got amazing transformations in their health and life. The patients that got great results said to me 'you've got to make this information available to more people' and I started to think about that.

At this point I made the realisation that not everyone wants to know this information. Sure, they all need to know it, but some aren't ready to hear it yet. I've found one particular group of people that are typically more motivated to act on this information and they are business owners and entrepreneurs. This is why I focus on helping business owners and entrepreneurs get more energy and maximise performance. If you want to be truly healthy then you need to eat well, move well and think well. This is what Ultimate Performance Formula is built around.

WHAT QUALIFICATIONS DID YOU NEED?

Well the beauty of the expert industry is such that you 'claim' your expert status rather than being awarded it! The fact that I am a doctor of chiropractic, a wellness practitioner and an NLP practitioner adds to my credibility and self-confidence. But even without those qualifications anyone else could still claim expert status and then build their knowledge and a business around the topic.

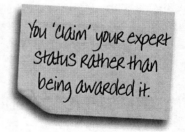

You 'claim' your expert status rather than being awarded it.

HOW LONG DOES IT TAKE DANNY?

When patients used to ask an old chiropractic mentor of mine, 'How long is it going to take for me to get better?' his response was, 'Well it takes two weeks for a cut to heal and nine months to have a baby and you're somewhere in between!' All joking aside, it takes time to start and grow a business. It takes consistent daily action, always moving forward one step at a time.

The monthly Expert Success Academy meetings help to keep me on track and also give me and the rest of the tribe added accountability so we follow through on and ultimately achieve our goals. The regular coaching calls help to solve problems and also celebrate successes along the way too which is important.

HAVE YOU MADE MISTAKES ALONG THE WAY?

Of course, I've made plenty of mistakes along the way. Can you show me a successful person who hasn't made mistakes? Exactly! You've got to make mistakes in order to be successful. Prior to developing the Ultimate Performance Formula I tried many different things, like many entrepreneurs, to get to this point and it's been a very interesting journey.

The irony is that the basis of the Ultimate Performance Formula was a direction I initially wanted to go down many years ago but I changed my mind. I went in a completely different direction and eventually went full circle and arrived back to where my gut instinct always knew was the right place for me. You could say that the other projects I did were mistakes and time wasted but the reality is they weren't mistakes, just very important learnings.

Before I started to focus solely on Ultimate Performance Formula, other projects I created were a Wealth Creation Interview Product and also a Chiropractic Business and Marketing Programme to help chiropractors grow their business. Whilst both ventures were relatively successful, I knew I had to do more to fulfil my purpose of transforming the health, energy and performance of business owners and entrepreneurs worldwide.

WHAT DOES THE FUTURE HOLD FOR YOU?

The future is looking very interesting indeed. My coaching business continues to grow as I enrol more and more new clients and when I get to a critical mass I will launch the Ultimate Performance Academy. The Academy launch will most likely coincide with the release of my book, which will further cement my positioning as the go-to peak performance expert in my niche. In the Expert Success Academy I have the perfect business model to model from which is very helpful!

HOW DID YOU MEET DANIEL WAGNER?

I first saw Daniel speak in September 2009 and instantly knew that at some point in the future I would be working him. He connected with the audience very well by sharing his story from the stage, as well as teaching some great marketing content. I later met him at a Marcus De Maria event I attended in February 2010. In April 2010 I joined Daniel's Internet Buddies Gold programme which eventually became the Blueprint Coaching Programme and I've been a member of his tribe ever since really.

WHAT ATTRACTED YOU TO THE EXPERT SUCCESS ACADEMY?

I've been working with Daniel and James for about three years now and I know, like and trust them so when the Expert Success Academy was launched it was a no-brainer for me: of course I was going to continue my education and coaching with them, I wouldn't go anywhere else now!

Being known, liked and trusted is important.

DID YOU ATTEND ANY OTHER TRAINING PROGRAMMES?

Yes, I have attended many training programmes over the last six to seven years and some have been good, some great and some terrible. Many of the courses tell you the What aspect of business and marketing and neglect the How aspect which is crucial to success. The Expert Success Academy delivers both the What and the How information which makes it head and shoulders above its competition in my opinion.

WHAT DID YOUR FAMILY SAY?

My family are well used to me coming up with new business ideas and other entrepreneurial projects as I have been doing that since I was a child. Some of the concepts and ideas I talk about don't make a lot of sense to my parents but they are always very supportive. Both my parents know that whatever I put my mind to I can achieve and I know they're both very proud of me, which is nice!

IS THIS SOMETHING YOU SAW YOURSELF DOING IN THE PAST?

Before I became a chiropractor I didn't see this coming to be honest! Previously I had said to my mates in Chiropractic College that I would one day be a world-famous DJ as music has always been my first love. The international DJ status hasn't happened yet but that will certainly be revisited so watch this space!

Anyway, so I remember when I first started practicing chiropractic my boss at the time said, 'So when do you want to do your first new patient health workshop? There's no pressure.' He was probably expecting me to say maybe in a few weeks and was very surprised when I said, 'how about tomorrow?!' I did the class the next day and really enjoyed the teaching, training and interaction with people. One of the definitions of doctor is 'educator' so I believe it's my duty to share with the world the real message of health.

I guess it makes sense that I love to perform as a speaker after many years of DJ-ing: it's a beautiful thing to be able to connect with the audience in both roles. The more speaking gigs I have done, the more I have fallen in love with it; I get such a buzz out of it and I always do my best to make sure the audience gets great value too.

HOW ARE YOU FINANCING YOUR LEARNING WITH THE EXPERT SUCCESS ACADEMY?

Cash flow from Ultimate Performance Formula clients finances my Expert Success Academy ongoing education.

His Academy membership is funded by his client income.

WHERE DO YOU PUT YOUR ENERGY?

I put my energy into helping my clients get the transformation that I know they can. I believe we all need coaches and mentors to help us get to where we want to be.

WHAT ARE YOUR GOALS FOR THIS YEAR?

To publish my first book Ultimate Performance Formula and also to continue to expand my coaching business. One of the ways I'll do this is by running Monthly one-day live events. The next step after that is to launch the Ultimate Performance Academy next year.

HOW WILL THE EXPERT SUCCESS ACADEMY HELP WITH THAT?

Well the Expert Success Academy business model is a perfect fit for my business. I already have several Ultimate Performance Formula coaching clients, both one-to-one clients and group coaching as well. The next step is to put on regular one-day live events where I will initially sell my coaching programmes and eventually membership to the Ultimate Performance Academy from stage. This is a similar idea to what Daniel does on his Discovery Day events.

In the future my Academy members will also receive monthly newsletters and a CD of the month, which is also inspired by Daniel and James's work! It's great because I can model my business on all levels of Expert Success Academy and Daniel and James actively encourage members to do that which is a breath of fresh air in this field.

APART FROM THE ACADEMY, DO YOU GO TO ANY OTHER NETWORKING EVENTS?

I do indeed. I attend a BNI chapter on a weekly basis for a breakfast meeting.

ANY PLANS TO DO ANY JOINT VENTURES?

Yes I do have plans to joint venture with several entrepreneurial groups in the coming months. I am also very keen to speak with CEOs of SMEs about staff health and vitality programmes delivered through the Ultimate Performance Formula framework.

KEY LEARNINGS

- You need a coach and mentor, whether it be to improve your health or the health of your business.

- Model your business on a successful business.

- Have a plan and take consistent daily action on that plan.

- Creating a product staircase offering a mixture of No Access and Full Access to me is important.

- Surround yourself with like-minded successful entrepreneurs like we have at the Expert Success Academy.

VICTORIA ROSE PERSONAL DE-CLUTTERING EXPERT

Clearing the Way for Your Future

Victoria-Rose (includes Eat that Elephant and Victoria Rose Coaching)

www.victoria-rose.org
victoria@victoria-rose.org
07773 503026

Victoria helps people organise and sort out their possessions, their systems and their lives: in doing this they achieve greater clarity, space and vitality. From a background of employment in project management, administration and training, alongside motherhood, she evolved into an independent coach and de-clutter expert. Victoria has many years' experience in project management, administration and training. For over 18 years she has been an expert facilitator, coach and mentor. She combines all her professional expertise and private experience with insight and compassion – and a strong practical streak – to help people clear and transform their inner and outer landscapes.

- **Qualifications:** BA (Hons) York University. Licensed Mentor with the More to Life Foundation. Certified Coach, personally trained by Katherine Woodward-Thomas in two transformative coaching programmes, *Calling in "The One"* and *Conscious Uncoupling*.

- **Credibility:** Almost 20 years facilitating, supporting and mentoring experience. Studied with Karen Kingston (author of *Clear your Clutter with Feng Shui*).

- **Lifetime Achievements:** Two happy, fulfilled adult sons. Being named as one of the top 1% most endorsed people in the UK for personal development on LinkedIn.

" I HAVE A PROVEN BLUEPRINT AND STRATEGY.

INTRODUCTION BY DANIEL WAGNER

Victoria has been working with me in the Expert Success Academy for just a year now. In that year I've seen a true transformation as she embraces what it takes to become an entrepreneur.

Reading her biography you can tell that she is smart, very smart, but entrepreneurship and running an expert business require a very special intelligence.

Because of Victoria's ability to intellectualise concepts, she was able to create multiple businesses, but without deciding on an overall strategy, resulting in overwhelm and inefficiency.

I actually believe that it is harder to create simplicity than it is to create complexity. A good part of my job is to create simplicity and streamline processes to help maximise businesses potential.

This is especially true in the startup phase, where it is so hard to get traction and to produce results that count.

As a coach, Victoria values and understands the power of accountability, and one of my highlights of the year was seeing Victoria take charge and run our LinkedIn project as a group leader.

Because it was a clearly defined project with a clear deadline, Victoria was really able to shine and impress the group with her leadership style. As business owners though, we have to set our own clear deadlines and define projects ourselves.

It reminds me of the little joke that goes: Q: What's the best thing about running a business? A: You're your own boss. Q: And what's the worst thing about running a business? A: You're your own boss. So there you have it!

I believe strongly that Victoria's de-cluttering coaching helps people to not just let go of the past, but – as her wonderful strapline states – clear the way to the future.

I am sure we all have discovered already how a spring clean of the house or even just our desk can increase effectiveness and efficiency.

Daniel Wagner

AN INTERVIEW WITH VICTORIA ROSE

VICTORIA, WHAT DID YOU DO AT UNIVERSITY?

I have a BA (Hons) in English and Education from York University. This reflects my lifelong interest in the humanities and people. I got a double first for my final dissertation, 'Becoming a Student'. I have always been fascinated about how and why people do what they do and how they relate to each other.

IT'S QUITE A JUMP FROM THERE TO THE CORPORATE WORLD — HOW COME?

I joined as a graduate into the International Computers Limited (ICL) training division. I have a very logical, organised mind with a fine attention to detail. I like to develop simple transparent systems to get things done and keep them running smoothly – so we can get on to the more interesting and enjoyable things in life. But I'm most interested in developing people so the technical side had limited appeal, compared to the project management and systems analysis parts. I went on to develop that in other organisations.

SO WHAT HAPPENED NEXT?

The short answer is children! I had (have!) two gorgeous sons who play a massive part in my life. Early parenting was a particularly challenging time for me as learning difficulties were identified and provision had to be sought (and fought for). Alongside this my step-father and my mother both got cancer and died within a short space of time. It really threw into relief what is important in life. And with inheritance issues (they had left no wills which was a nightmare – beware everybody and don't let that be you!) and the most enormous amount of 'stuff' to clear out, the theme of organising, letting go and prioritising became ever clearer for me.

SO, FAST-FORWARDING, WHEN DID YOU DECIDE TO SET UP A BUSINESS DOING DE-CLUTTERING AND ORGANISING?

Well, I had been doing it for many years with friends and acquaintances who would ask for help so I was developing my skills and deriving a tremendous amount of satisfaction from it – but no pay! My paid work was at that time with small businesses where I created smooth-running systems and events and they created what they were good at – designer retail outfits, delivering corporate arts based initiatives and so on.

She wanted to do more of what she really loved.

Then my dad died and that makes you look at your own life. I decided it was time to do more of what I really loved and to reach more people.

WHAT ARE THE MAIN CHALLENGES YOU HAVE EXPERIENCED?

Alongside my passion for de-cluttering physical space I have been involved for over 19 years with an international programme of personal development now called the *More to Life* programme. I have also studied and contributed to many other similar arenas. So I have trained and spent many years mentoring, coaching and supporting people to clear the mental blocks that are preventing them living the lives they want. Internal clutter and external clutter both weigh us down and drain our creativity and our lust for life.

So to answer the question, the biggest challenge by far was how to combine these so that potential clients could get a clear idea of what I am about and what services I provide. I was pretty much a rabbit in the headlights in terms of defining my business which is a stressful place to be.

HOW DID YOU MEET DANIEL WAGNER?

I went to a coaches' conference. When Daniel did his presentation on Personal Online Branding it was a proverbial light-bulb moment for me. It was so clear that this was the way forward and, most importantly, I would have a road map and a support team to help me achieve this. It was very exciting.

She had a light-bulb moment!

WHAT HAS HAPPENED SINCE?

First of all I attended the Online Brand Masterclass and I took my older son along to learn too. She was also going to become part of my support team; so it was a great thing to share.

I am thrilled with the pictures that John Cassidy took that weekend and they have become a key part of my brand. One image across everything. Previously my brand was 'Eat that Elephant' and I was known as the Elephant Lady! I had to choose between 'Hello Victoria Rose' or 'Hello Elephant Lady'. Not much of a decision really!

Then I joined the Expert Success Academy. The monthly structure has supported and focused me to build everything I do around this identity. I am now more confident with my expert status.

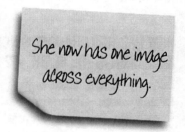

She now has one image across everything.

WHAT SORT OF EXPERT WOULD YOU SAY YOU ARE?

I am an expert in how people relate – to themselves, to their possessions, and to other people. At helping them identify and clear out the crap.

WHAT DO YOU ACTUALLY DO?

I work with individuals, couples or small businesses to help them to clear out and organise their home or office space – it's very hands-on.

I run workshops on different topics: clutter clearing; personal effectiveness and purpose; self-esteem.

I coach individuals to break through anything they are struggling with and support them to create and sustain something different.

Very often 'clutter' involves incompletions – I coach people to do this for themselves, we do it together, or sometimes I do it for them. Whichever way, it brings much satisfaction and relief.

And last – but far from least – I coach people through two very profound and effective programmes devised by Katherine Woodward-Thomas.

Nothing brings up our "stuff" like relationships, so when I saw an opportunity to go to the US and train with the founder and author Katherine Woodward-Thomas, I jumped at the opportunity of the adventure. She created the first programme, *Calling in 'The One'*, for people looking to attract a new or deepen an existing relationship. Her second programme, *Conscious Uncoupling*, is an exciting, revolutionary way to navigate the trauma of a relationship breakdown and to help re-create your life. I am also a regular volunteer coach on the online delivery of both these programmes.

At the risk of sounding like a plumber, it's all about clearing blockages – real and imagined. And creating something new.

HOW HAS THIS CHANGED SINCE YOU HAVE BEEN IN THE ACADEMY?

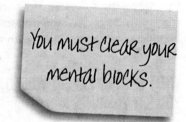

You must clear your mental blocks.

Actually that's also pretty much what the Expert Success Academy has helped me with – clearing my own mental blocks: bringing it all together in my personal brand; clearing my blocks and resistance to and fear of using social media. I have learnt different ways to identify and reach people and to keep in touch with them. My network is much bigger and I have a much more professional presentation all round which properly reflects the level of expertise and service I provide. Everything is much more congruent. I have one website to point people at and one email address. Less clutter!

WHAT DOES ALL THIS MEAN?

My time is better spent, I feel excited and more positive. This feeds in to my passion for clutter-clearing and coaching so I achieve even better results with my clients. My energy and focus is on my bigger purpose – to make a positive difference to as many people's lives as I can touch. With the help and support here, I have created a business centred around me so whatever aspects I focus on, pick up or drop, it is all linked through me as my brand, and it is easily maintainable and updateable.

I have a proven blueprint and strategy for me to develop products and services in the future to develop my business.

Overall I am more professional, more confident and so more fulfilled – and I earn more money too!

WHAT ADVICE WOULD YOU GIVE TO OTHERS?

You only have one life and it is a tragedy not to use it to live your purpose (whatever that is – money, make a difference, social reform etc.). The Expert Success Formula will help you structure and create your unique contribution to the world, and you'll have some fun along the way. Focus on what you can give – and you will get more back than you dream of.

I would recommend having a chat with one of the wonderful folk at the Academy and ask any and all the questions you may have. It is a substantial investment of time, money and attention so get everything out of it you possibly can – there's an awful lot there to be had.

KEY LEARNINGS

- Come with Focus, not with Fear.

- JFDI (Just F***ing Do It!).

- Don't sweat the small stuff.

- Ask for help and you'll get it.

- Implement what you've learnt as quickly as you can.

- Make yourself accountable as well as count-on-able.

- Don't use too many clichés!

EVA DALGETY
ONLINE PROFITS EXPERT

Helping Small Business Owner, Entrepreneurs and Self Employed Individuals to Unlock Online Profits in their Business

Dalgety Marketing Solutions

www.evadalgety.com
info@evadalgety.com
07572 847543

As the owner of Dalgety Marketing Solutions, Eva helps small businesses and self-employed individuals to unlock online profits in their business. For over three years, Eva has increased the sales and profits of her family business by over 217%, simply by building its online presence and unlocking a profitable new stream of sales traffic using her three-step proven process, and has since helped others to do the same with their businesses. Eva is able to guarantee a return on investment by following her processes and recommendations.

- **Qualifications:** BEng Chemical Engineering. PGCE in Secondary Mathematics.

- **Credibility:** Eva has increased the sales and profits of her family business by over 217%.

INTRODUCTION BY DANIEL WAGNER

Eva is a classic example of an expert who is not aware of their own qualities. I commonly refer to this as 'unconscious competence'. She has helped in her family business, building a fully-fledged e-commerce store, but thought that her achievements were nothing special and that anybody could do what she had done.

And that naturally led to a situation where she didn't sell her services at the correct price, even offering her expertise and services free of charge wherever she could!

Eva has been helping many people but most of the clients she helped were not able to afford her services, which led to frustration for both parties and created a price conditioning in Eva's mind.

The personal branding process that Eva went through helped her to be recognised and positioned as the go-to expert for e-commerce solutions for small businesses, allowing her to finally get paid what she deserves.

I see so many people, especially solo-preneurs and small business owners, that don't charge their true value because they are talking to the wrong prospect.

Eva has been a dedicated and fantastic member of the Expert Success Academy, breaking out of her comfort zone and achieving tremendous results for her new clients and, of course, growing her own business.

Her newfound confidence also helped her to renegotiate the deal she had with her brother's business, finally rewarding her for her contributions on the e-commerce side of the business.

Because of her many qualities it was easy for Eva to do too many things and not focus on one core set of skills. The single biggest breakthrough for Eva was when we decided to 'niche' her, both in her offering to the market and her target audience.

Eva has to juggle being a single parent with running her own business, which is no small feat, and it is testimony to her character that she has managed to grow her business in such a short time.

I am convinced that Eva's business will grow dramatically in the next 12 months, as her knowledge and expertise are in a high growth area.

Daniel Wagner

AN INTERVIEW WITH EVA DALGETY

EVA, WHAT DID YOU DO AT UNIVERSITY?

I studied chemical engineering and after graduation I found my first job in the IT industry. I spent the next 10 years working as an IT analyst involved in the various stages of the project cycle. This included project management and supervisory roles overseeing small teams, to later taking full responsibility for a complete project. This gave me valuable insight into how a project works, from the moment an agreement is signed to reporting on the project specification at the final review stage.

After offering private tuition in maths for many years I then studied for a PGCE in mathematics and began teaching in a secondary school in London. I then left my job to work in my brother's business and to set up my own consultancy business. Now I utilise my teaching and IT skills with online marketing strategies to generate an income from the internet.

WHAT DO YOU ACTUALLY DO NOW?

Currently I help small business owners and solo-preneurs who lack the time, technical knowledge and/or marketing expertise to generate leads for their businesses and build a list of prospects. I help them develop and optimise their websites and implement marketing strategies tailored to their business needs to generate more enquires, more sales and more profits through the internet.

WHAT ABOUT PREVIOUSLY?

Previously, I worked in my family's herbal tea business, utilising my programming background to develop an ecommerce platform and website to gain more sales and more profits: over 217% for the business. I also implemented processes and systems to streamline the ordering and fulfilment process to boost our orders, grow our customer base and increase our profits using online marketing strategies.

SO WHAT'S SPECIAL ABOUT THE WAY YOU WORK WITH YOUR CLIENTS?

Well, I have a discussion with my clients to first discover where they are now in their business and where they ideally would like to be. We then work on a strategic marketing plan following my three-step proven process for unlocking online profits in their business. We work through how they are establishing their online presence, look at creation of irresistible offers for their products and services and how they can nourish their buyer audience. The design of the marketing plan is to propel their business profits skywards.

A good marketing plan is essential.

WHAT WAS YOUR MAIN GOAL FOR THIS/LAST YEAR?

My goal for last year and the next few years is to help more businesses increase their profits, to grow my consultancy business by nurturing my clients to give them more time, more money and more freedom. So like me, they too can do the things they enjoying doing whilst working on their business and not in their business.

HOW DID YOU MEET DANIEL WAGNER?

I met Daniel late 2009 at a seminar in London when I had just left my job and started working for my brother's business. I joined Daniel's group which was then called the Internet Buddies programme. This programme helped me set up my family's initial ecommerce site selling herbal teas and I was able to implement online strategies to generate an income. I left the programme due to personal reasons but remain on Daniel's list.

Fast-forward to 2011 when I received an email from Daniel inviting me to a webinar. The webinar showcased the success stories of people who I had met on the Internet Buddies' programme. These success stories propelled me to attend his seminar in Sept 2011.

I attended the seminar and immediately signed up for the Platinum programme with plans to launch my own business while still working for my brother.

WHAT ATTRACTED YOU TO THE EXPERT SUCCESS ACADEMY?

I was attracted to the Expert Success Academy initially because of the successes of the people who continued on the programme after I had left. I joined because

I did not have a clear strategy of how I wanted to grow my consultancy business. I was running an ecommerce business and wanted to help others to also make money online. Also, I was working very much on my own with nobody to bounce ideas off so I was looking for group of like-minded people to associate with. Working alone, I had no accountability.

YOU CREATED A PERSONAL BRAND?

Yes. Attending this programme enabled me to clearly outline and define my promise to my audience. Even just building the website helped me to look at where I am now and where I ideally want to be. It also gives my prospects and clients the opportunity to find out more about how I can help them achieve their goals.

WHAT HAS CHANGED SINCE YOU JOINED THE EXPERT SUCCESS ACADEMY AND COMPLETED THE ONLINE BRAND MASTERCLASS?

Since joining the Expert Success Academy and completing the Online Brand Masterclass I have created a framework, started mapping out my product and service offerings and implemented automated strategies to increase sales for my audience. This framework will help my customers to skyrocket the profit in their business.

WHICH MEANS?

It means that I can help my clients to unlock online profits in their business by following my three-step, proven process. As my clients gain more leads, more sales and more profits, they, like me, will have more money, more time and more freedom to enjoy the things they want to do.

Create a multi-step, proven process.

This year I will continue to work to keep up to date on strategies and continue to offer more support systems for my clients and prospects. I will also continue to implement support systems such as running social media seminars and webinars that will give knowledge to my clients on how to continue to grow their businesses.

WHAT ADVICE WOULD YOU GIVE TO OTHERS?

I believe that anyone who is looking to grow their business should join the Academy. They will gain value and advice from the monthly Academy meetings and webinars. They will be able to associate with like-minded people and build real friendships, have accountability, gain personal growth and encouragement. The group helps you to expand your network, so expanding your resources. Also you have access to different experts who can help you to see things in your business from a completely unique vantage point. Isn't that cool?

So, if given the opportunity, I would highly recommend you join with the Expert Success Academy and take action on their recommendations.

WHAT WOULD BE A GOOD FIRST STEP?

My first suggestion would be to get a copy of the *Expert Success* book and use it as a reference book.

 **KEY LEARNINGS**

- Once you have your vision or goal, don't leave it in your head, write it down so that you can begin to believe that you can achieve it.

- Set your goal and then make a plan working backwards.

- Even though you may have a long-term goal, break it into smaller goals over shorter periods of time, say quarterly, and make them measureable.

- Plan SMART daily tasks the previous day/night and follow the plan today. It is very easy to get distracted and caught up in unimportant tasks if you are trying to plan and implement on the same day.

CHRISTINE WESTWOOD HOLISTIC HEALTH AROMATHERAPY EXPERT

Reducing Stress Through Natural Therapies

Meta-Aromatherapy
and Better Off

christine@betteroff.info
07712 833567

Christine helps people improve their health and fitness through natural therapies. Previously, she recognised stress in her city trader colleagues so, as they kept asking for help, she retrained and established her own natural therapy business. Christine is now one of the UK's leading aromatherapists, a broadcaster and author of three books, including a million-copy best seller. Her expertise spans three decades. The founder of Christine Westwood Training and the Meta-Aromatherapy process, her client base has included Boots plc., Holland and Barrett, Pepsicola, PA Consulting and universities.

- **Qualifications:** Massage, London and County Society of Physiologists. Tisserand Diploma in Holistic Aromatherapy. Emotional Intelligence, Master Hypnotist. Intergenerational Healing and Clean Language, with David Grove. Accelerated Learning: Training for Trainers. Life and Performance Coaching, Newcastle University. Business Counselling Certificate, Durham University.

- **Credibility:** My book, *Aromatherapy: A Guide for Home Use*, has sold over a million copies.

- Achievements: Helped Boots the Chemist set up their aromatherapy range and fronted their media campaign. Created an aromatherapy centre to provide recognised qualifications for practitioners. Part of a UK tour giving presentations for women with cancer and their families.

PUBLICATIONS

Aromatherapy: A Guide for Home Use, Amberwood Publishing Ltd, 1991 (sold over a million copies).

Aromatherapy Stress Management: A Guide for Home Use, Amberwood Publishing Ltd, 1994.

Aromatherapy for Healthy Legs and Feet: A Guide for Home Use, Amberwood Publishing Ltd, 1995.

Her book sold over a million copies!

" I'M A BEST-
SELLING AUTHOR.

INTRODUCTION BY DANIEL WAGNER

Christine Westwood and her partner Ian have been around me and my work for over five years, but it is only in the last 12 months that Christine has revealed some of her talents and her unique expert skills.

Initially joining me at my Make Money Online course, Christine and Ian were looking for quick wins in making money on the internet. But like so many they have found it difficult or impossible to make the affiliate model work for them.

I even lost touch with Christine and Ian for a few years, and was pleased to see them re-emerge last year. They joined the Expert Success Academy together and this is when Christine revealed her secret!

It was during one of the sessions when I spoke about the power of publishing a book or indeed authoring any form of work, when Christine told me that she was the author of the best-selling book on aromatherapy.

So it was only natural for me to help Christine establish herself as a full expert, which included authentic personal online branding and building a loyal following. This will ultimately make her the money she deserves and give her and Ian the lifestyle they desire from her expert business.

The problem with being a published author with a traditional publisher is that unless you sell hundreds of thousands of copies, the financial rewards are meagre.

So it is of critical importance that you establish other forms of revenue, which could include online membership sites, webinar courses, one-to-one and group coaching programmes or retreats.

The power of expert positioning is truly amazing, and it is important for anyone reading these success stories to understand that your expert positioning has to be claimed by you.

No one will come and award you an expert badge, you have to go out and claim it. This is possibly one of the biggest and most important distinctions and teachings of the Expert Success Academy.

So no matter what your skill or expertise, you have to claim that expert space in the market by enabling people to find you and then clearly tell them who you are and what you can do for them.

Daniel Wagner

AN INTERVIEW WITH CHRISTINE WESTWOOD

CHRISTINE, WHAT WAS YOUR MAIN GOAL FOR THIS YEAR?

My current personal goal is to be the fittest and healthiest ever in my life. This includes recovering fully from ME, which I have experienced in the last year, and to share how I've achieved this so others can benefit through online media.

WHAT SORT OF EXPERT ARE YOU?

I'm a holistic health aromatherapy expert.

HOW DID YOU GET INTO/STARTED WITH NATURAL HEALTHCARE?

During my work as a qualified accountant in the 1980s I became interested in researching and developing strategies for coping with stress and helping people reach their full potential.

I have helped companies such as Boots the Chemist and Holland and Barrett introduce their range of essential oils and train their staff.

I created meta-aromatherapy and established Christine Westwood Training to qualify therapists.

WHAT QUALIFICATIONS DID YOU NEED?

Because I wanted to work with the interaction of both body and mind I chose to qualify in each discipline:

*   Massage, London and County Society of Physiologists.

*   Tisserand Diploma in Holistic Aromatherapy.

*   Emotional Intelligence, Master Hypnotist.

*   Intergenerational Healing and Clean Language, with David Grove.

*   Accelerated Learning: Training for Trainers.

- Life and Performance Coaching, Newcastle University.

- Business Counselling Certificate, Durham University.

I registered my centre with the Complementary Medical Association and for National Vocational Qualifications and became an Assessor and Verifier for natural therapies and business management.

WHEN DID YOU LEAVE YOUR JOB?

I left a full-time accountancy career in 1985, although still taught management skills which I provided as part of the training for my students.

WHAT DID YOU DISLIKE ABOUT IT?

The lack of professionalism in the fledgling industry at the start of my career.

WHAT DID YOUR FAMILY SAY?

When I was first made redundant from my well-paid accountancy job, my parents would bring me adverts for accountancy positions and everyone thought I was mad, apart from a good friend who said, 'That's great, you are doing what you love.'

IS THIS SOMETHING YOU SAW YOURSELF DOING IN THE PAST?

I had a feeling that accountancy would not be my ultimate work, but it was not until I took a year out that I began to find my vocation. I explored an alternative lifestyle that included time at the Findhorn Foundation in Scotland and at the Siddha Yoga Ashram in India. During this year I qualified as an accountant and choose to return and work in the city. I could see the level of stress that people were experiencing. As individuals started to ask me how I remained so calm I began to see that there was a definite need for help.

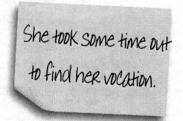

She took some time out to find her vocation.

WHAT WOULD YOU DO DIFFERENTLY IF YOU STARTED AGAIN?

I did not link my passion for helping through healing with an awareness of internet marketing to reach a wider field and help more people.

WHAT DOES THE FUTURE HOLD FOR YOU?

As a best-selling author I plan to ensure my three books are available online and to create an online academy programme to reach a wider audience.

HOW LONG HAVE YOU KNOWN DANIEL WAGNER?

I have known Daniel since 2006 and have always been struck by his sincerity and keenness to find a way to help others succeed in their businesses.

WHAT ATTRACTED YOU TO THE EXPERT SUCCESS ACADEMY?

Daniel, James and their team's dedication to finding and sharing the best and most ethical approaches to an online presence.

DID YOU ATTEND ANY OTHER TRAINING PROGRAMMES?

Yes, professional CPD programmes and networking events. I never stop learning.

HOW DID YOU RAISE FINANCE?

I was made redundant from my accountancy position in the city and once qualified in natural therapies, I set up my practice, which took off and blossomed.

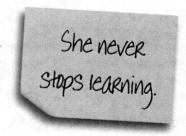

She never stops learning.

WHAT HAPPENED NEXT?

Very soon I was asked to give talks and training as well as media interviews. I was terrified of public speaking but used to spur myself on by the thought that it was worth it if I could help even just one person on each occasion.

Because I came from a professionally trained background I wanted to bring the same professionalism to aromatherapy. So I created Meta-Aromatherapy and set up Christine Westwood Training accredited by the Complementary Medical Association and as an NVQ registered training school.

WHAT CHALLENGES HAVE YOU FACED PERSONALLY IN YOUR 30 YEARS OF PRACTICE?

I have needed to address my own and my family's health: my mother has had cancer twice and fully recovered. However, sadly my father could not be helped when he developed Parkinson's.

I had a pre-cancerous diagnosis from which I recovered fully but more recently developed ME following farm chemical exposure and a virus. So it has been a case of 'healer, heal thyself'.

I firmly believe everything happens for a reason and as a result I am stronger and able to offer a more comprehensive solution.

HAVE YOU HAD ANY BUSINESS CHALLENGES?

Early on in my business I acted as guarantor for a business partner and lost half my investment.

When I needed to outsource elements for an EEC funded project to train 125 people in four months, I had to ensure that the people I worked with shared the same ethics, professional standards and were able to grasp my vision.

In 1994 I won a runner-up prize for Investing in Technology. I based it on the paperless office – not yet achieved – a shame, considering I'd rather see paper stay on trees.

HOW ARE YOU FINANCING YOUR LEARNING WITH THE EXPERT SUCCESS ACADEMY?

Whilst looking after my parents, I saw the need to secure my future and invested in property, which now provides an income in addition to my businesses.

WHAT CASH FLOW DO YOU HAVE NOW?

I receive royalties from my published books as well as income from property and other linked businesses.

WHAT ADVICE WOULD YOU GIVE TO OTHERS?

Learn as much as you can about running a business as well as your passion. Learn from everyone and go beyond your normal research. Do not limit yourself e.g. I spent time at Warwick University learning from scientists; I led a group in France at a top perfume house; I went on a historical tour of Egypt to learn about the roots of aromatherapy. Most of all, enjoy what you do.

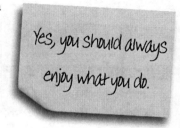

Yes, you should always enjoy what you do.

ANY TIPS YOU'D LIKE TO SHARE?

- Never be too proud to ask for advice and learn from the experts.

- Always be the best you can.

- Always work with the best.

- Outsource whatever you can.

- Learn from your mistakes and move on.

DID YOU HAVE A UNIVERSITY EDUCATION?

I chose a practical professional qualification which I studied for whilst working. I attended university vocational courses for which I obtained sponsorship e.g. Business Counselling at Durham University.

The best education is from the 'University of Life'.

My best education is from the 'University of Life', particularly spending time in foreign countries. I've learnt a lot about different cultures and their natural remedies.

WHAT IS YOUR MAIN FOCUS NOW?

In the last year I have focused on healing myself of ME using essential oils and a primarily a natural, green raw food approach to nutrition and sourcing food state supplements.

I now focus on healing and world consciousness. I use Ama-san healing as well as aromatherapy.

I also help locally as a tree warden for ancient woodland and a local country park.

HOW MANY JOINT VENTURE PARTNERSHIPS DO YOU HAVE?

I am a founder member of the Complementary Medical Association and a member of Bartercard, I'm happy to explore joint ventures with like-minded souls.

WHY/HOW DID YOU WRITE YOUR BOOK?

Initially I was asked for a comprehensive pamphlet to cover specific essential oils. This turned into 64 pages of information and it was decided to release it as a self-help book.

I meditated and received the inspiration for the cover.

I used a mind map overview and did one for each chapter. It took a month to write. At the end, knowing the book needed another perspective I sat and prayed at 2am for help. In the next few days a friend who had worked as a film editor on Tomorrow's World called in and we spent three days revising the book, during which time he informed me that I must be dyslexic. I dictated my next two books!

HAS YOUR BUSINESS BEEN A SUCCESS?

My offline consultancy and training business has been one of the most successful in aromatherapy. I now want to recreate that success online so that more people can be helped.

DO YOU HAVE ANY OTHER BUSINESSES?

I offer natural healthcare products and support clients through holistic health and wealth challenge programmes. I also have a managed property portfolio and related business.

WHAT ARE YOUR GOALS FOR THIS YEAR?

I want to:

- Publish my books and others that I have prepared online.

- Expand my client base and reconnect online with existing clients.

- Launch my online brand and to offer an online training programme.

HOW WILL THE EXPERT SUCCESS ACADEMY HELP WITH THAT?

The Expert Success Academy provides structure and keeps me up to date. The monthly network meetings are really good to learn what not to use as well as what to use and how to go about it.

Daniel and James' team are dedicated, ethical people; they are kindly patient and are always at the end of an email or phone to help.

APART FROM THE ACADEMY, DO YOU GO TO ANY OTHER NETWORKING EVENTS?

I run healing and health networks locally and attend national meetings.

Until last year I was chair of the local Southern Landlords Association but have stepped down to concentrate on healthcare.

WHAT DID YOU LEARN ON THE ONLINE BRAND MASTERCLASS?

- How to create my online business plan and model.

- The nine building blocks to a successful online brand.

- How to optimise my message.

- The importance of specialised portrait photography to create the right image.

WHAT IMPACT DID IT HAVE ON YOU?

- I felt more confident about creating and managing an online presence.

- I gained an understanding of what I could have done differently offline which would have supported an online brand e.g. protection of my intellectual property.

- I learnt ways in which I can share my expertise.

- I realised what a craft it was to present me as the professional I am.

- I liked the precision of the approach. I have always thought it was good to have another professional review my work for articles, books and presentations, so why not with an online brand presence. Over the course my confidence grew as the formula unfolded.

- I learnt how to reach a wider audience and develop a larger client base.

- I discovered the value of joint ventures in online business.

- I learnt how to professionally put together the elements of an online presence.

WHAT DID YOU LEARN FROM THE EXPERT SUCCESS BOOK?

- How to create my online business model and plan.

- How to create strategic partnerships and joint ventures.

- The importance of offering something remarkable and solving problems.

- Authority and value.

- How to create a compelling offer and use scarcity and contrast frames.

- How to leverage contacts to support a cause.

- How to re-purpose content.

- The importance of list segmentation and text marketing.

- How to track, measure and improve my online presence.

WHAT IMPACT DID IT HAVE ON YOU?

The Expert Success Formula has given me a clear framework to replicate my offline success, online. I now feel more confident that I can manage my online presence to reach a wider audience.

 **KEY LEARNINGS**

I have learnt the value of:

- Systems.

- Adding value.

- Outsourcing.

- Contrast frames to aid choice.

GILLIAN FOX
WEB COPY EXPERT

Winning You Sales With a Waterfall of Words

The Copywriting Fox

www.gillianfox.com
www.thecopywritingfox.com
gillian@thecopywritingfox.com
01993 702285

Gillian Fox writes creative sales copy for online and offline businesses and runs copywriting workshops in Oxfordshire. She originally trained as a secretary and went on to become PA to the MD of a recruitment and advertising agency before getting married and running a company with her husband. Gillian is a sales copywriter with a wide portfolio of clients in the coaching, training and personal development fields. She's been around long enough to have experienced the ups and downs of life that show us we all have far more strength inside of us than we think. Her message 'never give up' sings out loud and clear in her book, *Promise Me: A Personal Journey.*

- **Qualifications:** Studied Interior Design and Decoration at Ivy House Design School in 2006 and gained a highly commended certification.

- **Credibility:** Studied with Nick James at his exclusive Copywriting Academy in 2009.

- **Personal Lifetime Achievements:** Runner-up in Daniel Wagner's *'Better Your Best'* competition in 2011.

PUBLICATIONS

Promise Me: A Personal Journey, CreateSpace, 2011.

"MY BOOK ALSO GAVE ME CREDIBILITY AS AN EXPERT.

INTRODUCTION BY DANIEL WAGNER

Gillian is simply amazing. She has overcome so many challenges that we could fill a whole book just with her story! As a matter of fact I helped Gillian publish her own book a few years ago, which tells her tremendous life story and the many challenges she has overcome.

Her book was never meant to be an expert piece, it was never meant to help her authority processioning, it was mainly meant to just tell her life story; a cathartic and wonderful process that I have been through myself and with many of my students.

But of course a natural side effect of being a published author is that people accept your authority.

Gillian is an example of an expert who has developed a new skill from scratch at a later time in her life. As a matter of fact, Gillian wasn't even aware that the industry that she is now an expert in even existed.

Through studying with the right mentors and being part of the right groups along with sheer perseverance, Gillian was able to build her business, her way, to suit her lifestyle.

And that is what the Expert Success Academy is all about. Helping people achieve their dream lifestyle through their expert business.

Gillian didn't set out to build a multimillion pound empire, she doesn't want world domination, but she loves what she does and she helps people with her great skill of being a wordsmith – a copy writer.

As you might be aware by now, the Expert Success Formula has three distinct parts. And part three: cultivating a buying audience, has a lot to do with copywriting and using words to influence and persuade.

Expert businesses can take any shape or form, from running big enterprises and worldwide businesses, all the way down to running your business alone from home. And there is no right and wrong, there is just what you want out of it.

That is possibly one of my favourite parts of what I do: helping people get out of life and business exactly what they want and on their own terms.

Daniel Wagner

AN INTERVIEW WITH GILLIAN FOX

WHAT DID YOU STUDY AT COLLEGE?

I took an OND in Business Studies, but left early to join the BBC as a clerk/typist at Broadcasting House. This was the swinging 60s when Radio 1 had just gone on air, so it was an exciting place to start work.

WHAT DID YOU DO NEXT?

I worked my way up the secretarial ladder, moving jobs frequently and widening my experience. Along the way I also worked for Hertz Rent-a-Car at Heathrow Airport as a rental rep, which I loved until they issued us with badges bearing the immortal words 'Hertz Girls Say Yes'. Time to go!

I wanted to buy my own property, so I looked around for areas I could afford and found a flat in Saffron Walden in Essex. I applied for a PA job with a local company and started work for the MD, a guy called Geoff Fox.

Little did I know what fate had in store!

THEN WHAT HAPPENED?

Seven years later I was married to Geoff and we had formed our own recruitment and advertising company, with branches in Manchester, Birmingham and Milton Keynes.

We lived on a farm, had horses, cattle, dogs, a cat and a wonderful lifestyle. Our head office was in the barn opposite our farmhouse, so our commute to work was about two minutes!

However, when the recession descended in the early 90s we took the decision to retire early, sell up and sail around the world. For the next couple of years we lived the dream, even buying a plot of land in rural Portugal to self-build a home.

Sadly life had other ideas, and half-way through the build Geoff was diagnosed with a brain tumour. He died two months later.

After Geoff's death I spent a few years finishing our self-build project before returning to the UK to rebuild my life.

WHAT DID YOU DO NEXT?

I went into property and rode the wave; buying, doing up and selling in a rising market. My mantra was 'if I can do it in Portugal I can do it in the UK'. Then I started a letting agency in Suffolk on the advice of a so-called business advisor.

HAVE YOU MADE ANY MISTAKES ALONG THE WAY?

Oh yes – my business advisor turned out to be a conman, and I lost a six-figure sum of money and spent a year sorting out the wreckage before eventually selling the business as a going concern.

After that I decided to play small and safe, taking various part-time jobs where someone else paid my wages. Never again was I going to run my own business!

SO HOW DID YOU MEET DANIEL WAGNER?

My journey with Daniel started over four years ago when I went along to a property meeting in Milton Keynes. Yes, despite the mess I'd made of it I still kept in touch with trends.

Daniel was the guest speaker and there was something about him that sparked my interest in his topic of online marketing. Although I had little technical experience of the internet (sending an email was the summit of my achievement at the time) it felt right, so I signed up for his weekend course and then joined his Platinum group (the fore-runner to the Expert

Sometimes, just sending an email can be a challenge.

Success Academy), going along to the monthly meetings and applying the lessons step by step. I remember the excitement when I made my first online sale, an affiliate ebook costing $26!

Little did I know this was the start of a whole new business journey.

HOW DID YOU START THE COPYWRITING FOX?

Through Daniel's group I met Nick James and was accepted on to his Copywriting Academy. Although I'd gone along to learn about copywriting for my own website, Nick mentioned that copywriting for others may prove to be a good business model.

Daniel encouraged me to pursue this idea and I presented my first ever offer to his group – I would write 10 emails for the princely sum of $97. To my delight several people paid me and that really was the start of *The Copywriting Fox*.

WHAT SORT OF EXPERT ARE YOU?

I write sales copy. That is sales letters, squeeze pages, landing pages, and email sequences, all of which help businesses sell more of their products and services. I now also run hands-on copywriting courses coaching small business owners to polish up their copywriting skills.

WHAT QUALIFICATIONS DID YOU NEED?

English has always been my best subject, so I had a good command of the written word. All I had to do was adapt it to the more colloquial, less formal style used in sales copy and study the language of influence and persuasion.

HAVE YOU HAD ANY CHALLENGES?

Loads – this has been, and continues to be, the road to personal as well as professional development.

For example, being invited to be one of the contestants in Daniel's first 'Better Your Best' competition to win £10,000 at the conference was a huge challenge – I'd never spoken to a large audience (over 200 people) before, but when I stood on stage and shared my story and business progress it was humbling to find out how powerfully that story connected with members of the audience. I will never forget the lady who came up to me afterwards, with tears in her eyes, and thanked me because what I said had really helped her at a difficult time in her life.

HOW DID YOU WRITE YOUR BOOK?

That experience was the prompt I needed to finally set down my story. If my life experiences could be of help, even to one person who found themselves in a similar situation, then it was time to write the book.

It was also another way of putting the past to rest. I liken it to the moment in the Harry Potter story when Professor Dumbledore takes his wand, puts it to his head and draws out silver threads of memory and deposits them into a 'memory bowl' where they can be accessed if needed. My book served the same purpose for me.

Write your 'story' to put the past to rest

HOW DID BEING PART OF THE EXPERT SUCCESS ACADEMY HELP YOU?

Being accountable to the group as well as to Daniel and James is one of the reasons I love being part of the Expert Success Academy Mastermind group. It's a very powerful motivator to do what you said you'd do by when you said you'd do it.

Daniel and James encouraged me to have the book published for their next conference, and it was great to have the accountability of sending a chapter a week to them to ensure I met the deadline. I also owe a debt of thanks to James's wife Licia who read some of the material whilst feeding their newborn twins in the early hours!

The book also gave me credibility as an expert – as a wordsmith, having a book published was an integral part of my product staircase, both showcasing my writing skills and hopefully entertaining people at the same time.

A book gives you credibility as an expert.

Without the Expert Success Academy I would not have had the understanding of how online marketing works, or the mentoring to build a successful personal brand to the level where I'm now recognised as *The Copywriting Fox*.

WHAT ARE YOUR GOALS FOR THIS YEAR?

As one of the Expert Success Academy Masterminders, I recently spent several days on a retreat (bootcamp) in Portugal with the rest of the group. Each of us gave an hour's presentation on our business achievements over the last six months and the challenges we faced as we moved our businesses forward.

It's an invaluable part of the Mastermind membership to receive honest feedback from both fellow group members as well as our mentors, and to brainstorm new ideas as well.

It was also great to have time in the evenings to socialise with everyone, and enjoy the food at the excellent local restaurants.

I returned from Portugal with a cunning plan to build more revenue sources into my business by way of copy critiques and webinars, as well as my main goal to expand my hands-on copywriting workshop to a larger audience.

Copywriting is such a basic and important skill for any business really wanting to put their marketing message over either online or offline, so I'm opening up my copywriting workshops to larger numbers of business owners over the next few months, and have found the ideal business centre venue which has just opened and is only five minutes from where I live – now that's serendipity!

HAVE YOU GOT ANY TIPS FOR OTHERS?

You know, four years ago my confidence was on the ground and I never thought I'd run another business again. With the coaching from Daniel and James, plus the support of my peers in the Expert Success Academy Mastermind group I've built up a successful copywriting business which now brings me in a four-figure income each month, and if I achieve my goals for the next six months I'll have trebled my income in comparison to the last six months figures.

I'd encourage anyone who is either starting, or already running their own business to seek out the Expert Success Academy and learn from the rich source of experience, technical knowledge and regular updates that come from being part of a very special group of people who want to succeed and know they are in the right place to do it.

Attending the regular monthly meetings and hearing other people's successes and challenges is a great way to learn, as well as being a source of inspiration. The 'hot seat' individual coaching slots have yielded sound business ideas that I can apply to my business as well.

Sometimes it's one of the seemingly smaller tips that can make all the difference. Recently we learnt about a website contact form that syncs with a calendar and enables potential clients to fill in their details and book a phone consultation time. Within a week of putting this on my website I gained a new client who paid me £397 for writing an email sequence.

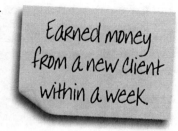

Earned money from a new client within a week.

And of course the networking at the Expert Success Academy meetings means I can offer my fellow members the benefit of my copywriting expertise with full endorsement from Daniel and James.

WHAT WOULD BE A GOOD FIRST STEP?

Get yourself along to an Expert Success Academy event and meet the people involved. If I hadn't gone to that meeting in Milton Keynes I would not have met and been inspired by Daniel and taken my first steps towards the successful business I now run.

Ask questions and talk to people in the group and find out what they're like and what they've got from being part of the Expert Success Academy. You'll meet a diverse group of people from many different businesses but all with a core desire to be successful doing what they love.

When anybody asks me what marks the Expert Success Academy out as different from other business groups, I always say 'integrity' and a 'genuine desire to help people build sound and successful businesses'. Daniel will tell you it won't happen overnight and it takes some hard work on your part, but these guys walk the talk and their unique blend of insightful personal and business coaching will give you the opportunity to carve out your own *expert success*.

KEY LEARNINGS

- You are more than you think you are – so get a mentor to help you recognise and develop your strengths, and a peer group of like-minded people to hang around with.

- Keep up to date with what's current in both online and offline marketing. Being on the ball will give you the edge over your competitors, and being in the Expert Success Academy will give you access to a wealth of information and expertise.

- Goethe allegedly said, 'Whatever you can do, or dream you can, begin it. Boldness has genius, power and magic in it.' Give up on procrastination and opt for action – just do it.

- Joint ventures and alliance.

PHIL HAMPTON
ANIMATED VIDEO EXPERT

Creating Animated Promotional Videos that Help your Business Attract and Engage Customers and Boost Sales

Cartoon Media Ltd.

www.cartoonmedia.com
phil@cartoonmedia.com
01227 362211

Phil runs Cartoon Media, creating animated 'doodle' videos for businesses. His videos are designed to engage, entertain and educate your potential customers. Phil has almost 20 years' experience as a project manager delivering software developments in the insurance industry. Via his company, Cartoon Media, Phil Hampton uses his twin loves of comic book art and online marketing to produce animated promotional videos. Cartoon Media's videos will help you attract new customers and sell more products and services online, all without you having to stand in front of a camera.

- **Qualifications:** Diploma in Personal Performance Coaching, The Coaching Academy, 2009.

- **Credibility:** 20 years' experience as a project manager.

" MY 3-MINUTE 'DOODLE' VIDEO INCREASED DANIEL WAGNER'S OPT-IN RATE BY 100%

INTRODUCTION BY DANIEL WAGNER

It's not easy to start a business while being in a full-time job, yet that is a position that most budding entrepreneurs find themselves in. Phil is no exception.

When I met Phil he had already spent many years trying to make money online building a product funnel, building a list and going after a niche market vigorously.

It is hard sometimes to determine if you should be more persistent or if you should actually give up, because what you try to achieve is just not going to work or is simply going to require too much effort.

So when Phil told me about his existing business, trying to help comic book artists to learn marketing, I just had this feeling that we were trying to sell to a market that wasn't able to afford the products that Phil had to offer.

He had pretty much done everything right, apart from offering his product suite to the wrong market!

But that is why I knew that I could help Phil to become successful very fast, because he has shown all the ingredients of taking action and implementing ideas.

The success story you're about to read is a great big sample of becoming a player in an already busy niche. But one of the great aspects of the internet is that a new player can take market share almost overnight.

The strategies we used and use are applicable to almost any market or niche, and they are almost a guaranteed way to make money and establish authority.

What I love about running your own business is that every stage of your business has different challenges. So now that Phil's business has taken off, he is dealing with challenges of delivery, operations, and handling growth!

So there will always be challenges, but I personally prefer to deal with the challenges of growth compared to the challenges of a stagnating or shrinking business.

Daniel Wagner

AN INTERVIEW WITH PHIL HAMPTON

PHIL, TELL US ABOUT YOUR EARLY EXPERIENCES IN BUSINESS PRIOR TO JOINING THE EXPERT SUCCESS ACADEMY.

I worked in the insurance industry after leaving college, and having had a bad experience working for an overbearing boss close to retirement, I'd had enough and decided to be my own boss for a change. But I couldn't quit my job until I had developed an independent income stream that could still pay the bills.

In 2009, I achieved a Personal Performance Coaching Diploma from The Coaching Academy and thought that an advert in the *Yellow Pages* was all that was required to generate a stream of enquiries as a coach. I quickly discovered that nothing could be further from the truth!

Mistakenly relied on Yellow Pages for clients.

I then set up a website to market my coaching skills to corporate managers, but failed to generate any traffic or enquiries. I also created an online product helping people to get promoted at work, but didn't sell any copies.

HOW DID YOU FEEL AT THAT POINT?

Very frustrated and disheartened, especially since I was trying to juggle a 9-5 job, family life and work on the business in the evenings. The business was impacting my home life, and I hated my job more than ever.

SO WHAT DID YOU DO NEXT?

As I had failed at 'do what you know', I then moved onto 'do what you love'. One of my lifelong hobbies was reading comics and studying the comic book industry, and I knew that there were many comic book writers and artists who would benefit from improving their own marketing skills.

After failing to market myself sufficiently in the past, I studied a number of marketing audiobooks and courses. I found that I loved learning online marketing techniques, and soon set up a new website called The Comic

Academy, helping people to become a success in the comic book industry. By using some simple but effective Twitter marketing techniques, I gained 1,000 targeted followers in six weeks, and used this to drive traffic to my website. I created two information products over the year, which I sold for only $27 and $37, but despite growing an email list of almost 1,000 writers and artists, my total sales barely covered the set-up costs. It seemed that my followers loved my free content but weren't willing to pay me for the advice that would help them succeed in the comic book industry.

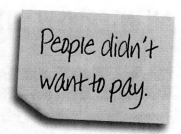

SO WHAT HAPPENED NEXT?

At the end of January 2012, I was made redundant from my job at the insurance company. I was over the moon! However, I'd only worked there a few years, so my redundancy package was only going to last a few months. A month later I was hired as a consultant by a different insurance company on a temporary contract. My month of being jobless and the new contract gave me some breathing space to consider whether or not The Comic Academy was worth continuing, or whether I should change my niche. I started reading books on deciding your life's purpose, but ended up getting more confused than enlightened. I knew that I didn't want to work in insurance for the rest of my life – I just didn't know what my next step should be. Then I met Daniel Wagner.

HOW DID YOU MEET DANIEL?

At the end of March 2012, I attended a coaching conference at which Daniel was one of the presenters. I had previously seen Daniel speak and he was someone I looked up to, having managed to turn his previous business failures into huge successes through determination and hard work.

At the end of Daniel's presentation, I signed up for the Expert Success Online Brand Masterclass in June. I knew that this was a workshop for those who already had a good idea of their niche, but I just felt that it was right for me to attend; that I would gain some sense of what I should do next from it.

I bought the *Expert Success* book, and had a quick chat with Daniel. After seeing my Comic Academy website he said, 'That's a great looking site, but I'm not sure about your niche. Writers and artists don't usually have a lot of money to spend on information products or coaching.'

He had pinpointed the major flaw in my business in less than two minutes. I had created powerful products and a growing reputation, but I didn't have a paying audience.

> *A mentor can pinpoint a major flaw within two minutes.*

WHAT HAPPENED AT THE ONLINE BRAND MASTERCLASS?

In the run up to the Masterclass, I read the *Expert Success* book from cover to cover and thought it was one of the best books on setting up a successful business that I had read. It was very honest and revealing about the nuts and bolts required to set up a successful business.

I spent the three days of the workshop working on my personal brand under The Comic Academy banner, as I still had no other ideas in mind. However, working through the various exercises definitely got me thinking more deeply about what I should do next. After creating the wording of my personal brand website, I felt that I didn't want to continue with The Comic Academy as a business. I had begun to realise that it was more a hobby than a business.

DID YOU COME TO ANY DECISION ABOUT YOUR FUTURE DIRECTION AT THE MASTERCLASS?

At the end of the three days, Daniel's business partner, James Watson, had a look at the Comic Academy website with me and suggested that I look into creating animated 'doodle' marketing videos (also known as whiteboard animations). This would involve changing my focus from being an information marketer to a service provider, but my target audiences would be businesspeople who had more money to spend than comic book writers and artists!

I needed to research more about how to set up such a service, and my potential competitors before making a decision on the niche. However, James invited me to join the Platinum level of the Expert Success Academy, and work out the next steps together. I could see that Daniel and James had a variety of business skills and technical knowledge, and were both invested in making their clients a success, so I gladly accepted the offer to join. By the time of my first Platinum meeting mid-July, I had decided to focus on creating animated marketing videos.

WHAT WERE THE FACTORS THAT MADE YOU DECIDE ON THIS NEW NICHE?

I already had 20 years' experience managing the delivery of technical software products in insurance. Cartoon Media would combine my project management skills with my marketing knowledge. My decades of reading comic books, and studying the marketing techniques of comic book companies, enabled me to judge how best to convert a marketing video script into pictures, and I knew some great cartoonists whom I could work with on the videos (since I can't draw to save my life). It seemed that the stars were aligning!

WHAT WERE YOUR FIRST STEPS IN SETTING UP THIS NEW BUSINESS?

I registered www.cartoonmedia.com, and got a logo and mascot designed by a great cartoonist that I know in Hungary. He is also one of the cartoonists who create the images for our videos. I wanted a business that enabled me to work from home, using the skills of talented cartoonists and voiceover artists from around the globe. I decided against creating the videos by filming the cartoonist 'live' drawing on a whiteboard (the method used by some whiteboard animation companies), as this would mean bringing the process in-house to get the lighting perfect.

Then I came across software called Videoscribe which simulates the drawing of the images by hand, and this was perfect for my needs. I first trialled the process by creating three promotional videos for Cartoon Media, using different cartoonists and voiceover artists, and posted them on YouTube to help drive traffic to my website. I also created a three-minute promotional video for Daniel and James for the *Expert Success* book, and used this experience to hone the project process.

WAS THE VIDEO YOU DID FOR THEM A SUCCESS?

Yes – Daniel and James found that the video increased the opt-in rate for the free chapter of *Expert Success* by 100%. James recorded a great video testimonial for me, and I placed this on my website shortly after I launched it on 1st October 2012.

HOW HAVE YOU FOUND THE PLATINUM EXPERT SUCCESS MEMBERSHIP USEFUL?

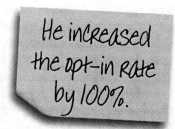

He increased the opt-in Rate by 100%.

I have found the weekly telephone group coaching by James every Monday has been great to get regular advice in case I'm stuck on something or need to talk over a problem without having to wait for the next monthly meeting. James knows a great deal of different tips and tricks to help grow an online business, and I've implemented a number of them over the last few months. The monthly Platinum group sessions with Daniel and James have helped me focus on the next best tasks to grow my business. The Facebook group has also been a great help, since there is a large variety of business skills and knowledge in the Expert Success Academy. I recently posted a query that generated over 20 useful pieces of advice from various members.

WHAT HAVE YOU LEARNED AS AN EXPERT SUCCESS ACADEMY MEMBER THAT HAS HELPED YOU TO GROW YOUR BUSINESS?

I think the main exercise that helped me in the early days was deciding on my various packages and pricing levels prior to launching the site. My packages were based upon video length and number of images rather than just length, which differentiated me from the competition. They were also priced at levels that would appeal to different customers, and positioned strategically to highlight the middle package as being the best value, whilst still generating a decent profit. I've since seen my pricing table copied by a couple of new animated video businesses, which proves that it was a good idea!

James also recommended the vCita contact software, which is a pop-up that allows clients to contact me, or book an appointment in my online diary, and this has generated a number of enquiries since adding it to my site. Finally, Daniel and James have encouraged me to regularly track my numbers (Google Analytics tracks visitors to my site, plus number of enquiries, conversions, sales and profit), which helps me to decide upon the areas to improve in any given week.

WHICH MEANS?

Fewer than six months after launching the Cartoon Media website, I am now making as much profit each month as I made working in insurance. It's taken me over four years, but I can now finally say that I am my own boss. I walk my son to school every morning, and spend more time with him in the evening. I have implemented effective project delivery procedures, and have a great 'power team' of freelancers helping to create the videos, so that I

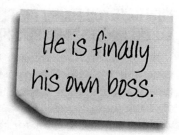

He is finally his own boss.

can now concentrate on growing the business further and developing customer relationships. This wouldn't have been possible without the great advice and support provided by Daniel, James and the Expert Success Academy members over the last nine months.

WHAT ARE YOUR GOALS FOR THE COMING YEAR?

Currently I'm not ranking on the first half of page one of Google for any of my 10 target keywords, so I'll be putting measures in place to achieve that within the next six months for at least the top five.

My financial goals are to at least double my current monthly income in six months' time.

HOW WILL THE EXPERT SUCCESS ACADEMY HELP WITH THAT?

The primary aim of the Expert Success Academy is to help business owners position themselves as go-to people in their niche. I've already done the initial work to set up a profitable company, and the best way to improve my profits is to improve my positioning. The advice that Daniel and James have given me, and continue to give me, will help me achieve that.

WHAT ADVICE WOULD YOU GIVE TO PEOPLE?

Get a business mentor and join a group of success-oriented business owners. By joining the Expert Success Academy, I've benefited from having two great mentors in Daniel and James, and become part of a friendly, helpful and knowledgeable group of business owners.

WHAT WOULD BE A GOOD FIRST STEP?

I'd definitely recommend that people read Expert Success, by Daniel Wagner. It's got everything you need to know to position your business as the number one in its niche.

KEY LEARNINGS

- Ensure that you have a hungry audience willing to pay significantly for your products or services.

- If you spot a 'gap in the market' it's usually because there's no 'market in the gap'!

- Don't do everything yourself. Find people with the skills you need, who enjoy the jobs you hate.

MICHAEL VEAZEY
PERFORMING ARTS EXPERT

Inspiring Choirs and Soloists to Sing Better; Inspiring Orchestras to Play Better

Michael Veazey and
Orchestra Eroica

www.michaelveazey.com
www.orchestra-eroica.com
info@michaelveazey.com
07946 495639

Michael Veazey coaches solo singers (musical theatre/opera), conducts choral societies (musical director, Godalming Choral) and orchestras (musical director, Orchestra Eroica). He started piano at age seven and conducting at 16, and studied music for seven years full-time at college and university. Michael has conducted Godalming Choral Society since 2007. Michael conducted professional and non-professional orchestras for more than 15 years and accompanied at the Guildford School of Acting for five years.

- **Qualifications:** Music Degree BMus (Hons). Post-Graduate Diploma in Advanced Performance (Royal Northern College of Music). Post-Graduate diploma in Conducting (Royal Welsh College of Music and Drama). Dip. ABRSM (Piano) with distinction.

- **Awards:** Highly Commended in the Weiz 2009 International Conducting Competition.

&& INSTEAD OF WORRYING AND STAGNATING, I'VE TAKEN ACTION.

INTRODUCTION BY DANIEL WAGNER

I have known Michael for a few years now, but I never got to know him properly until a few months ago. Michael is an artist, and traditionally artists and business success don't really go hand-in-hand. I am convinced that this commonly-held belief is turned on its head and Michael is determined to make sure that it is.

Michael decided to join the Expert Success Academy, because he felt understood, welcome and part of a tribe he could relate to. You see, even when your vision is to create an orchestra, marketing and business knowledge comes in handy.

So Michael attended a Platinum meeting of the Expert Success Academy as a VIP guest, and has since then made tremendous progress in making his dream a reality. And I know that Michael is not alone in tackling those challenges!

Too many people have a dream or a plan but never get round to putting it into practice. Not until they join a group that makes them accountable and supports them and gives them the self-belief to go out there and make it happen: to just go after the dream.

Only a few months ago I was stuck at a hotel at Heathrow because of an accident on the motorway. I decided to stay behind after the Platinum meeting to enjoy dinner with my team and some Academy members, including Michael, stayed behind and joined us at the round table.

I will remember that evening for a long time, as we had the most invigorating, humorous, and spiritual conversation. I really connected with Michael that evening, as my past as a musician meant I could relate to him very well!

That is what I love about the Academy, it is a fantastic group of like-minded people who help and support each other to achieve their dreams using a proven process.

I am very much looking forward to seeing Michael's orchestra perform and fill the concert halls of the UK and beyond. And who knows, it might be the next TV success story like that achieved by the military wives only a few years ago!

Daniel Wagner

AN INTERVIEW WITH MICHAEL VEAZEY

MICHAEL, HOW DID YOU GET STARTED IN MUSIC?

My mother was always playing the piano or singing at home so I guess that's where I got my love of both of those things from.

When I was five, I started playing the recorder then I started piano aged seven and continued into my teens. I really enjoyed it and it seemed to come quite quickly. I was lucky enough to have a good teacher with high standards musically and technically.

At 11 I took up French horn, which is where my love of orchestras started.

WHAT ABOUT WORKING WITH SINGERS? WHEN DID THAT COME IN?

I was quite a late starter there. I really started in the sixth form chamber choir at school. I then sang in a very good chamber choir at university.

But actually I came to choral societies via being a professional orchestral player in my early twenties. I played in over 100 choral society concerts in about five years. And I realised that I would be able to conduct better than 90% of the conductors without even thinking about it. That's when my serious ambition to conduct came back to the fore.

SO REALLY IT WAS PLAYING FOR OTHER CONDUCTORS THAT INSPIRED YOU TO CONDUCT?

A mix of inspiration and disgust!

I had been very inspired by my music teacher at school, who was a seriously talented musician: a talented pianist (classical and jazz), a great singer and a talented conductor (the skills, not coincidentally, I most admire and use daily).

My youth orchestra conductor was a truly excellent conductor (scary but with high standards), and my conducting teacher and conductor at university was a very warm and inspiring man. But my belief at the time regarding conducting was 'You have to be a genius to do it'. My respect for the profession got in the way of me actually doing it. Playing for some conductors, and being a competent orchestra player that judged incompetent conductors, combined into an over-critical belief around conducting.

It was only when I saw how incredibly badly most other people were doing it, that I felt I had the right to conduct.

WHAT QUALIFICATIONS DID YOU NEED TO CONDUCT?

Most conductors have at least an undergraduate degree in music so I did that, including an exchange year studying conducting in Germany. I had a truly excellent teacher in technical and musical terms but as a person, he reinforced my perfectionism.

So after graduating, I went to the Royal Northern College of Music as an orchestral player rather than as a conductor, feeling I lacked the experience to be a professional conductor.

WAS THAT YEAR IN GERMANY THE END OF YOUR CONDUCTING STUDIES?

Well, no. After my experiences with incompetent choral conductors, I decided to study conducting full-time again to start a career in conducting.

DID STUDYING CONDUCTING AGAIN PRODUCE THE CAREER PROGRESSION THAT YOU WERE WANTING?

In all honesty, no! It's true I had a more positive teacher and I believe that I learnt a great deal about the craft of how to actually conduct. However, I hadn't really planned how to go from college to an actual professional career conducting. So after that course, I thought 'Now what?'

WHAT DID YOU DO TO TRY AND SOLVE THIS PROBLEM?

Again I tried to follow a conventional route and copy others by applying for conducting competitions and kick-starting high-level work that way. Nearly all competitions rejected my entries – it's probable that my application videos were not very inspired or professional. Also I think I underestimated the importance of the positioning power of having truly famous mentors on my CV, which I lacked.

Sadly, I reached the age of 35, the cut-off age for international competitions, without even participating in one! So that route was definitely closed to me, to my distress!

He underestimated the importance of positioning.

WHAT WAS YOUR NEXT MOVE AFTER THE AGE OF 35 TO TRY TO GET YOUR CAREER TO THE NEXT LEVEL?

I didn't really have a clear answer at that stage. I kept applying for conducting jobs although they were now at a much lower level, mostly amateur choirs and orchestras, than I'd originally dreamt of.

DID YOU HAVE ANY SUCCESS WITH THAT?

Yes but only once, really! I was very happy to win the position of musical director with Godalming Choral Society in 2007, against 62 other applicants. And I have been there at ever since and have conducted over 15 concerts there. It's been a great success and although it has had its challenges, I've really enjoyed it.

WHAT HAVE BEEN YOUR MAIN SUCCESSES WITH GODALMING CHORAL SOCIETY?

In my first concert we sold over 600 tickets and at the end of the performance we had a standing ovation - the first one in the history of the choir, apparently. In our last concert we did a sell-out performance of Mozart Requiem which was another great success.

A standing ovation is a great place to start.

WHAT HAVE BEEN YOUR MAIN LEARNINGS FROM CONDUCTING THIS CHOIR?

Obviously I've honed the art of conducting, including the physical technique (waving!).

Also, choir vocal training that works for people after a hard day or week at work. But I've also learnt non-musical skills: leadership; inspiring people; getting and keeping attention; structuring the learning process; working with a board of trustees; forward planning, etc.

YOU SAY YOU ALSO WORK WITH PRIVATE SINGING STUDENTS — HOW DOES THAT WORK?

Yes, I've been fortunate enough for my work at the Guildford School of Acting to work for hundreds of hours over five years with what I would describe as a genius level teacher of singing, a wonderful singer and teacher named Rob Forbes.

WHAT WAS SO AMAZING ABOUT HIS WORK THEN?

Rob has great warmth and charisma. Also he is passionate about the importance of learning for singers, as a reaction to his own experiences of mediocre teaching as a young singer. He was effectively forced to go and seek out truly excellent mentors.

Fortunately he found them, became fascinated by the process, and absorbed the lessons deeply.

THAT SOUNDS LIKE HE HAD QUITE A PERSONAL JOURNEY HIMSELF. SO HOW DOES THAT RELATE TO YOUR OWN WORK AS A SINGING COACH?

I have a mental model of anatomy to relate singing to, and a tool bag of exercises to correct bad habits or create certain sounds.

In addition, though, I bring my pianistic background into play. In the realm of musical theatre, my hundreds of hours of accompanying have given me insight into the dos and don'ts of preparing for West End auditions and performances.

As a student, I had great lessons in opera coaching from the staff of the Welsh National Opera, and have since developed thanks to my contacts in the London-based opera world and daily contact with top-level opera pianists/coaches.

HOW DOES THAT TIE IN WITH YOUR CHOIR CONDUCTING WORK?

The technical approach from Rob Forbes, enhanced by other singing teachers I work with, means I can very quickly find a more comfortable and more exciting way to sing for choir members.

I have also learned a great deal from other choral conductors, including the UK's best: Adrian Partington, Paul Spicer, Mary King and Robert Dean, all of whom I've played for and/or worked with.

COMING BACK TO YOUR ORCHESTRAL CONDUCTING AMBITIONS, DID YOU HAVE ANY SUCCESS APPLYING FOR JOBS IN THE NORMAL WAY?

No! I underestimated the sheer importance of positioning as an expert as a conductor. I knew I was competent, and I had a certificate saying that I had been trained to a high level. That proved not to be enough even to get invited for auditions for amateur orchestras, never mind my original dream of professional orchestras.

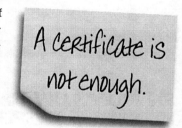

A certificate is not enough.

WHAT DID YOU TRY INSTEAD?

I lost my way for a while and, while still wanting to conduct in the long-term, was seduced by the idea of life coaching as a way of making a more immediate living. I was attracted to a taster session day, very much like the one that the Expert Success Academy runs.

AND WAS THAT A SUCCESS IN TERMS OF GETTING YOU WHAT YOU WANTED?

Not really. Although the guy running the group was (and is) a very brilliant marketer and I believe also a good teacher in some aspects, in reality I did not seem to achieve any major career or business movement.

It would be unfair to just blame the Mastermind group or the mentor. I was still in an unhelpful mindset regarding conducting – and money! Also, I was unclear in my own mind what I did want from the group. It didn't relate clearly to my skills or values.

I guess I had got seduced by the idea of earning money, and I'd forgotten to link the idea of 'more money' with what Daniel Wagner calls 'more purpose'.

I did gain a really broad knowledge of some great marketing strategies but nothing more.

HOW DID YOU HEAR OF DANIEL WAGNER?

I actually met Daniel when he came along to become a member of the same Mastermind group. In fact, James Watson joined around then, and I worked a little with him for a while too.

Both James and Daniel seemed to me to be very honest, trustworthy and focused and I liked them immediately.

Daniel left a lasting impression with me. I think it was a combination of a natural charisma and energy, business success and self-belief.

SO IF YOU JOINED A MASTERMIND GROUP ONCE AND IT DIDN'T HELP YOU IN YOUR GOALS, WHAT MADE YOU TAKE THE PLUNGE AGAIN AND JOIN THE EXPERT SUCCESS ACADEMY?

Good question! My experience made me wary of such groups (rightly so in most cases) but after following him online for a long while, I decided to go with Daniel's group because of Daniel's personal energy and integrity.

As a musician, I combine a rational, analytical side, with strong intuition. I trusted my intuition that Daniel was the person to be with. Thanks to his constant marketing approach, I felt that I knew Daniel quite well by the time I ordered his book. I read it cover to cover and was very impressed.

I based my decision to join the Academy on both a try-out day and the Expert Success Summit. The inspiration, warmth and clarity of structure of the Academy sold me on becoming a member.

WHAT WERE YOUR MORE 'RATIONAL' REASONS FOR BEING A MEMBER OF THE PLATINUM GROUP?

Firstly, if you feel inspired, you take more action, and so get results. I have absolutely noticed a difference in my action-taking on my career-related projects since I joined.

Secondly, there is a very vibrant community of members, many of whom have had very successful careers in their own right. The Facebook group is amazing – if I have a question, rather than worrying I just pop it on the group page, and within 48 hours, I'll have multiple responses.

Inspiration led to action and then results.

Thirdly and not least, it creates a powerful peer group with whom to share successes (aka boasting) – and also be accountable (aka shame as motivator!).

WHAT BIG WINS HAVE YOU HAD SINCE JOINING THE ACADEMY?

I've had a goal of setting up my own orchestra for years now.

The main block was fear of losing money and of empty concert halls – pretty much a pure marketing issue.

Being a member of the Academy has given me the confidence to get on with forming the orchestra and setting up the first concert.

Instead of worrying and stagnating, I've taken action: I've booked the venue for the first concert and set up a website, Facebook page and Twitter feed; run our first marketing meeting; had meetings with about five different advisors and, just today, I registered a limited company!

Obviously I didn't get all the information I needed for that from the Academy; that's not the point. In the age of Google, information undersupply doesn't really exist. What is lacking is clear structure, and the feeling of belonging to a tribe who have your back and will help when you really need it. The Academy gives me both.

WHAT ARE YOUR GOALS FOR THIS YEAR?

This year is going to be focused mostly on my orchestra (Orchestra Eroica).

The first goal is simply to sell at least 200 tickets for our July début concert.

I am in conversations with media contacts exploring pitching a concept to TV and/or radio producers for a fly-on-the-wall documentary about creating an orchestra.

We also have future plans for combining comedy with conducting, in live events and on film.

HOW WILL THE EXPERT SUCCESS ACADEMY HELP WITH THAT?

The *Expert Success* book should be perfect as a basis for brand and marketing work. And the Academy members will support me with encouragement and advice as they have so far.

WHAT ADVICE WOULD YOU GIVE TO PEOPLE CONSIDERING JOINING THE EXPERT SUCCESS ACADEMY?

Just try it out! There are many levels at which you can get involved. Daniel and James don't use high pressure tactics so relax, just pick one and try it out.

WHAT WOULD BE A GOOD FIRST STEP?

Obviously it is very inexpensive to join the Silver or Gold level and gain some exposure to Daniel and James and their strategies so that is a good place to start.

However, if you are ambitious or you're stuck, I would urge you to get to a live event as soon as you can.

Start with Daniel's website and check out a couple of his videos, that will give you a great idea of what he is really like (Daniel is exactly the same in person as on these videos – what you see is what you get!).

Then, buy the *Expert Success* book for peanuts and book in for a massively discounted 'try-out day'.

After doing that, you will definitely know if it is for you. If it is, I look forward to seeing you at the next meeting!

- A penguin out of its element is clumsy but in its element, effortlessly powerful. Know yourself – be honest! Then lead like-minded people.

- Choose one thing to be known for. Clarity is power!

- Expertise is 80% context and 20% technical ability.

- Isolation kills dreams. Powerful peers boost dreams.

SOPHIA JAMES AND NIGEL BENCH ONLINE MARKETING EXPERTS

Making You Shine Online

Internet Power LLP

www.internetpower.co.uk | www.sophia-james.com
www.nigelbench.com | connect@internetpower.co.uk
0117 230 5350

Sophia James and Nigel Bench both have over 20 years professional, business and marketing experience. Together they create powerful online brands and integrated online marketing solutions for business success and successful business people. They will make you shine online. They make successful people shine online – creating business and personal online brands and websites, with integrated online marketing, for professional and service businesses and people. Sophia was a solicitor for over 20 years, including management, quality and marketing and then set up a fitness centre. Nigel spent 30 years in management in the hotel industry.

- **Sophia's Qualifications:** Sophia has an MBA, LLB, and a list of other qualifications and achievements as long as your arm, from marketing and entrepreneurship to coaching, NLP, hypnosis and much more – she's competed successfully against Olympic and world champions in eventing and even has a black belt in judo.

- **Nigel's Qualifications:** Nigel has degrees in hospitality and business management, as well as numerous specialist marketing and other industry qualifications.

- **Achievements:** We are proud and delighted to have won the Expert Success High Achiever Award at the Expert Success Summit in 2012. Our more personal recent achievements include walking on fire and on broken glass, breaking boards and time travelling (we all create our own reality) while creating our dream business and lifestyle.

“ WE INCREASED TURNOVER BY 400% LAST YEAR.

INTRODUCTION BY DANIEL WAGNER

I just love Nigel and Sophia's story! When people come to see me for the first time, they have often been on my list or followed my teachings or stories for many years.

Nigel and Sophia have both had corporate careers before, and now in the prime of their life, decided to run their own business on their own terms. The internet seemed the obvious place to start, but as many of us experienced, the path to internet riches can be treacherous and confusing.

So helping Nigel and Sophia build their business, was a true exercise in business and marketing coaching, which is what the Expert Success Academy does best.

Nigel and Sophia have been part of the inner circle Mastermind group for four terms, and their change and transformation has been nothing short of amazing. And as always, business growth and business success goes hand-in-hand with personal growth and personal success.

They now live and work from their dream home, on their own terms, and are doing a tremendous job of increasing their already established expert positioning. This is by no means an easy feat in their industry, which is web design.

But they have mastered the art of packaging a unique set of services and skills to avoid falling into the trap of dirt-cheap bargain websites. As a matter of fact, they have been able to multiply their price, which has also helped them to attract a better level client.

Their business has, in just a few short years, developed the very important passive recurring element, which many business owners can only dream of.

I know they have ambitious goals and already mapped out their exit plan, which is such a joy to behold! They are indeed a great example how you can run a business any way you like, combining a successful enterprise with spiritual and alternative values.

Nigel and Sophia have also provided services for many members in the Expert Success Academy, a wonderful side-effect of this fast growing community. If you need a service to move your business forward, you should always look in your tribe first!

Daniel Wagner

AN INTERVIEW WITH
SOPHIA JAMES AND NIGEL BENCH

NIGEL AND SOPHIA, WHAT SORT OF EXPERTS ARE YOU?

Sophia: We are experts in online marketing and specialise in business and personal online brands, integrated online marketing strategies and implementation.

Nigel: In practical terms this encompasses web design, copywriting, social media and email marketing, plus advanced online marketing tools and techniques, including landing and sales pages, membership sites and text message marketing.

Our clients include professionals such as vets, doctors and alternative health practitioners; property investors; coaches and consultants; lawyers and accountants – providing specialist expertise and knowledge-based advice and/ or training services and products.

HOW LONG HAVE YOU BEEN IN THIS BUSINESS?

We've been running our business together for four years now, but it wasn't always this way, we both have corporate business backgrounds, with long and successful careers in different industries.

SO, WHAT DID YOU DO ORIGINALLY?

Sophia: Well, I started out as a lawyer. When I qualified, the only form of advertising solicitors were allowed to do was to put up a brass plaque on their door. So marketing was all about building personal relationships.

I began in the city, working for one of the top international law firms and later moved to Bristol. Originally I specialised in commercial litigation, shipping, banking and insurance and later in professional negligence.

I was always interested in business and I've always liked to stretch myself and learn new skills, so after 10 years I did an MBA and moved into law firm management. I was on the executive board of a large law firm, ran the marketing department for a while and also specialised in quality, client care, professional ethics and risk management.

Nigel: My background is in hospitality. I worked in a 5-star hotel in Berlin as part of my degree and then in my twenties I ran a small hotel in Sussex with my family.

Since then I have run everything from luxury country house hotels to a chain of pubs – and even a gourmet café! I've looked after every kind of customer, from famous celebrities enjoying a break (Charlton Heston comes to mind), to builders and call centre workers on their tea break.

WHAT THEN?

Sophia: After over 20 years in law, I wanted to do something different. So I set up a gym with a business partner. It was so exciting, starting and building up a new business completely from scratch. I also discovered that I loved the marketing and sales side. Most solicitors hate marketing and sales – and think they are hopeless at it. This is actually a complete misconception – just look at the huge and hugely profitable city law firms, built entirely by the lawyers. It's changing now, but they've never allowed their marketing teams to do much more than tinker around the edges.

In our gym, we focused on great service. We knew every single one of our gym members personally – and made many lasting friends. It was amazing: helping people get fit, lose weight and transform their lives, I loved it.

Get to know your (ideal) customer personally.

Nigel: I ended up as finance director of a large conference centre and wedding venue. In a way it was a mistake. I'm good at the numbers, but I always preferred dealing with people – both customers and staff. Delivering a great experience to people for their special occasion is so rewarding.

And I always enjoyed the marketing side. I ran and promoted events from lawn concerts to murder mysteries! I just wish I'd known then as much as I know now about online marketing and really effective website design!

HOW DID YOU END UP GOING FROM LAW, GYMS AND HOTELS TO AN ONLINE MARKETING BUSINESS?

Sophia: First of all, we met! Then the credit crunch began and my gym business was still growing, but too slowly. Nigel's business was under pressure too.

Nigel: Then we decided to get married – and we wanted to spend time together. We'd both spent many years working very long hours and Sophia commuted too – we both had previous relationships that had suffered from long hours and ties. We also wanted to explore something new – we both enjoy new challenges, learning and exploring new ideas and activities. As we both had great business experience, it made sense to look at doing something together.

WHAT MADE YOU CHOOSE ONLINE MARKETING?

Sophia: Like many others, we started off simply going to an internet marketing event. We looked at other options too, but we liked the idea of being flexible and working from home. The business model appealed too – with low overheads and the opportunity to harness low cost modern technology and connect with people anywhere, easily and quickly.

Nigel: We started off just trying the usual internet marketing models – affiliate marketing, ClickBank etc. It was fun and we learnt a lot. We signed up for a few different courses and learnt from all of them – including how to build WordPress websites.

I'd been involved in websites before, in my previous roles, and was amazed how accessible WordPress is. Of course, it becomes quite technical when you do more advanced work, but you just don't need to know all that geeky code to build a simple site – and certainly not to edit and update it.

We were looking at local business models, so we could immediately see the opportunity for businesses to use the same online marketing technology and techniques the internet marketers were using. I knew all about offline marketing costs so the possibilities for reaching new people and developing relationships with existing customers, at a fraction of the cost was very exciting!

HOW DID YOU MEET DANIEL WAGNER?

Sophia: We originally met Daniel at a Mark Anastasi internet marketing event in London. He was selling a course, from the stage, and we really liked his presentation. I talked to him afterwards and although we didn't in the end sign up for his course, I was impressed. I really liked his approach and his energy.

Nigel: I was struck by Daniel's blend of a very clear business focus combined with a spiritual awareness. It's very similar to our own approach to life and business.

SO WHAT DID YOU DO THEN?

Sophia: We started doing a few websites and online marketing set-ups for friends and for other local businesses.

Nigel: We wanted to contribute to our local community, so local business marketing seemed a great direction to go in. It gave us an opportunity to share the new skills we were acquiring. At the same time we carried on exploring other internet marketing options, so we set up various online businesses – more of that later...

> Start by trying things out on friends and other local businesses.

WHAT HAPPENED NEXT?

Sophia: I've always been very interested in ongoing personal development and while we were learning more online marketing skills, we also went on other, more personally orientated courses. We were both always well aware of the benefits of mentoring and coaching and knew the right coach would help us progress.

We'd been thinking of joining a different Mastermind group and then the opportunity to join Daniel and James suddenly came up. It was obvious this would be a far better match for our business and what we wanted to achieve, so we applied.

WHAT ATTRACTED YOU TO THE EXPERT SUCCESS MASTERMIND GROUP?

Sophia: In those days the Expert Success Academy didn't yet exist, as such! When we discussed the Mastermind programme with Daniel and James, there were a number of things we particularly liked. Daniel and James are very complementary, they bring different skills and experience and they make a great team. Their in-depth approach was exactly what we were looking for to really bring clarity and accelerate our business.

Nigel: We also really liked the Mastermind format – a group of 12 different businesses, meeting every month, working together and sharing ideas, skills – and challenges. You all learn a huge amount from the other members and their businesses, as well as from James and Daniel.

Sophia: Most important of all was the integrity and energy Daniel and James brought. We instantly felt they were the right people for us to connect to and work with. When you choose a business coach, it's obviously important to find someone with the right skills and experience but the intangibles are equally important. If your values and energy are not aligned, you won't connect effectively and the relationship will ultimately be limited in what it achieves, for both of you.

HOW DID YOU FINANCE IT?

Sophia: To be honest, it was a stretch. A real stretch. At the time we had very limited income and diminishing funds. But we just knew it was the right thing to do and that it would more than pay off. You simply progress so much faster when you have this kind of support. So we didn't hesitate. We found the money somehow.

Nigel: Investing in your business is essential if you want to progress. We knew this was a unique opportunity – and success is all about taking opportunities when they arise.

HOW DID YOUR BUSINESS BENEFIT FROM JOINING THE EXPERT SUCCESS MASTERMIND GROUP?

Sophia: Wow, where to start! When we joined the Mastermind group we didn't really have a proper business as such – we had lots of different strands and we weren't sure which to focus on.

Nigel: We had literally hundreds of websites. Many were affiliate sites. We also had sites on personal development, fitness and weight loss, astrology and gastro pubs – reflecting a few of our (diverse!) interests. Some made a little money, but most didn't. We also had our fledgling local online marketing business, Internet

Power, which we hadn't done much with over the previous few months.

Sophia – With Daniel and James's help, plus feedback from the group, we very quickly decided to focus on Internet Power – helping mainly local businesses with their online marketing and websites. We also decided on a couple of niche markets to start concentrating on – professional services (reflecting my background) and also local gastro pubs (reflecting Nigel's).

Nigel: Once we had that clarity and focus we put all our efforts into developing Internet Power. It wasn't easy to start with, we had a few existing clients, but none was very active – and none of them needed a new site. Really we were starting from scratch.

HOW DID YOU PROGRESS FROM THERE?

Sophia: We began building contacts and started to get new business. Early on we also started working with one of our fellow Mastermind members, Alan Robinson, who is a very successful business consultant to the veterinary industry. He was impressed by our work and we began a project together, developing a marketing and website package for vets.

Nigel: I also developed the prototype for what is now our own unique product, our Online Dashboard. This gives our clients fast, easy access to all their online marketing tools – including their website, social media profiles and email marketing.

Sophia: Shortly afterwards, Daniel and James asked us to produce and deliver the websites and online marketing packages for their first Online Brand Masterclass. This was a fantastic opportunity for us – and a great illustration of how they have always gone out of their way to support us – as they have with all the members of the Mastermind group. We can't thank them enough.

Nigel: The next major success was when we started to work with Del Brown, a very successful property investor in Bristol, who was also starting to run property investment meetings and training. We set up his entire online presence, including his personal brand website, his main business website, a tenant website and his online booking systems – including all the copy and free reports. We also run all his online marketing campaigns on an ongoing basis.

Since then we have found an increasing number of clients looking for a 'done for you' solution, where we use all our marketing expertise to write the copy for their websites and other online marketing communications, as well as the main design and set up – and we now specialise in providing this service to busy professionals.

SO, WHERE IS YOUR BUSINESS TODAY?

Sophia: It's now two years since we first joined the Mastermind group and our business is totally transformed. We have gone from a start up with almost no income or clients to a well-established successful and profitable business creating personal and business online brands and online marketing. We now have over 70 active clients – many of whom we have

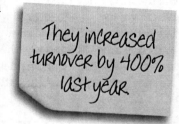

They increased turnover by 400% last year

worked with on several projects. We increased turnover by 400% last year and are on track to do the same again this year. We have also built regular recurring income through our ongoing marketing, Online Dashboard and hosting packages. Building recurring income is one of the important elements of a successful business and one of many key concepts highlighted in the *Expert Success* book.

Nigel: We have also just completed a series of presentations to a local business group and a property group and are now just setting up a series of workshops. We find the expert positioning approach that is fundamental to the Expert Success Formula works exactly as Daniel explains – experts attract customers. As an expert, you do not have to chase clients: they come to you. We are constantly busy and over the last few months we have also been approached by several very successful business people, who want us to set up personal coaching programmes for them.

Sophia: We have just sold out a series of £3k packages to vets, which were sold via a webinar run by our fellow Mastermind member, Anthony Chadwick – our first experience of selling via webinars. It's a long way from the £99 websites we were doing two years ago! We are also working on a similar, bespoke package for Alan Robinson's clients.

We also have a professional business structure – Internet Power LLP was set up over a year ago. We have well-documented systems and processes, ready to move to the next stage and we are using outsourcers to streamline our production, leaving us free to concentrate on customer service and our specialist skills.

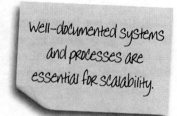

Well-documented systems and processes are essential for scalability.

Nigel: Most important of all, we have built our dream lifestyle business. We have moved to a beautiful, remote part of the country (Exmoor) where we live in a lovely old farmhouse with our horses and cat, Boris. We run our business and deliver great service to our clients, using online technology – and have time to spend together. We can travel abroad, which we both love, while working as usual – our clients have no idea that as we get their latest project live, we may actually be enjoying the sunshine in Spain, Italy, Portugal or St Lucia.

DO YOU HAVE DIFFERENT ROLES IN THE BUSINESS?

Sophia: Nigel is more technical than me, so he does more of the complex technical set-ups. He's also very creative on the design side, so he does most of the key visual design and liaises with the graphics experts. He is the main contact with our outsourcers and suppliers and has built great relationships with them – they are all key members of our team.

Nigel: Sophia is a great writer, so she does a lot of the copy for websites and for ongoing marketing materials and communications. For some clients we write and deliver their blogs and emails and even their free reports and guides etc. Sophia does most of this, plus the social media side and much of our own marketing – she's great at staying in touch with contacts and clients. For our business and our clients' businesses, building relationships is the key to successful marketing.

Generally though both of us can, and often do, cover the vast majority of what our business entails. We usually both speak at presentations (which is actually much harder than doing it alone!) – and on one project we wrote a series of emails to clients and even Daniel and James couldn't tell who wrote which.

HOW MUCH HAS THE EXPERT SUCCESS ACADEMY CONTRIBUTED TO YOUR SUCCESS?

Sophia: Daniel and James have been amazing. Of course we have worked very hard too, but they have played a huge and invaluable role in our business. They are supportive and insightful – and they always provide great feedback and ideas.

Nigel: The other members of the Mastermind group have also been incredibly helpful and supportive. They are all successful business people in their own right and their contributions at every meeting are exceptionally valuable. One member calls the Mastermind group his 'Strategic Board' – and he's exactly right. It's very powerful.

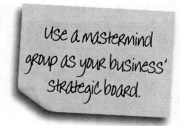

Use a mastermind group as your business' strategic board.

We've also been very fortunate to have worked with many of the members of the Expert Success Academy and especially the Mastermind group – we're proud and humbled that so many have become our clients, as well as our colleagues – and our friends.

WHAT IS DIFFERENT ABOUT THE EXPERT SUCCESS ACADEMY?

Sophia: The Expert Success Academy is quite simply unique. It's an extraordinary group of extraordinary people, sharing great business ideas and information in a very open, supportive, positive and ethical environment.

Daniel and James work tirelessly to help each and every member succeed and reach their goals. They are also passionate about maintaining the integrity and values of the group.

Nigel: The collaboration, support and joint working within the group are exceptional. We have made many friends – and are in touch with virtually every single member of the Mastermind group, including those from the very first group we joined.

Sophia: This isn't a group that is right for everyone. It's essential that you share the core values and approach. If you do, then it is a fantastic experience.

WHAT DO YOU RECOMMEND AS THE NEXT STEP?

Sophia: I'd encourage anyone to contact Daniel and James and go to one of their events and find out if the Expert Success Academy is for you. If it is, you are very fortunate – you will learn a huge amount, but most of all you will be part of a group that will make sure you achieve the success you desire.

Nigel: The most important step is to take action. So, open the door, step through and create a new reality reflecting your own dreams and desires.

KEY LEARNINGS

- Clarity – leads to focus.

- Contribution – add value, based on your own unique values and skills.

- Commitment – keep learning and keep going.

- Consistency – delivery is a key part of your brand.

- Connection – love what you do, where you do it and who you do it with.

HELEN TURIER ULTIMATE WELLBEING AND RESILIENCE EXPERT

Creating Ultimate Wellbeing for Women in Business

www.helenturier.com
helen@helenturier.com
07920 026884

Helen helps businesswomen to transform their wellbeing and performance by learning to manage stress and develop their resilience. She has 28 years' experience in healthcare and wellbeing, first as a Registered General Nurse, then as company director of a multimillion pound healthcare IT company and six years as a reflexologist specialising in stress management. Surviving the rollercoaster of her own life has given her the knowledge and skills to develop

The B.O.U.N.C.E. Model of Resilience. Learning and implementing this model guarantees that Helen's clients develop the resilience needed to effectively cope with the demands of modern life.

- **Qualifications:** Registered General Nurse, trained by The Queen Alexandra's Royal Army Nursing Corps in 1987. Completed the Institute of Directors Director Development Programme in 2003. Awarded a Diploma in Reflexology in 2007. Achieved a PTLLS teaching qualification in 2011. Became a Certified NLP Practitioner in 2011. Became a Certified Thought Field Therapist in 2011.

- **Credibility:** Was simultaneously running one multimillion pound company (MDS Ltd) as managing director while on the board of another multimillion pound company (CAS Services). Published author of four books.

- **Achievements:** Developing The B.O.U.N.C.E. Model of Resilience. My proudest personal achievement is going from being on social benefits (with three children under three years old) to becoming a company director of two multimillion pound companies within five years. But raising those three wonderful young people at the same time was, by far, my greatest achievement.

PUBLICATIONS

Bounce-back Ability: Developing Resilience on the Rollercoaster of Life, 90-Day Books, 2012.

Get Back on Your Feet Again. Fifty-five tips to improve your resilience after a setback, 90-Day Books, 2012.

Managing Pressure & Change Effectively Using The B.O.U.N.C.E. Model of Resilience, 90-Day Books, 2012.

Do You Always Catch a Cold on Holiday or at Christmas? Discover How Your Lifestyle Could be Killing You, 90-Day Books, 2013.

INTRODUCTION BY DANIEL WAGNER

Without doubt, Helen is a high achiever. She came to my Discovery Day, signed up for my Online Brand Masterclass, and straight away joined the Expert Success Academy.

She was already a published author when we met and had created a teaching framework, but somehow the level of success she deserved and desired was still eluding her.

I guess she immediately saw that the concepts we share as part of the Expert Success Formula – which are Authentic Personal Online Branding, the creation of a Strategic Product Staircase, and using automation to Cultivate a Buying Audience – would lead her to her goal.

Helen's message of increasing one's resilience is so important in today's world and society, as all of us have to juggle a multitude of roles and challenges simultaneously. In Helen's case bringing up teenage children, building a business, and promoting her book!

Because Helen wants to expand her reach, she faces the natural challenge of leverage, which every business owner faces when they become successful. So the creation of the Strategic Product Staircase, including online learning and facilitation, plus large group engagement will help Helen achieve her vision.

One of the many advantages of being part of the Expert Success Academy is that you can literally copy and paste our model and apply it to your own business.

So when Helen talks about building a multitier mentoring and coaching business, she can adapt the proven model of the Expert Success Academy, allowing her to progress faster, make fewer mistakes, and become more profitable.

I believe that all of us should look for tested and proven shortcuts, and to do whatever we can to share our message with the largest possible audiences!

There are thousands of people out there like Helen, who have a life-transforming message; who need to share that message with the world. And if you're one of them, then it's not just your right, it's your duty!

Daniel Wagner

AN INTERVIEW WITH HELEN TURIER

HELEN, WHAT WAS YOUR MAIN GOAL FOR LAST YEAR?

My main goal for last year was to balance the pressures of promoting my book, piloting my resilience training courses and building up my business on the one hand, while supporting my teenage children through their GCSEs, A Levels and university applications on the other.

WHAT SORT OF EXPERT ARE YOU?

I'm a wellbeing and resilience expert and have published four books on the topic.

WHAT DOES WELLBEING AND RESILIENCE MEAN, EXACTLY?

You know how many successful businesswomen fall ill whenever they take a break or go on holiday? Well this is not as harmless as it seems. It's a heads-up that they could be headed for a more serious illness like heart disease, cancer and immune problems like ME. I work with these women to help them develop a more resilient lifestyle that revitalises their health, boosts their energy, and increases their performance at work and home.

She's already published four books!

HOW DID YOU GET INTO RESILIENCE?

I believe that as a business owner I have a duty of care to my clients. That duty of care means I must ensure that I can perform to an optimum level. When I was simultaneously running one company (MDS Ltd), and on the board of another (CAS Services), I experienced first-hand the importance of the energy, performance and attitude of the leaders on the performance of my employees and the business. As a small company we were growing rapidly whilst maintaining a number of government contracts. It meant that many of our staff were in a prolonged state of personal challenge and growth. So I learnt a huge amount about supporting personal growth and development in a high-pressure environment in a holistic way that was mutually supportive to the business and the employee.

I like to lead by example but as a lone parent I was struggling with getting the balance right myself at home. As a result the lifestyle choices I was making impacted on my health and I was diagnosed with an endocrine disorder. My consultant told me that I would have it for life and that drugs would not help. I needed to change my diet and manage my stress. If I did

It's not easy to juggle a multitude of roles and challenges simultaneously.

not then I ran the risk of developing serious life-limiting health problems like diabetes, heart disease or cancer. Of course as a nurse I knew far more than the average person about those risks and it was a scary and sobering thought. However asking me to lower my stress levels at a time when I was in the process of helping the owner of the two companies to sell them was not good timing: it would have been easier if the consultant had asked me to organise a flight to the moon. I could have handled that far more easily!

I decided that I needed to understand more about stress and wellbeing from a more integrative approach than my more traditional nursing and medical model of healthcare.

So, I made it my mission to learn about stress and resilience, to understand it and to implement changes into my business and personal life so that I could complete the sale of the companies - and get my health back on track.

One of the tools I used to manage my stress was reflexology. This therapy helped me to understand a true holistic approach to health and wellbeing. I also learnt about and used life coaching to help me achieve my goals.

WHEN DID YOU LEAVE YOUR JOB?

Such is my passion for health and wellbeing that in 2005, after the two companies had been sold, I decided to focus on helping other businesswomen to learn how to manage their stress, develop resilience and create their ultimate wellbeing.

Focus on what you already know!

Since 2006 I have trained as a reflexologist, coach and NLP (Neuro-Linguistic Programming) practitioner and extensively researched resilience and wellbeing. I set up a practice working with clients to help them to manage their stress and to create greater wellbeing. The tools and strategies that I applied with clients to help them deal more effectively with the ups and downs and challenges of modern business life have transformed the wellbeing of their lives.

WHY DID YOU WRITE YOUR FIRST BOOK?

Writing my first book in 2012 was a great way for me to put down on paper the strategies that I had learnt that had helped me become resilient in the face of adversity. My B.O.U.N.C.E. Model of Resilience is a simple-to-use tool that helps you develop your resilience and can also be used as a check-up tool when life has dealt you a curveball and knocked you off balance, enabling you to get back on track again quickly and easily.

Based on this first book I developed a training programme for business people that I piloted last year with over 100 people. Then that led on to publishing three other books.

WHAT DOES THE FUTURE HOLD FOR YOU?

My mission is to see a more resilient approach to health and wellbeing that is led by women, who are traditionally the nurturers in society. Research has shown that women make the best company bosses, but many women's health suffers as a result of the demands modern life places on them. By being resilient I mean that we each step up and learn how to live and work to an optimum performance level and that our

Experts help others to achieve success too.

work environment, our lifestyle and our healthcare support and empower us to do this. By helping women to learn how to develop their resilience I believe that I can help businesswomen achieve the success they deserve without sacrificing their wellbeing or their health.

HOW DID YOU MEET DANIEL WAGNER?

Having studied personal development for a number of years I had heard about Daniel's business success. So when my friend invited me along to a one-day workshop being run by Daniel I leapt at the chance to hear him speak first-hand.

WHAT ATTRACTED YOU TO THE EXPERT SUCCESS ACADEMY?

There are many personal development and business growth organisations out there that promise huge rewards to their followers but do very little to help those people to implement the learning. As a qualified trainer I know that acquiring knowledge is easy; the real growth actually comes from implementing that knowledge. What appealed about The Expert Success Academy is that each month we delve deeper into the practical implementation of Daniel's formula. And there is also support from the community on the Facebook group when we encounter challenges in implementing it in our own businesses. The community helps to keep you on track and supported but ultimately of course it's down to me as a businesswoman to actually do it.

WHAT ARE YOUR GOALS FOR THIS YEAR?

My goal for this year is to develop my resilience and wellbeing programme into an online learning version, as well as setting up a multitier mentoring programme, so that my B.O.U.N.C.E. Model of Resilience becomes accessible to businesswomen worldwide.

HOW WILL THE EXPERT SUCCESS ACADEMY HELP WITH THAT?

The Expert Success Academy has shown me an effective way to structure my mentoring programme that will allow me to earn and to grow in a way that is manageable and achievable.

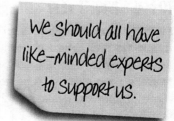
We should all have like-minded experts to support us.

In addition, the Academy has given me access to many like-minded business people who are all experts in their own right. So I have great resources at my fingertips when I need them.

WHAT DID YOU LEARN ON THE ONLINE BRAND MASTERCLASS? WHAT IMPACT DID IT HAVE ON YOU?

The Online Brand Masterclass was great because it helped me to focus on my core strengths. It's tempting to want to help everyone, but I now know that my skills and experience will, initially, be best used to empower businesswomen to develop their resilience. The rest of the world comes in stage two!

The Online Brand Masterclass also meant that I have a professional website that has the right look and feel. It makes a great starting point for businesswomen who are committed to improving and optimising their wellbeing and their performance.

WHERE DO YOU PUT MOST OF YOUR ENERGY?

My energy is currently focused on getting the first part of my sales pipeline completed and on networking with the Academy members so that I can build the support network that is essential to operate a resilient business and lifestyle. I am also piloting workplace Lunchtime Learning Sessions for small and medium businesses, based on my Three Simple Strategies for Managing Stress.

HOW MANY JOINT VENTURE PARTNERSHIPS DO YOU HAVE?

I don't currently have any joint ventures but it is my goal to form them with other Academy members so that I can provide my membership programme with huge value.

HAS YOUR BUSINESS STARTED TO MAKE PROFIT YET?

She's on a mission!

My reflexology business is profitable but is very much 'trading time for money'. By building a business with The Expert Success Academy formula I am aiming to be generating income more efficiently, whilst simultaneously helping to spread the learning about resilience and wellbeing. For me it's as much about building a financial future for myself and my family as it is about changing the way people think about stress and health. I'm a woman on a mission.

APART FROM THE ACADEMY, DO YOU GO TO ANY OTHER NETWORKING EVENTS?

I am a regular guest speaker at networking and business events across Sussex and Surrey. My personal monthly goal is to speak at a networking or business event and publish an online or printed article. This will help spread the word about resilience and its importance. So far, I'm on track this year.

WHAT DID YOUR FAMILY SAY ABOUT WHAT YOU DO?

As a parent to three young people, it is important to me that I show them how to effectively juggle the conflicting demands of work and family without compromising on values and beliefs. They are very supportive of my work and proud that their mum is a published author and businesswoman. However I know I can be an embarrassing mother – for example, I once showed a group of dancers at my daughter's ballet class how they could use visualisation and positive pre-play techniques to improve their pirouettes!

“ MY B.O.U.N.C.E. MODEL IS BASED ON MY YEARS OF EXPERIENCE IN HEALTH CARE AND WELLBEING.

KEY LEARNINGS

My key learnings are embodied within my B.O.U.N.C.E. Model of Resilience:

- Believe you can do it. This is vital to being an expert: if you don't believe in yourself then how can anyone else?

- Set goals and maintain an optimistic outlook. Running your own business is hard work and it is easy to get bogged down in the thick of it. By setting goals you keep on track and focused even if life throws you a curveball.

- You are your business. Make sure you practise what you preach. Integrity is one of my highest values and I know my clients appreciate and understand this.

- Nurture yourself. You are the linchpin of your family and your business and if you do not balance work and home, eat healthily and exercise regularly, and manage your stress properly then your business and your home life will be damaged. In some cases that damage will be irreversible. Don't learn the hard way. Learn to become resilient.

- Being connected and supported is an integral part of being human, so make sure you build supportive networks both at work and home.

- Enjoy and celebrate your success along the way, both big and small. At the Academy meetings each month we all share our wins for that month. Sometimes they are huge in financial terms sometimes they are huge in personal growth terms and sometimes they are little wins that take us a micro step closer to our dream.

KAM DOVEDI
PROPERTY PORTFOLIO
BUILDING EXPERT

**Delivering Great,
Low Risk Returns
Through Property
Portfolio Building**

Premier Portfolio Builder

www.kamdovedi.com
www.premierportfoliobuilder.co.uk
kam@kamdovedi.com
07970 173 899

Kam specialises in helping busy people who do not have time but could benefit from his portfolio building service. He actively invests in residential and commercial properties and in the last 20 years Kam has accumulated a significant property portfolio which is worth millions. He began by sourcing properties for himself, and after discovering a foolproof method of investing, he started to build portfolios for others. Property has allowed him to live a life of freedom and choice.

- **Qualifications:** BSC (hons) in Business Development.

- **Credibility:** Property Mentor with a number of the UK's largest property education companies. Angel Network and Mastermind Alliance Investors Club award winner.

- **Personal Achievements:** Built a significant personal property portfolio worth millions over 21 years.

> **I PLAN TO PROVIDE THE NUMBER ONE PROPERTY PORTFOLIO-BUILDING SERVICE.**

INTRODUCTION BY DANIEL WAGNER

I first noticed Kam and his son at one of our Intensive Training days. They talked about their clothing business and seemed to be mainly interested in some of my online marketing expertise.

I only learned later on that Kam was a very experienced and successful property investor who would be a prime candidate to build an Expert business. He signed up for my Online Brand Masterclass and joined the Expert Success Academy on the Platinum level.

A keen contributor, he always tried to catch some extra time with me in the breaks. Then, at the beginning of 2013, he finally had enough of waiting around I guess! So he upgraded to the Academy's Diamond level and booked some 1:1 coaching time with me to kick things into gear.

Kam has successfully refined a hands-free investing model for busy professionals, but was concerned about the marketing aspect and the scalability. I am pleased to see progress in both these areas after just a few short months.

One of the interesting aspects of Kam's expert-positioning is his unconscious competence and natural humility. A high achiever with a great work ethic, he always juggles a lot of different projects, not giving himself all the credit he is due. We're working on that!

This is part of why the Expert Success Academy does so well. We make sure people get recognition and feedback on successes, while striving to solve their business challenges.

Kam has called himself a 'course junkie' and it's true that he has spent a few years on the circuit doing all kinds of trainings and courses. I would disagree with this self-description, as my definition of a 'course junkie' is a person who gets his kick out of attending a course but doesn't take much action.

I can testify that Kam is an avid course buyer and attendee, but he's got a lot to show for it! I'm convinced that much of his recent success story was only possible because of the new knowledge he'd acquired, alongside the new peer group he was exposing himself to.

I, for one, am glad that he attends all these courses, because that's how we met!

Daniel Wagner

AN INTERVIEW WITH KAM DOVEDI

KAM, WOULD YOU TELL US A BIT ABOUT YOUR BACKGROUND?

My full name is Anoop Kumar Dovedi, but all my friends and colleagues know me as Kam, and I am a professional property investor.

I was born and grew up in the east end of London. My parents were immigrants from India, my mother a simple village girl and my father very well educated, and very well versed in English with almost a regal aura, but also with a serious alcohol problem. I found out I had to grow up very fast and found myself from the age of 11 having to make major financial decisions within the household with my mother. We were extremely poor and it was so painful to see my mother struggle to keep everything together. It was at that point I told myself I can be a better man, and the need to be a decent person and to help other people then arose.

I vowed that I would never be in a position of financial helplessness like my mother was, and I would do everything I could to ensure that she was never in that position again. From that point onwards began an indescribable passion to make a success of my life, which made financial freedom of a high importance.

WHAT MADE YOU GET INTO PROPERTY?

I remember at the age of 15 I started working for a large department store in the east end of London, which was run by a family. One of the partners in the business took a liking to me. He was a very powerful and influential man in his business but on occasions he took the time to talk to me. He sowed the seeds that property would be the way to create massive wealth. It's amazing how the right people come along in your life when you need them the most!

The right people come along when you need them most.

I realised then if I believed in myself life's doors would open for me. I juggled my jobs around school. After college I made the decision to go to university. In the second year of university where everyone else was renting accommodation, I used my grant money, and money I had saved from my jobs, to fund the deposit for my first house. I was still short of funds for the deposit though and I worked day and night shifts for 36 hours a day to make up the shortfall. I realised I could create the life I wanted through working hard.

HAVE YOU MADE MISTAKES ALONG THE WAY, AND HOW HAVE OTHER PEOPLE'S OPINIONS IMPACTED YOU?

Yes, of course but hindsight is a wonderful thing! At 21 I was buying my third property - even before the times of *buy to let*. I explained to others what I was doing. The bank manger looked at me as if I was insane, as did my friends and a couple of the property surveyors that I knew. Thinking that their 'professional opinions' mattered; I sat on the fence for a long while. I hadn't had any property education and soon found out that I had three properties in negative equity, with bad tenants and high debts. These properties were on the brink of repossession. To compound this, I had bought properties that were hundreds of miles away from each other.

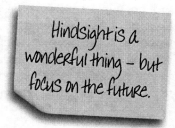

Hindsight is a wonderful thing – but focus on the future.

DID YOU GET ANY PROPERTY EDUCATION?

Up to this point I had a very limited property education but I rapidly realised I needed help. And it was just by sheer coincidence that I came across some literature about property investment education. Then my property journey really began. Reading books, such as biographies of major, influential business people and on self-development, all perpetuated my desire to do and become more than I was at the time. I completed a range of property and business courses and seminars which have since opened many doors for me. For example, I was mentored by many millionaires and even a billionaire. I have invested over £100,000 in my property education to date and it has definitely been worthwhile.

WHY DO PEOPLE REGARD YOU AS AN EXPERT?

I don't think I'm an expert - yet! People perceive me as an expert simply due to the fact that I constantly work smart, hard and fast and achieve results while finding ways of moving forward. Those who get to know me realise that property is on the brink of an obsession for me! And it's the one area that people find I am really good in.

WHY BUILD PROPERTY PORTFOLIOS FOR OTHERS?

I was sourcing a large amount of properties by investing in one the most prolific, highest yielding, best discount producing areas in the South East of England. I had developed trusted relationships with Estate Agents and was working collaboratively with professional refurbishment teams but I had sourced more properties than could logistically be bought. Therefore, I started to buy properties for other people, and as the deals continued to flow we started to provide outstanding results for investors.

WHY DO PEOPLE COME TO YOUR BUSINESS RATHER THAN OTHERS?

We differ from our competitors because we offer services which are simple to understand, and we don't over-complicate our procedures and processes. We communicate very well with our investors, and we are generous in the terms we offer. We also provide a high quality service with the most cost effective, performance-related fee. While some of our competitors are too large to care, others are too small to have economies of scale and have no proven track record. Basically the service we offer is an extension of our personality and our brand: personable, delivering beyond expectation, and driven by results.

WHAT ARE THE GOALS FOR THIS YEAR?

Our goal this year is to make Premier Portfolio Builder the number one UK-specific property portfolio-building service for hands-free investors. However, because we are buying discounted deals for our investors, we only take on a small number of investors each month, and pride ourselves with the quality of the deals we bring to the table; there is a limited supply of such deals. So this may be a huge challenge, as the deals simply need to be first rate.

HOW DID YOU MEET DANIEL WAGNER?

I first came across Daniel Wagner when he was working with a well-known property expert in the UK. It seems strange now, but I remember thinking how great it would be to work with him. I realised that the level that he was working at was on a much larger scale compared to me at the time and it would be fantastic to work on the same level as him. Little did I know that Daniel would become a good friend and mentor.

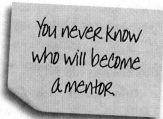

You never know who will become a mentor.

WHAT ATTRACTED YOU TO THE EXPERT SUCCESS ACADEMY?

It's amazing how a sequence of events can take place in such a short time. I had heard a great number of Daniel's talks, and when he offered the Online Brand Masterclass, I knew that this was the opportunity that I was looking for. After the Masterclass, Daniel offered a ticket to attend the Expert Success Summit. At this event I had two hugely inspiring moments which dramatically changed the direction of both my business and my life. If we ever meet in person I shall tell you if you ask about them, because we just don't have time now.

HOW HAS THE EXPERT SUCCESS ACADEMY HELPED?

The Expert Success Academy has helped my business dramatically. Firstly, you can choose what level you want to work at - as the courses are almost tailored specifically for everyone's business - which I found helpful. It has also helped me because the monthly meetings give a constant reminder of the small steps that need to be taken in order to excel. So that gives me a constant push in the right direction, which ensures that I work consistently. The weekly calls are a fantastic way of making sure that you are constantly moving forward, and also help with implementing new practical steps in your business. Also, the fact that the same group of people comes to the meetings, helps hold you accountable.

The quality of people in the Academy provides another benefit because it is good to improve your brand alongside others, and to make sure that certain, very important tasks are completed. Also, the relevant information I receive during the courses is easy to implement. However, to ensure that we can apply what we learn, practical exercises are carried out during the

Knowledge is a great start, but practical exercises make things happen.

course, and this is vital for actually using what we learn and applying it to our business. So as a result, my business has improved massively.

WHAT IMPACT DID AN ONLINE BRAND HAVE ON YOU?

An online brand positions you head and shoulders above your competition. In the process of building my online brand, I have noticed an increase in the number of people who consider me as an expert. Also I find that my online brand website looks professional and gives a true reflection of the services I provide. The information about the portfolio building business is given clearly and concisely on our website so it's easy for people to find and read it. The clearly displayed information makes it easier for people to read and make a decision. Therefore, online branding has impacted me by increasing the business opportunities that are available.

WHAT'S THE ONE MOST IMPORTANT PIECE
OF ADVICE YOU WOULD GIVE PEOPLE?

I would definitely say that if you are sitting on the fence, get off it and make a decision. Of course ensure that you do your due diligence; however do not get into analysis paralysis. I would go one step further and say that you may find it useful to work outside of your comfort zone because this is what is really going to allow you to grow. If you find it difficult, you may want to choose to do what I do - which is simply make a consistent habit of gradually working outside your comfort zone. Take small steps, one step at a time, and before you know it you will have just taken a giant leap.

KEY LEARNINGS

- Solutions recommended by Donald Trump or Richard Branson cannot be applied to your business straight away. So find mentors who are just two to five years ahead of you. Because, they can make you aware of pitfalls and challenges that are more appropriate to your situation.

- Aim to delegate as much of your workload as possible. This will enable you to simply concentrate on your income producing tasks - let others do the rest.

- Do your due diligence to check out whoever you choose to work with. Make sure that they are really doing what they say they are. If their results are proven, do not procrastinate; make a decision and work with them.

CONGRATULATIONS AND NEXT STEPS

I want to personally thank you for reading this far and exploring these Expert Success Stories. I hope you have enjoyed them and that you were able to draw inspiration from specific stories of transformation.

I also hope that it has encouraged you to explore the teachings of the Expert Success Academy and to discover the Expert Success Formula for yourself.

SO HERE IS WHAT I'D LIKE YOU TO DO NEXT....

If you want to learn more about the Expert Success Formula, then simply go to www.expertsuccessformula.com where you can purchase the *Expert Success* book and take advantage of some exclusive bonuses that are waiting there for you.

I would encourage you to find out more about our next Discovery Day. We'll share how you can build a six-figure business in the next 12 months and explain how the Expert Success Formula and the Expert Success team can both help you to grow your business and give you more clarity. Simply go to www.expertsuccess.com/events to find out more.

> ...Simply go to
> WWW.EXPERTSUCCESS.COM/EVENTS
> to find out more.

Alternatively, just go to www.expertsuccess.com to learn more about the people behind Expert Success and the Expert Success Academy and how they can help you to the next level.

You can also request a free 20-minute consultation with one of our Expert Success Coaches to help you explore your options further. Simply go to www.expertsuccess.com/coaching to book your slot now.

If you want to find out more about how the Expert Success Academy can help you and your business, then simply find us online or on Facebook. Search for 'Expert Success'. Otherwise shoot us an email to office@expertsuccess.com and one of our Expert Success Coaches will touch base and see how we can help and serve you best.

❝ I HOPE YOU HAVE ENJOYED THESE EXPERT SUCCESS STORIES.

Lightning Source UK Ltd.
Milton Keynes UK
UKOW032336290513

211401UK00004B/21/P